D1084487

For Pam —

THE DOCTOR BROAD

Thanks for your
support — Enjoy!
Barbara Roberts
AKA
The Doctor Broad

THE DOCTOR BROAD

A MAFIA LOVE STORY

Barbara H. Roberts, MD

Heliotrope Books
New York

ISBN 978-1-942762-67-6

Cover photograph by Brittany LeClerc

Cover design by Mike Plunkett, Barbara H. Roberts, MD, and Naomi Rosenblatt

For Joe
and
for Dory, Archie, and Meagan

CONTENTS

PREFACE

There are people in the know who will tell you that I caused the downfall of the New England Mafia. I managed this not by killing anyone or putting someone behind bars, but by keeping a man alive and out of jail for about a year too long. At the time, I was a slim young physician, a single mother of three, a feminist, ex-antiwar activist, and former Catholic schoolgirl. The man I kept alive and out of prison was Raymond L. S. Patriarca, the "alleged" head of the New England Mafia.

Thirty and more years on, it is easy to forget the fear and respect his name commanded. From a grimy office on Federal Hill in Providence, Rhode Island, his tentacles reached into every nook and cranny of the six New England states—wherever men gambled, loan-sharked, robbed banks, cars, or homes, or ran insurance scams. I was Patriarca's cardiologist in the last three and a half years of his life. My testimony that he was too sick to stand trial on charges of accessory and conspiracy to murder allowed him to live out his last years, if not in peace, then at least in his own home.

On the frigid December night in 1980 when I agreed to become his physician, I knew that my life had arrived at a crossroads, but I had no inkling of the deluge of publicity that would result, of the costs to me and my children that this decision would entail, or of the love that waited, not many months hence, to ambush my heart and cause pain beyond my capacity to imagine.

This is not just a Mafia story. I don't pretend to have any inside information about organized crime, although I came to know and care for several men who were identified by the media as "alleged organized crime figures." This memoir traces my life's trajectory from a now-vanished world almost to the present.

We look back on America in the decade immediately after World War II with nostalgia for a lost innocence. It was a world that had yet to experience the scourges of widespread drug addiction, AIDS or foreign terrorist attacks on American soil. But it was also a world where racism and sexism stunted millions of lives. A woman's place was in the home (once she was no longer needed for the war effort). Women who aspired to anything other than marriage and motherhood were looked at askance and thought unfeminine. Birth control was haphazard, and abortion was a crime. Trying to end an unwanted pregnancy meant putting one's life in the hands of criminals and risking pain, mutilation and death—but the stigma of out-of-wedlock motherhood was so great that countless women were driven to take those risks. Those who didn't were herded into punitive homes for unwed mothers where they were treated like pariahs. Their children were torn from them at birth and given up to strangers for adoption, their origins hidden under a veil of secrecy.

In this era, women were completely absent from the boardroom, the executive suite, and from professional sports, excepting tennis and golf. The number of women and blacks in medicine and law was a tiny percentage of what it is today. In that first post-war decade, television was in its infancy, a Catholic had never been elected President, Vietnam was France's problem, and Communism was our only enemy. Rock-and-roll had not yet been born. The dictates of religion and the government were largely unquestioned.

And then, everything changed. For many of my generation, John F. Kennedy's assassination marked the end of our childhood; the ensuing decade saw the birth of a new world—one altered almost beyond recognition from what we'd known. And we changed with it. In 1963 I was a devout, observant Catholic; by 1973, I was an outspoken feminist, a speaker at mass anti-war demonstrations, a pro-choice activist, and an atheist. Two things remained of the girl I once was: a love of children and a desire to heal.

I grew up the oldest in a family of ten children, and caring for them was as natural to me as breathing. My love for these numerous younger siblings was fierce, protective, and reflexive. When I became a mother myself, that love devolved onto my own three children. In the turmoil that characterized much of their childhood, I strove to protect them from the consequences of my mistakes—and I was not always successful. For this I will carry regret to my grave.

My commitment to feminism and medicine has led me into unexpected byways. I have traveled a path I never foresaw into moral dilemmas I never envisioned. It has been a journey rich in love and laughter, tears and heartache, labor and study. So, I repeat: this is not just a mafia story. It is the story of a woman born in mid-twentieth-century America who was raised in one world but came of age in another; who expected to live one life but found herself ad-libbing something very different; who faced challenges undreamt of by her mother, while providing a new paradigm for her daughters. It is dedicated to my husband and my children, who have anchored and centered and blessed me with their presence in the world.

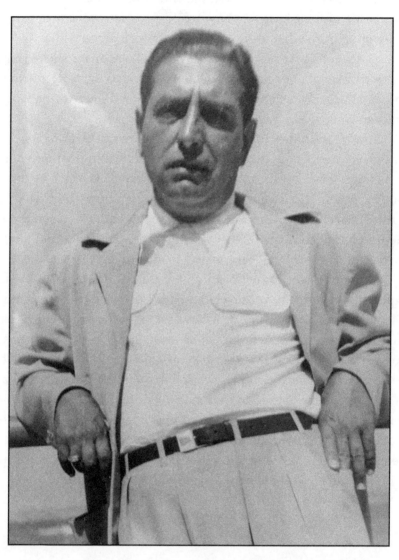

*Raymond Patriarca, longtime head of the New England Mafia.
Courtesy of Raymond J. Patriarca.*

PART ONE

A teenage Raymond Patriarca.
Courtesy of Providence Police Department.

Raymond Patriarca Senior, young Raymond, and
unidentified man. Courtesy of Raymond J. Patriarca.

Right:

Young Christopher Patriarca, Raymond's grandson, at New York Military Academy. Courtesy of Raymond J. Patriarca.

Below:

Raymond Senior and his son Raymond J. Patriarca, when Junior was attending New York Military Academy. Courtesy of Raymond J. Patriarca.

Raymond Patriarca in the 1950s. Courtesy of Raymond J. Patriarca and the Boston Globe.

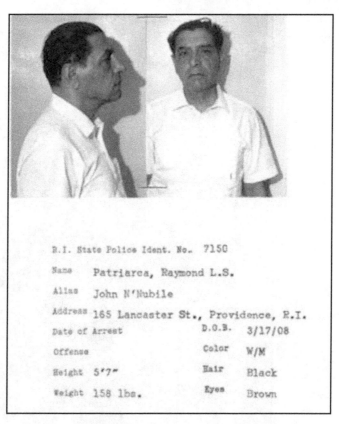

R.I. State Police Ident. No. 7150

Name   Patriarca, Raymond L.S.

Alias   John N'Nubile

Address 165 Lancaster St., Providence, R.I.

Date of Arrest   D.O.B. 3/17/08

Offense   Color   W/M

Height 5'7"   Hair   Black

Weight 158 lbs.   Eyes   Brown

Mug shot of Raymond Patriarca using an alias (John D'Nubile, misspelled). Courtesy of RI State Police Department.

1 · PUBLIC ENEMY #1

A coward turns away, but a brave man's choice is danger.
—Euripides

Picture this: it's the night of December 4, 1980. The temperature during the day barely edges above freezing; right now, the thermometer hovers around 15 degrees, a harbinger of the bitter cold that will grip the state for the next two months. The waning crescent moon has already set, and the darkness is palpable.

I'm hurtling through the backwoods of northwest Rhode Island in a late model Ford driven by a young associate of my friend, the notorious "mob lawyer" Jack Cicilline. We're on our way to check on his even more notorious client, Raymond L. S. Patriarca, the long-time head of the New England Mafia. We race by crumbling dry-stone walls, stone-ender homes built in the style of the seventeenth century, and deer munching on frozen grass.

Raymond had been arrested at his home in Johnston, Rhode Island, while eating dinner that evening. A diabetic for many years, he was too distraught to finish the meal despite having already taken his insulin. His son, Raymond Patriarca Junior, and his wife, Rita O'Toole

Patriarca, are afraid he'll react badly to the excess insulin, or that he'll have an angina attack (he's also neglected to take his nitroglycerine with him). He's being taken to the Rhode Island State Police Barracks in Scituate. Settled in 1710 by families from Massachusetts, the town's name was derived from an Indian word meaning cold river.

I'm thirty-six years old but look younger. I have dark brown hair reaching my shoulders, dark brown eyes, and a sprinkling of freckles across my nose and cheeks. I am slim, five feet four inches tall, and I weigh in at a whopping 107 pounds. I'm the first female adult cardiologist to practice in Rhode Island, having arrived here in 1977, three years earlier. Prior to Raymond's arrest, I had agreed to consult on the ailing crime boss's health at the request of his son—but I had not yet met the man who was to be my patient in person. Now his need for medical attention has become urgent.

The charges he is facing, based on an informant's testimony, include accessory and conspiracy to murder. These are just the latest in a string of legal entanglements Raymond has dealt with since he was a teenager. They will not be the last.

As I'm driven to the fateful meeting, I muse on the little I know of the man.

≫✧≪

My earliest memory of Raymond Patriarca dates back to the 1950s. Always an avid peruser of newspapers, I had read about his testimony before Arkansas Senator McClellan's committee investigating organized crime. In 1958, Raymond denied using strong-arm tactics to promote his cigarette vending-machine business. A year later, he was the only alleged mobster who did not take the Fifth Amendment in front of what was popularly known as the "Senate Rackets Committee." Under questioning by committee counsel Robert F. Kennedy, Raymond described himself as an "honest businessman," saying, "I have been a goat around Rhode Island for 20 years." Just eight years before my current car ride, in 1972, he'd again denied mafia connections in front of the House Select Committee on Crime. It would be hard to find a person in Rhode Island who had not heard of the infamous crime boss, and now I had agreed to take on his medical care. I knew instinctively that my life had arrived at a crossroads. I wondered, briefly, if I was making the right decision, or whether I had lost my mind.

Cloistered in the car as we rushed through the bare New England countryside, I was seized with panic. I felt as if I were about to take center stage in some long-running hit play without knowing my lines and with only the foggiest notion of what the playwright intended. Flashes of old mobster movies ran through my head: Guns roared, brains spattered against windshields, mothers, wives, and children wept beside caskets, while killers offered hypocritical condolences, their faces betraying nothing. Did I really want to take on a patient who was a notorious mobster? A man who, in addition to suffering serious vascular disease, was now facing capital charges? How would doing so affect my custody struggle with Ned Bresnahan, the father of my youngest daughter? How would it affect my other children, my practice, and my other patients? It wasn't farfetched to fear that I'd be ostracized professionally, and I depended on other doctors for patient referrals.

But I'd already consented to see Raymond as a patient before his arrest. How could I turn my back on him now, when the stress of impending trial and incarceration likely would exacerbate his illness?

And niggling in the back of my mind was another consideration. Not many years before, I'd experienced government harassment first-hand. I'd almost lost custody of my two older children because of my political beliefs. If Raymond's arrest was based on the word of an informant, then I was not inclined to automatically believe in his guilt. Informants had provided information on me to the FBI when I was active in the anti-war movement. I learned this when I was questioned by the FBI about my politics and associates in the early 1970s. Informants had played a particularly sinister role in the McCarthy era, when I was growing up. As I saw it, the judicial system was far from infallible.

And in fact, his guilt or innocence was irrelevant. Part of a doctor's training involves learning to set aside judgments. Ideally, a physician renders the same care to the bag lady turned up by a snowplow on Main Street as she does to the CEO of the largest company in town. A patient's behavior before entering your care is only important insofar as it influences his or her health. During my career, I'd ministered to wife-beaters, alcoholics, drug addicts—even to a member of the dreaded Savak, the Shah of Iran's secret police. What these people had done in the past was not something I allowed myself to dwell on. It didn't matter what crimes Raymond was or wasn't guilty of. What mattered was what medical ethics dictated. All of these conflicting thoughts and feelings warred within me.

"Forget the movies," I told myself. "This is real life. Just pretend he's a patient like any other." And as I thought this, I knew what I had to do. Morally and ethically, as a physician, I had no choice. Raymond was, without question, an ailing, elderly man, one to whom I'd already made a commitment. But did I have what it took? And what exactly would be required of me if I accepted the notorious mobster into my care? Time would tell, but I reminded myself that the Hippocratic Oath I'd taken to put each of my patient's interests ahead of my own was not only for those patients without criminal records or those not facing capital charges. It was for everyone who came to me as a patient.

In addition to that, there was still a lot of the "good Catholic girl" in me no matter how profoundly I'd rebelled against the Church. During my long years of Catholic schooling, I'd been instructed to visit the imprisoned, comfort the afflicted, and treat the most wretched person as if he were Christ in disguise. The impulse to martyrdom inculcated by this upbringing, though deeply buried, was very much alive, and I felt its power that night.

After getting lost a few times, we pulled up at the State Police headquarters. The reception area was packed with people, but Jack Cicilline was the only one I recognized. I'd expected the scene to resemble a wake—long, funereal faces and hushed conversations—but it was more like a tailgate party at a rowdy college Homecoming Weekend. Jack seemed in great good humor and introduced me to several of the lawmen: "This is Raymond's cardiologist. I want her to check on him.

He's only recently out of the hospital." This was, in fact, truly the case. Raymond had developed a gangrenous toe—a common complication in diabetes—which had been amputated at Fatima Hospital, where his vascular surgeon, Dr. Robert Indeglia, had admitting privileges.

Raymond himself was nowhere to be seen, and there was no opportunity to talk to Jack privately. I said as little as possible, trying to pick up some cue from Jack as to how he wanted me to act and what he wanted me to do. After a few minutes, he told me to wait in the reception area while he went back to talk to Raymond, who, he told me, was being held in Major Lionel Benjamin's office. Benjamin was second in command to Colonel Walter Stone, the superintendent of the Rhode Island State Police. (My son Archie would play on the same high school football team with Benjamin's sons a few years later.)

When Jack returned he motioned me to follow him into Benjamin's office, then left and closed the door behind us, leaving me alone with Raymond and Colonel Benjamin.

My image of a Mafia don, like that of so many other Americans at that time, was Marlon Brando's raspy-voiced Vito Corleone from *The Godfather*, with his hooded gaze and menacing presence. What confronted me that night was something radically different. Raymond looked more like a wizened Italian cobbler than an all-powerful mafioso. My first thought on seeing him in the flesh was, "My God, he's so tiny." The second was, "Holy shit, he looks like he's going to have a cardiac arrest any second, and I'll never be able to resuscitate him here."

The man I beheld was a short, shriveled seventy-two-year-old with a greasy sheen of perspiration coating his brow, an alarmingly cyanotic complexion, and the generalized muscle wasting of the chronically ill. I approached him, but he took no notice of me. I later learned he thought at first that I was a reporter.

"Mr. Patriarca," I said, "I'm Doctor Roberts. Your son wanted me to check on you."

At this, he made eye contact with me but still didn't speak. His breathing was labored, and I asked him if he was having any chest discomfort. "Yes," he admitted, somewhat reluctantly. He added that he had left his nitroglycerine at home. Major Benjamin piped up, "Hey, Doc, do you want me to give him one of mine?" I declined, not knowing if they were the same dose as Raymond's.

Raymond agreed to let me take his pulse and listen to his heart and lungs. Doing so only increased my alarm. His pulse was extremely erratic, which can be a warning sign of sudden cardiac arrest. His chest pain had lasted for over two hours. Quite aside from any legal considerations, I was now convinced that the only place he belonged was in the cardiac care unit of a hospital. His own nitroglycerine pills were brought from his home, and I gave him one. This eased his pain over the next fifteen minutes, but he continued to look ashen and to have an irregular pulse.

I told Major Benjamin that Mr. Patriarca needed to be admitted to the hospital immediately, arrest or no arrest.

"No way," he said. "You're going to have to talk to Colonel Stone."

Although I did not know it at the time, there was a long-standing public antipathy between Raymond and Colonel Stone, but Jack would later tell me that his own impression from private conversations with both men was that they had more respect for each other than might be expected, given their respective occupations. Whatever the truth of their relationship, that night, it seemed to me that Colonel Stone wanted Raymond's arrest and subsequent conviction to cap his long and distinguished career in law enforcement.

After introducing myself to him over the phone, I informed the colonel, "Mr. Patriarca is suffering from angina and an unstable heart rhythm. It is my professional opinion that he needs to be hospitalized immediately." He was not all happy with this recommendation and insisted that I speak to the police surgeon. I telephoned the police surgeon and reported my findings to him. He promptly agreed with me that hospitalization was indicated. I then called Colonel Stone back, and he agreed, albeit reluctantly, to allow Raymond to be transferred to the hospital. However, he insisted that Raymond be brought to Fatima Hospital because, he said, "it's the only hospital where we can keep him under 24-hour-a-day armed guard." I needed to have him admitted to the Miriam Hospital where I practiced; I didn't have admitting privileges at Fatima. Luckily, at that moment, I had a Eureka moment.

A few weeks before, one Anthony Sfameni, coincidentally another client of Jack Cicilline's, had been found in the trunk of a car, shot in the head, rolled up in a rug, and left for dead. At the time, he was out on bail on a murder charge himself, and his attempted murder was thought to be a revenge shooting. He had been admitted to the Miriam Hospital and kept under continuous armed guard for his own protection. I reminded Colonel Stone of this to convince him to authorize Raymond's transfer to the Miriam Hospital. Jack said he would meet us there. He seemed extremely pleased. He later told me he was shocked that I'd been able to whisk Raymond away from the police barracks. In truth, so was I.

Raymond's arms and legs were shackled, and he was put in the back of a police cruiser. I was allowed to sit next to him. I remember little of that ride except praying that I would not have to perform CPR en route—yes, even atheists pray when terrified. Two rifle-toting policemen rode in front, with another beside us in the back. There was a fleet of a half a dozen cars accompanying us filled with cops, lawyers, and by now, reporters. We took off into the night, lights flashing, sirens wailing—the first of a number of similar rides Raymond and I would take in the ensuing months.

With police flanking Raymond on either side, we approached the triage desk in the Miriam Hospital Emergency room. Feigning a calm I was far from feeling, I told the nurse, "I am admitting Mr. Patriarca to the Coronary Care Unit with unstable angina, and I want him hooked up to a monitor and an IV immediately." The nurse rushed off, goggle-eyed, to find the charge nurse. I obtained an electrocardiogram, which only increased my unease: It showed unmistakable signs that Raymond's heart muscle was starved for oxygen, and he was having frequent extra heart beats—both atrial premature beats, which indicate a danger that the lungs may fill up with fluid, and ventricular premature beats, which may be a prelude to ventricular fibrillation, in which the heart's electrical impulses becomes so rapid and irregular that effective circulation ceases and the patient dies if his heart is not shocked back into a normal rhythm.

I summoned the Coronary Care Unit resident and gave him a brief history, then told him what measures I wanted him to take to stabilize the patient. He looked at me with equal parts mesmerized fascination and abject terror, like a prairie dog confronted by a rattlesnake. I assured him that he could call me at any time with questions if there was any change in Raymond's condition. After another hour or so, when I was somewhat encouraged that Raymond was stabilizing, I left the hospital and drove the short distance to my home. Someone, I cannot remember who, had brought my car to the hospital from Jack's office, where I'd been meeting with him and his brother about another matter when all this started. Favors like this became routine during the years that I was Raymond's physician.

The children were asleep, but my live-in boyfriend, George Gregory, greeted me with, "You're late. Where have you been?"

"You're not going to believe this," I replied, "but I am now taking care of Raymond Patriarca. His family asked me to check on him after he was arrested tonight. I wound up admitting him to the hospital."

George was not thrilled. He was already unhappy about my friendship with Jack Cicilline. He made very little money at his job as a boat builder and was aware and resentful of the difference between his income and Jack's. It was bad enough that I made so much more money than George did. Added to this was the toll taken by the constant, not always petty, harassment we endured from the estranged father of my youngest child, Ned Bresnahan, who was suing me for common-law divorce, palimony, and custody of our four-year-old daughter. A love of sailing was the only thing George and I had in common. Now that winter was upon us and we could no longer sail together, our differences were thrown into stark relief. My becoming Raymond's doctor was not going to be a salutary ingredient in the stew of our relationship, and the circumstances of our lives took on an astonishing similarity to Alice's adventures down the rabbit hole.

I fell into an uneasy sleep, only to be awakened at 2:30 a.m. when the resident called to tell me that Raymond was having an increased number of ventricular premature beats. I decided not to put him on additional medication since he was not having any chest discomfort, but the call left me wide awake and worried. I had only just fallen back to sleep when I was roused by another call at 4:30. Raymond was having angina, shortness of breath, and more of the worrisome extra beats. I instructed the resident to start him on intravenous lidocaine, a medicine to control his abnormal heart rhythm, and nitroglycerine ointment, a long-acting form of the medicine that dilates the coronary arteries and decreases the work of the heart. After this second call, Raymond stabilized, and I was able to catch a few hours of sleep.

In the morning, knowing Raymond's arrest would be front-page news—and that my name might be mentioned—I told my two older children, Dory and Archie, what had happened. "You might hear that my name is in the newspaper today. I'm taking care of an organized crime figure, and he always gets a lot of press. I just wanted to tell you before anyone else did."

They seemed to take the news in stride. Dory was then fifteen, a striking brunette at Classical High School, the college preparatory high school in Providence, and Archie was a tow-headed eleven-year-old in the sixth grade at the private Wheeler School. They were both good students and had made many friends in our three-plus years in Rhode Island. As they had in each of the previous three years, they were acting at Providence's Trinity Square Repertory Theater, where Archie was appearing in *On Golden Pond* and Dory played one of the Cratchett girls in *A Christmas Carol*.

When I arrived at the Miriam Hospital to make rounds that morning, Jack Cicilline was waiting for me in the lobby with a large entourage. I didn't recognize any of the people who accompanied him. Again, the mood was bizarrely festive.

"This is the little lady who pulled off that coup," Jack said gleefully, as I shook hands with a collection of people whom I gathered were somehow connected to Raymond.

"Gee," one of them said, "I expected someone much bigger and older."

I heard those sentiments expressed often over the next several months. Apparently, something about the pairing of the slight, young lady doctor with the aging don did not compute, but we would be linked forever in Rhode Island mythology. In fact, I told people that no matter what I wanted it to say—which was, "Here lies Barbara Roberts, Spinster, Mother of Three"—my headstone would no doubt read: "She was Raymond's doctor."

One-inch headlines on the front page of the *Providence Journal* on Friday, December 5, 1980 proclaimed "Patriarca Arrested in 1965 Slaying" over a head shot of Raymond with eyes almost shut, a cigar stub in his mouth. The *Journal* reported that he had been arrested shortly before 5:00 the evening before and charged with ordering the 1965 execution of a "small-time hood," Raymond "Baby" Curcio, a thirty-one-year-old drug addict who "had incurred Patriarca's wrath by burglarizing the home of the mob chief's older brother, Joseph, who has since died." The article also indicated that "Rudolph Sciarra, one of Patriarca's most powerful mob associates, was being sought for providing the guns used in that killing but is believed to be in hiding out of state." Rudolph was indeed making himself scarce, but he turned himself in within a few days.

At the time, I hadn't met Rudolph, but years later, he would become another one of my AOCF (alleged organized crime figure) patients, of whom there would be many. He was quite the colorful character. A very muscular man of medium height, he used to smoke five packs of cigarettes a day, and in addition to chronic lung disease, suffered from recurrent bouts of pancreatitis and high blood pressure. His skin had the deep wrinkling of the chronic smoker, and his voice was also a smoke-cured rasp. He still had a full head of light brown wavy hair when I met him. He'd been a criminal most of his life, and I imagine he had more than a passing acquaintance with firearms, but he was also one of the worst hypochondriacs I've ever met. Even in prison, he checked his own blood pressure every few hours. In his seventies he developed angina, which I treated medically for as long as I could. Like many of my AOCF patients, he was terrified of invasive procedures, but finally, after his angina became unstable, he consented to my doing a cardiac catheterization to determine the extent of the blockages in his coronary arteries. He was a total wreck despite sedation, but everything went well and when we were finished, he croaked in his gravelly voice, referring to a mutual friend, "Doc, Louie told me you were the best, and he was right."

There were a number of law officers as well who, for whatever reason—and I could think of a few—chose me as their cardiologist. At times, my waiting room resembled a mini-Apalachin, the town in upstate New York where the chieftains of all the mob families met back in the 1950s; the meeting was broken up by the police, and such a conference was never attempted again, as far as I know. But I never heard anything except cordial chit-chat engaged in by the cops and their sometime quarry as they waited to see me.

2 · Old MacDonald Had a Farm

Music hath charms to soothe the savage breast.
—William Congreve

The Coronary Care Unit where Raymond was admitted took on the appearance of an armed camp. Two prison guards sat directly outside Raymond's cubicle, and another was parked at the entrance to the unit. All were fitted out with rifles and kept a wary eye on everyone who entered the vicinity of the notorious don. I instructed the nurses not to allow anyone but Raymond's wife, son, grandson, daughter-in-law, or lawyers to visit. Despite this, I was infuriated one day to find another physician, who had no connection to Raymond's case, praying over Raymond as he lay helplessly in bed, urging him to repent and "give your soul over to Jesus."

Another time, one of the nursing supervisors, Sandy Stamoulis, walked onto the unit carrying a large guitar case, exactly like the ones that countless movie mobsters use to conceal automatic weapons. The guards paled as Sandy sauntered up to the nurses' station toting the ominous case. They made her open it on the spot. It contained only a guitar, and we all (except the police) had a good laugh.

After a week in the Coronary Care Unit, Raymond was transferred to a private room on the fourth floor of the Miriam Hospital, where cardiac patients were sent after their stay in the unit. The armed guards now sat just outside the door to his room. The question of whether I should perform a cardiac catheterization to document the extent of his coronary blockages was often on my mind, but Raymond was opposed to this, and I could not disagree. He was so unlikely to be a good candidate for surgical revascularization—that is, a bypass operation—that there was little justification for subjecting him to the risk of the diagnostic procedure.

I believed catheterization would document severe, diffuse blockages in all his coronary arteries; in this situation, bypasses often close within a short period of time. Added to that was the fact that even a diagnostic catheterization carries a greater-than-normal risk in diabetic patients. Diabetic patients also have a higher incidence of poor wound healing, post-operative infection, and congestive heart failure. The dye used to outline the coronary arteries not infrequently causes kidney damage. All in all, I believed that the risks of catheterization and surgery outweighed the possible benefits.

I knew that the various prosecutors who were eager to put Raymond on trial would not rely solely on my testimony about his health, since it was counter to what they wanted to hear. I decided to ask my former professor and mentor, Dr. Bernard Lown, to consult about Raymond's condition. If a world-renowned cardiologist who was a full professor at Harvard Medical School concurred that Raymond should not be subjected to the stress of a trial, it would carry a lot more weight than the word of a young, unknown woman doctor. In addition, the state was already lining up other, more senior cardiologists in Rhode Island and Massachusetts to examine Raymond and render an opinion as to whether or not his cardiac condition was as grave as I was making it out to be. When I called Dr. Lown and explained the situation, he readily agreed to come to Rhode Island.

My early experience with Dr. Lown was not auspicious. The week

I started making rounds in the Levine Cardiac Unit at the Brigham, where Dr. Lown was the attending physician, my babysitter quit. Every day that week, I was later and later for rounds, as I scrambled to make childcare arrangements. Dr. Lown was a well-known stickler for punctuality, and I could sense that he was losing patience. Finally, on Friday, I came rushing through the swinging doors of the unit just as he was leaving, with his entourage of other fellows, residents, interns, medical students and nurses. He stopped, fixed me with a steely glare, and said, "Dr. Roberts, if you were a man, you'd have been fired by now."

That was it—my Irish temper went off like a firecracker, and I snarled, "Dr. Lown, if I were a man, I'd have a WIFE looking after my children." There was a collective gasp of horror from my colleagues, and I thought, "Oh shit, Barbara. You're going to be fired, you'll never be a cardiologist, your children will starve…" After what seemed like an eternity but was probably just a few seconds, he shook his finger at me and said, "That's a very good retort." I almost fainted with relief, and we remained friends from that day forward.

On December 17, 1980, I rode up to Boston in a white stretch limousine that Raymond's son, "Junior" Patriarca, had hired to transport the illustrious consultant to Providence. We picked up Dr. Lown at his home, and on the way back to Providence, I filled him in on more of the medical and legal details of Raymond's case. I waited at the hospital while Dr. Lown took a history and examined Raymond. During the course of his interview, Raymond had two more episodes of angina, both of which responded to what Dr. Lown described as the "carotid maneuver." In fact, this was something he had impressed upon his fellows when we were trainees as an almost fool-proof way to determine if a patient's chest discomfort was angina, the symptom caused by insufficient blood supply to the heart. Rubbing on a patient's carotid artery in the neck causes a reflex slowing of the heart rate. Since lowering the heart rate causes the heart to require less oxygen, this alleviates the symptom of angina.

What Dr. Lown taught us to do was to perform the carotid massage and ask the patient: "Does this make the pain worse?" If the patient responds, "No, Doctor, it actually makes it better," you could be certain that the symptom was arising from a lack of blood supply to the heart. And this is how Raymond responded during his examination by Dr. Lown that evening.

Afterwards, Jack, Junior, Dr. Lown, and I had dinner at the Grotto Azzura, one of the many superb Italian restaurants on Federal Hill, just down Atwells Avenue from Raymond's business, National Cigarette Service. It was ironic that his "legitimate" business promoted cigarette smoking, a habit I'd come to loathe after seeing the tremendous toll in suffering and death it caused the hapless addicts who succumbed to the lure of nicotine. In my opinion, the tobacco industry, which causes the deaths of hundreds of thousands of people every year and cripples countless others with chronic lung disease, is truly an example of "organized crime." It just happens to have bribed our legislators into looking the other way.

Dr. Lown submitted a comprehensive report on Raymond's condition, which he concluded by writing, "Because of his fragile cardiac and emotional state, there is high probability that any incarceration would jeopardize his survival." He concurred with me that Raymond's cardiac disease was made more dangerous by his depression, and that the stress of a trial or jail would put him at an inordinately high risk of death.

I now had a powerful ally in my corner and was more confident that I might actually succeed in keeping Raymond out of the clutches of the law. There wasn't a shred of doubt in my mind that the stress of a trial, let alone a jail term, would kill him as readily as a bullet fired at point-blank range. Convincing skeptical cops, prosecutors, and judges would be another story.

I was gradually coming to identify very strongly with Raymond as an "underdog." This sounds bizarre, given his power, past, and reputation, but by the time I first laid eyes on him, he was very frail, very sick, and very frightened. He knew instinctively that a trial and jail term were tantamount to a sentence of death, even though he had kept secret the true extent of how disabled he really was. He was between a rock and a hard place. His pride and acculturation prodded him to deny the severity of his illness, but for me to succeed in keeping him from going to trial, he had to expose his fragility to public scrutiny. This he was deeply unwilling to do, at least initially. He also knew that I would pay a price for going to bat for him, and he made his gratitude clear, telling me more than once, "I know I owe you my life. I couldn't love you more if you were my own daughter."

How could I abandon him? I came to care passionately about his well-being. I would keep him from being put on trial; I would keep him out of jail. It had become a contest between me and the legal system, one I was determined to win.

A few days before Christmas, Jack's secretary called and asked if I could come to his office after my own office hours to discuss the report I was preparing on Raymond's condition. When I got there, Jack was grinning like the Cheshire cat, and Junior was there with his usual entourage of Nino and Nicole. These men were both from Italy and I rarely saw Junior without them. They were not obviously armed but were clearly functioning as guards and drivers. Dr. Robert Indeglia, a vascular surgeon who'd become a good friend of mine, had saved Nicole's life a few years before when a bullet had nicked his aorta, the main artery that leaves the left side of the heart. The mystery of who shot him and why was never solved.

Many years later, Nino entered the Witness Protection Program after shooting to death two men in the Silver Lake Social Club, one of the many clubs in Italian neighborhoods where men gather to play pinochle and presumably take bets. These are smoky, dingy dives where women are not welcome. The men use them as bolt holes to get away from their wives and mistresses, as much as a place to "do business." But in 1980, Nino was still a loyal soldier in the Patriarca crime family. A large, red gift box sat in the middle of Jack's office, tied with a garish white ribbon, the bow as big as my head.

"Go on, open it," Junior urged. "It's a Christmas present from me and my father." Inside the box was a gorgeous, full-length Blackglama mink coat, my name embroidered in script on the satin lining. It was exquisite. There was a card accompanying the coat from the owner of Tolchinsky Furs (an upscale furrier in Warwick, Rhode Island), informing me that if I wished, I could exchange it for any other coat in the store. When she heard about the gift, Jack's wife Sabra Cicilline urged me to return it and get a sable coat instead, but, of course, I didn't.

I had never even imagined owning a fur coat, never mind a full-length mink, one whose ad campaign pictured famous women posing in just such a wrap, the copy reading: "What becomes a legend most?" I thanked Junior and jokingly asked if this meant that I was becoming a legend. Jack said they were just embarrassed to be seen out in public with me wearing the old green cloth coat that was my usual uniform, and that I needed to spruce up my image for their sakes, if for no other reason.

There are no secrets in Rhode Island, and it wasn't long before friends told me that my daughter Meagan's father Ned had learned of this extravagant gift. He never mentioned it without calling it, disparagingly, "the Mob Mink" and implying that it was a payoff for my testimony about Raymond Sr.'s health. Fortunately, the *Providence Journal* either never learned of this gift or chose not to publicize it.

The holidays passed in a blur of parties, work, and ferrying the older children to their performances at Trinity. Ned stepped up his campaign of harassment. I later learned that he called the FBI and informed them that unnamed mobsters were making threatening telephone calls to him, demanding that he drop his custody suit. I didn't think there was a drop of truth to that allegation. Nevertheless, the FBI placed a tap on his telephone line, hoping to document the threats, but discontinued the monitoring after a few months when it was unrevealing. Our custody battle continued to wend its indolent way through the Family Court. And much like an indolent infection, it sapped my strength and periodically flared into malignant warfare.

On December 5th, the day after Raymond's first hospitalization, a scheduled Family Court hearing was postponed until December 18th. On that date, I went to court only to be told that there would be another postponement, this time until January 19, 1981. Ned was granted visitation in the meantime from December 26 until the 28th and on Wednesdays after December 31 from noon until 5:00 p.m. at my home.

These visits were always powder kegs waiting to explode as Ned became incensed at having to bring Meagan back to the house where my boyfriend George had replaced him, or to spend time in George's presence while visiting Meagan. On January 1, after the first ordered home visit, Ned called the Providence Police, claiming that George had kicked him. Although they had enough experience with Ned not to rush out and arrest George every time Ned called, the calls were duly logged and could be entered into evidence in the upcoming custody trial.

After I became Raymond Patriarca's physician, Jack withdrew as my Family Court lawyer to avoid any appearance of conflict of interest. Attorney John Bevilacqua took over. Bevilacqua's father was then on the Rhode Island Supreme Court, and his family's connection to the Patriarcas went back a long way. In 1973, Raymond had received an early parole from prison after Joseph A. Bevilacqua Sr., then Speaker of the Rhode Island House, wrote a letter supporting his release in which he described Raymond as "a person of integrity and, in my opinion, good moral character." The *Providence Journal* mentioned this letter frequently in articles about organized crime and the influence it curried with politicians. In later years, the *Journal*'s vendetta against Judge Bevilacqua contributed to his ultimate removal from the bench and impeachment. As I would come to learn from personal experience, the *Journal* rarely forgave anyone who offered assistance to the mob boss, whether they were doctors, lawyers, politicians, or ordinary citizens.

By this time, Raymond Junior had been apprised of my legal struggles with Meagan's father and told me how badly he felt that my role as his father's doctor was complicating the situation. I never learned exactly whose idea it was, or how it was arranged, but shortly after John Bevilacqua became my lawyer, a secret meeting was arranged between me and Judge Alprin, the judge who was then assigned to Roberts vs. Bresnahan in Family Court. On the evening of January 14, Matty Guglielmetti, a friend of Junior's, picked me up at my office and drove me to a store in North Providence owned by a man who was allegedly connected to the Patriarca crime family. The store had been cleared of customers and closed early.

Feeling as if I had wandered onto the set of a James Bond movie, I was directed to one of the curtained dressing rooms. This had another exit at its rear, through which I was beckoned a few minutes later. I was left alone in a tiny office for a short time, and then a small, dapper man entered the room and introduced himself as Judge Alprin. He had a jolly, round face and a kindly paternal air, the picture of a benevolent Kris Kringle. He asked me to tell him my side of the story, and I was only too happy to oblige. After hearing the whole sorry tale, he made no promises, but told me: "Don't worry. Rhode Island almost never denies mothers custody of their children, even if they're selling their bodies on street corners." He was risking censure at least for meeting with me like this, and I suppose, although I don't know it for a fact, that money changed hands, but in any event, by the time the custody suit came to trial in 1982, he was no longer the judge assigned to hear it, and I had gone through two additional changes of lawyers.

The *Providence Journal* continued to cover the story of Raymond's arrest and subsequent hospitalization with almost daily stories. It described the unseemly bickering between the State Police and the Providence police, with Providence Police Chief Angelo Ricci accusing the State Police of "glory-grabbing" and of "the worst case of professional misconduct in the annals of modern law enforcement." Apparently, the arrest and booking of Raymond and Rudolph Sciarra, his alleged accomplice, were supposed to have taken place at Providence Police headquarters, not the State Police barracks in Scituate—or at least that was the understanding of the Providence police. Governor Garrahy was brought in to arrange a truce between Chief Ricci and Colonel Stone.

It didn't stop there. The newspaper reported that the "Patriarca case also produced bruised feelings among members of the Rhode Island State Marshals who said they were furious that the State Director of Corrections declared an emergency yesterday morning and gave their responsibility for the bedside custody of Patriarca to prison correctional officials." These disputes were reminiscent of feral dogs fighting over a choice bit of road kill. It was only many years later that I learned some of the background of these unseemly tugs of war.

The evidence that led to Raymond's arrest was developed principally by State Police Lieutenant Vincent Vespia, working in conjunction with Providence Police Sergeant Richard Tamburini. Both movie-star handsome, they became as close as brothers in the course of working together. When Raymond's arrest was imminent, the appropriate warrants had to be applied for, based on affidavits supplied by the lead investigators. A joint meeting of the State and Providence police was held, during which all of the brass, with the exception of Colonel Stone, were present. The Colonel kept to himself in his office, which apparently was not unusual.

It was agreed at the meeting that Lieutenant Vespia and Sergeant Tamburini would arrest Raymond once the judge had issued the warrant, and that he would then be taken to the Providence Police Station. Ed Pare, then Captain of the State Police, left the room, conferred with Colonel Stone, then came back and gave his OK to this plan. But as everyone was filing out of the room, Captain Pare told Lieutenant Vespia to wait behind. Once everyone had left the room, Pare said, "I'm going to give you a direct order. When Patriarca is arrested, you bring him here." Much against his will, since he knew his professional credentials were on the line, Lieutenant Vespia agreed. However, he called Chief Angelo Ricci of the Providence Police to tell him about the order he'd received, countermanding what had been agreed upon. Ricci was furious, but knew that Vespia had no choice. As Vespia and Tamburini drove to Raymond's home on Golini Drive in the Providence suburb of Johnston to make the arrest, they received many radio calls, asking if the warrant had been signed yet. Once a warrant is signed, any policeman can make the arrest, but Vespia did not answer the radio until they were pulling up to Raymond's door, at which point he reported that the warrant was ready to be executed.

They knocked on a side door, and Raymond's wife Rita opened it, saying, "Vinny, I have a feeling I'm not going to be happy to see you." Raymond was in his pajamas, eating a dinner of sausage and potatoes. He looked at the two policemen and said, "That stool pigeon finally talked, didn't he?" Lieutenant Vespia replied, "Raymond, I have a warrant for your arrest." Raymond asked if he could finish eating, and they told him he could, but after a few more bites, he pushed the food away, too upset to continue. Within minutes of the arrival of Vespia and Tamburini, a whole slew of other policeman and FBI agents arrived at the house, but Rita told them, "Vinny's here already; you can't come in," and they left empty-handed.

Vespia followed Raymond into his bedroom while he changed into slacks and a shirt. Rita put a ski parka on him and placed a handful of cigars in his pocket, and Raymond, Vespia, and Tamburini left for the State Police barracks. As Vespia remembers it, within a short period of time, I arrived also, wearing a stethoscope around my neck—which isn't how I remember it, although I certainly had my stethoscope in my pocketbook. Jack introduced me to Vespia and Sergeant Tamburini, and after I walked away to examine Raymond for the first time, Vespia turned to his partner and said, "Richard, it's all over. You will never see this man in a court of law. It's all over."

Jack Cicilline told me that, on the night of Raymond's arrest, he was only hoping I could assure Raymond's son that his father was not going to have a heart attack in the police station—he was amazed when I was able to persuade the State Police that he had to be hospitalized. In truth, I was amazed myself. But there was no way I could assure anyone that Raymond would not have a heart attack, because I expected just such an eventuality—not just then, but on many other occasions over the next few years.

In other articles, the *Journal* pointedly ignored the affidavits that I and four other physicians wrote in support of Raymond's application for bail and reported that the Attorney General said he would not delay the State's case against Patriarca because of his illness: "If necessary, we will ask the Superior Court to conduct the arraignment of Mr. Patriarca in his hospital room to keep this case moving in the ordinary course of scheduling." A columnist for the newspaper wrote an article in which he said:

> ...it seems we have a new trend in Rhode Island, the chronically ill suspect. If it catches on it could alter our entire criminal justice system. Police Departments will soon have to trade squad cars for ambulances... Conversations among suspects will take on a new twist as well. 'Hey,

Louie, I'm in big trouble, they collared me on murder one. It sticks and I'm lookin at life'. 'Get Cicilline, best criminal defense lawyer I ever seen.' 'Hey, what are you talkin? Forget lawyers, I need a doctor...'

The general tenor of the articles was frankly skeptical that Raymond was as sick as I testified and suggested that his hospitalization was a ploy to keep him from having to face these latest charges.

By now, the *Providence Journal* had identified me as Raymond's doctor; back at the hospital, I was an instant celebrity. I could see people pointing and whispering as I made my rounds. Raymond's condition continued to be precarious. He developed redness and swelling around the amputation site in his foot, and a bone scan revealed evidence of osteomyelitis, or bone infection. This was a dreaded complication in a diabetic whose blood supply to the feet was already compromised, and it required that Raymond be treated with a six-week course of intravenous antibiotics. Prosecutors were fighting his application for bail on the accessory to murder charge, and it was unclear whether it would be granted. If it were not, he would be sent to prison to await trial once he was stable enough to be discharged from hospital. I was more certain than ever that incarceration would kill him.

On January 21, 1981, in his hospital bed, he was formally arraigned on the charge of being an accessory before the fact of the 1965 murder of Raymond "Baby" Curcio. Judge John Bourcier came to the hospital to hear him plead innocent to the charge; much to the dismay of the *Providence Journal*, the judge excluded the press. I was present in the event of a cardiac catastrophe, my eyes glued to the heart monitor during the legal proceedings. To my intense relief, within a few hours of the arraignment, Judge Bourcier granted Jack's motion to release Raymond on bail pending trial.

Eight days later, on January 29, 1981, I discharged Raymond from a hospitalization that had lasted almost two months. I had not told anyone but Raymond, Junior, and Jack of my plans in order to avoid having hordes of reporters waiting to lob questions at me or my patient. Junior arranged for an ambulance, which pulled up to the rear entrance of the hospital. We made our "getaway" without mishap.

On February 2, the *Providence Journal* published a story under the headline "Miriam Staff Had No Warning About Patriarca Discharge" detailing Raymond's departure. I never learned who the *Journal's* source was. I always refused to speak to reporters about Raymond's condition, although my secretary Donna Bechard was inundated with calls from them on almost a daily basis. In consequence, and because I was aiding a criminal they had long enjoyed castigating, the *Providence Journal* was not my friend. The newspaper stories about my role as Raymond's doctor, and my struggles with Ned, would cause my children—particularly Dory and Archie—much pain and subjected Dory to the taunts of classmates. One of them told her, "If my father was that close to Raymond, he'd be giving him poison, not trying to keep him alive." There was nothing I could do except hope that the experience would not leave permanent scars.

Not long after I was first mentioned in the newspaper in connection with Raymond Patriarca, I received a call from a man I had briefly dated shortly after moving to Rhode Island in 1977. He told me that one of his former customers from the bar he'd owned in Cranston had called to say, "Vinny, remember that doctor broad you used to go out with? She's the old man's doctor now!" I wasn't finding much to laugh at in those days, but I laughed at that. To me a "broad" was a woman with large tits and no brains, and here I was endowed with just the opposite. (At least, I was certain about the tits part of the equation. There were times I wasn't sure about the brains.) While I had traveled a long road from the devout Catholic virgin who was the valedictorian of her high school graduating class, I was about as far from being a "broad" as it was possible to be. Years later, this sobriquet would come to seem the perfect title for a memoir of those years.

Raymond was home from the hospital but hardly out of the woods, either medically or legally. He continued to be depressed and was liable to burst into tears at any mention of court proceedings. He was on multiple medications for which he needed to be monitored on a regular basis. Ordinarily, I would have scheduled a follow-up visit in my office shortly after the hospital discharge, but that clearly would not be so simple in Raymond's case. I pictured the scene in my waiting room if Raymond were brought there: Half the room would be busy trying (figuratively) to kiss his ring, while the other half would be having the vapors, if not cardiac arrests, at being in the presence of the infamous mob boss. Many of my patients were Italian-American, and Raymond was held in tremendous respect by a sizable proportion of Providence's Italian-American community. Many members of this community believed he was being hounded as much for the fact that he was of Italian descent as for his alleged crimes.

There was an additional reason why having Raymond come to my private office could be problematic. I worried prosecutors would claim that if Raymond were well enough to travel to the office, he was well enough to travel to court. I decided that I would make house calls rather than have him come for follow-up visits to my office.

Raymond and his wife Rita lived modestly because it was not in his nature to flaunt, and because he was well aware of the danger of being charged with tax evasion. Their ranch home was on a tiny corner lot in a development of similar, decidedly middle-class homes, bearing no resemblance to the grand mansions inhabited by mob bosses in Hollywood movies. In fact, their home was far smaller than my own, and in a "less desirable" neighborhood. There were no sweeping manicured lawns or elaborately landscaped gardens; no gates, no statues, no armed guards patrolling the premises, no obvious surveillance (though I didn't doubt it existed), and no other accoutrements of movie mobster residences. The furnishings were heavy and dark, with drapes covering all of the windows. Raymond spent most of his time in a recliner in the den/TV room just off the garage, reading newspapers and watching television. I began to make weekly house calls, during which his wife Rita, an excellent cook, fed us lunch.

At Case Western Reserve, where I attended medical school, there was a required course called Family Clinic in which we were assigned to be the student doctor to a pregnant woman and to follow her through pregnancy, labor, delivery, and subsequent well-baby visits. We made home visits to better learn the social situation of our patients and how it impacted their health. Almost all the Family Clinic patients were poor black women from the Hough ghetto in

Cleveland (which would erupt into rioting during the summer of my internship year). The lesson we learned was invaluable: Every patient's health was inextricably woven of many strands, and their home life, socioeconomic status, and intimate relationships all played vital roles.

I knew a little about Raymond's family. I knew he had two sisters, Grace and Ida, but by the time I met Raymond his brother Joseph had died. Grace, a tiny, timid woman who'd lost an eye in an auto accident, was soon to become my patient also. I knew about Raymond's testimony at Congressional hearings on organized crime in the 1950s because I'd read about them in newspapers and because the local television news often ran clips of him looking much younger and healthier than the man I knew, protesting that he was not a member of the Mafia. I knew that his first wife, Helen, had died of cancer, and that in 1975, shortly after being released from prison, he had married his long-term "cumara" (the slang term for mistress in the Neapolitan dialect), the former Rita O'Toole. Rita was a stout, blond, formidable Irish-American woman who brooked no nonsense from Raymond or anyone else. She bustled around the house cleaning, cooking, and caring for her pets, two toy poodles named Jabbo and Peppy. They were spoiled little fur-covered bladders on whom she doted.

I knew that Raymond had served time in prison on several occasions in the past and that he had achieved a mythic status with many of his fellow Italian-Americans in Rhode Island. Federal Hill, where his office was located, was considered one of the safest neighborhoods in the city. Women could walk the streets at any hour without fear of being molested. Muggings were unheard of, and burglaries or break-ins extremely rare.

While many revered him, it was also true that many people of Italian extraction loathed Raymond and all he stood for, resenting the fact that his criminal reputation cast a pall, by implication, over all his ethnic brethren, no matter how law-abiding they were.

By now, in addition to Junior, I had met Junior's second wife, Barbara, and his son Christopher, who was then nine years old. Christopher was an only child and Raymond Senior's only grandson. Junior told me ruefully that his first wife, whom he had met in college, had run off with her horse trainer. But other than these bare facts of Raymond's history and home life, I was unfamiliar with the details of his criminal past. Nor did I particularly want to know them. I didn't want to chance that such knowledge might influence my care of him. I didn't think it would, but I didn't want to risk it. I needed to deal with Raymond as I found him at that place and time. I felt the contradiction between the almost mystical power that people attributed to him and the crippled patient I saw, for whom the slightest stress could tip his health over the brink.

We both provoked strong feelings in others, and this was another reason I found myself identifying with him. My role was not to be his prosecutor or judge. My duty was to battle his disease with every weapon in the medical armamentarium and to do everything in my power to avert any stress that would endanger his fragile and fraught stability. William Osler, a pioneering physician in the nineteenth century, wrote: "The good physician treats the disease. The great physician treats the patient." My goal had always been to be a great physician, and while I rarely approached that goal, I think that in the years I was Raymond's physician, I, perhaps, came closest to achieving it.

⋙⋘

As 1981 slowly unfolded, starting with a bitterly cold winter, I had two overriding concerns: the ongoing custody battle with my daughter Meagan's father Ned, and the health of my most notorious patient. Without my asking, Raymond told me, tearfully, that he was innocent of ordering Curcio's murder. I neither believed nor disbelieved him. I thought that the informant could just as easily be telling the truth as making up stories and saying what he knew the police wanted to hear. Either way, it had no bearing on my duty as Raymond's physician. If it made Raymond feel better to tell me he was innocent, whether he was or not, then that was OK with me. I assured him that I would continue to be his physician no matter what, and finally told him, "Look, Raymond, you'll go to trial over my dead body!" At this, I won a rare smile from him.

On our weekly visits, I regaled him with stories of my past. It was clear we were not about to get into a discussion of his past. Like a latter-day Scheherazade, with the difference that he was the one facing an execution of sorts, not me, I told him about my childhood in Marycrest, my years as a pro-football wife and medical student, and my experiences in the anti-war and women's movement, all of which he at least pretended an interest in. And perhaps he really did find them interesting stories. I told him about my parents, my nine siblings, and about my Aunt Bea's sister-in-law who had been married to the notorious mobster Dutch Schultz's henchman, Marty Krompier. I occasionally teased him by saying, "You know, Raymond, I'm probably the only one of your doctors who has an FBI file as thick as your own."

In many ways, the doctor-patient relationship is a seduction; not a sexual one, but an emotional one. Unless a doctor can win a patient over emotionally, she cannot be effective in getting the patient to follow her advice. Particularly in heart disease, it is often necessary for patients to make radical changes in their life styles. This is impossible unless the patient enters into an alliance with the physician, and it's often difficult even then. I was lucky in that Raymond had already made the necessary changes. He had long ago stopped smoking cigarettes, followed a diabetic diet (Rita saw to that), and took his medicines faithfully. He still smoked cigars, but not as often as he had in the past. At one time, he'd been a heavy cigar smoker (hence one of his nicknames: Cigar), but by this time they were a rare indulgence. The legal proceedings that loomed were as dangerous to his fragile stability, if not more so, as any failure to follow the regimen I set for him—and his depression in the face of these trials only compounded his danger.

I cast about for ways to treat his depression and found one that always brightened his mood, at least temporarily. Meagan, a chatty four-year old, was now attending Montessori nursery school in the mornings, and on occasion I would pick her up at noontime and take her with me when I made my weekly house call on Raymond. In no time, she was calling him Uncle Raymond and chattering with him about all of her friends and their doings. Rita's younger pet poodle, Jabbo, took an immediate shine to Meagan and often tried to hump her leg. At this, Raymond would become apoplectic, shouting at the dog to stop and hurling rolled up newspapers at him until Rita rushed in to remove the offending canine. I was caught between wanting to laugh hysterically and fear that his anger at the dog would precipitate a cardiac arrest.

Meagan was unconcerned and soon looked forward to these visits, as Raymond took to slipping her a twenty-dollar bill when we left, telling her to take her mother out for a treat. Before long, Meagan would have her hand out as she went to kiss Raymond good-bye, which he found highly amusing, perhaps recognizing something of himself in the brash four-year-old.

One Sunday, fearing that he was going stir-crazy from being cooped up in the house twenty-four-hours-a-day with only the television and Rita for company, I insisted that we all go for an outing. He was reluctant at first, always wary of causing more problems for me than I already had and giving ammunition to those who claimed that he wasn't all that sick, but I told him that if I accompanied him, it was unlikely that one trip to a restaurant would prove he was well enough to stand trial. On a brisk, sunny day that winter, Rita, Junior's wife Barbara, Meagan and I all piled into his 1969 Cadillac and headed for the Coast Guard House, a restaurant located right on the ocean in Narragansett. The crowds that flock to its dining rooms and decks in the summer weren't there, and we managed to have a quiet lunch, attracting only a few stares and whispered comments from the other diners.

On the drive back, Meagan decided that we all had to take turns singing stanzas of "Old MacDonald Had a Farm," one of her favorites, and we each had to choose an animal when it was our turn. When it was Raymond's turn, if he hesitated and did not immediately come up with an animal, Meg scolded him, "Come on, Uncle Raymond, it's YOUR TURN!" It was hilarious to hear the four-year-old bossing around the Boss, as he did his best to keep up with the singing. It remains one of my favorite memories of that time.

The outing to the Coast Guard House would prove to be a brief respite. The forces of law and order were closing in for another go-round.

PART TWO

Left:

*Dorothea Farrell Hudson
and Alan Hudson
on their wedding day,
January 30, 1943.*

Below:

*Young Archie Roberts,
"Big Archie," and
Dory, 1971.*

Right:

Dory Roberts, young Archie, "Big" Archie, and Barbara at a Columbia University football game, 1970.

Below:

Barbara Roberts sailing Boadicea, *1980s.*

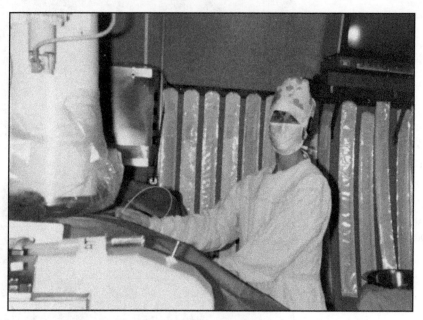

Dr. Barbara Roberts performing a cardiac catheterization.

Left:

Barbara Roberts speaking at the last mass anti-Vietnam war demonstration, January 1973.

Ned Bresnahan and Meagan, 1976.

Young Archie Roberts, Meagan, Ned Bresnahan and Dory, 1976.

3 · MARYCREST

Religion is the opiate of the masses.
—Karl Marx

Opiates are the religion of the masses.
—Ed Willock

I'm often asked why I became a doctor, and I always reply, "Because I couldn't become a priest." Of course, nothing is ever so simple. And now, decades after the Catholic Church and I parted company, it strikes me as inconceivable that I was a "believer" for so long. But throughout my childhood and for years beyond, the most powerful influence in my life was the Catholic religion.

I was born a month after the Normandy invasion in 1944 to Dorothy Farrell Hudson, a twenty-two-year old housewife in New York City, and Alan Hudson, twenty-four, who was then serving in the Navy. My mother was a slim, shy woman with an unmistakably Irish face and masses of wavy dark brown hair, which she sometimes wore rolled up behind her ears in the fashion of the 1940s. In pictures from that time, her eyes have a startled look, as if the camera had surprised her in some reverie she would have preferred to enjoy unobserved, but they reflect none of the sadness that would reside there in later years. There was a sweetness and an innocence in her face, with its wide hazel eyes and rounded cheeks that dimpled when she smiled. My father was thin and almost six feet tall. He, too, had dark wavy hair and regular features. As a young child I adored him, missing him fiercely when he was away, hurling myself at his legs whenever he returned from work to our one-bedroom apartment on Marion Avenue in the Bronx.

My mother was Irish on both sides, my father a combination of Irish, English, and German ancestry. During World War II, many of his friends were sent overseas, but my father spent the war years typing intelligence reports at the Brooklyn Naval Yard. In addition to his academic subjects, he'd studied stenography and typing at Bishop Loughlin High School in Brooklyn, and he was one of the hundreds of stenographers and typists recruited by the U.S. Naval Intelligence Service in the months before Pearl Harbor.

Over the next ten years, my parents had nine more children so that in a little over a decade my mother gave birth to ten children. Their first son was born eleven months after I was, but he was premature and died a few weeks later. They then had five more daughters, and my father began to run out of names. There's a Catholic prayer, the Litany of Our Lady, which was popular in my family. In it, Christ's mother is called by all her many titles; Queen of Heaven, Mystical Rose, Lady Mary, and so on. My father turned to the Latin version of the litany for girls' names, so I have sisters named Mary Regina, Donna Maria, Regina Coeli, and Rosa Mystica. When my mother became pregnant yet again, my parents' friend Frank Sheed, of the publishing firm Sheed and Ward, growled, "What's the next one going to be, Alan? Consolatrix Afflictorum?" (Comforter of the Afflicted). Luckily for the next one, it turned out to be my first surviving brother, who was named Edwin Duffy after our family priest. Edwin was followed by another son, Matthew, born in 1953, and another daughter, Victoria, born in 1954. My parents had their last child, my brother Mark, in 1959.

In my early childhood, my father was selling life insurance in an Italian neighborhood in the Bronx, where for the first time he was exposed to Italian food and culture, particularly opera. He fell in love with both. He bought an Italian cookbook, which he brought home to my mother and said, "Here, learn to cook these dishes." So, despite being mostly Irish, I grew up eating homemade pizza, chicken cacciatore, and spaghetti with meatballs and sausage.

By the time I was four, my parents had become friendly with a group of other young Catholic couples with growing families. They belonged to the Christian Family Movement whose members sought to live their lives in strict obedience to the dictates of the Catholic Church—particularly its prohibition on birth control—and who, like the earliest Christians, put a strong emphasis on communal prayer and communal life. United in their desire to raise their children in "the country" away from the dangers and temptations of the big city, they hoped to form a Christian community that would engage in subsistence farming and other cooperative ventures. They bought fifty-five acres of woodland in Rockland County, twenty-five miles north of New York City, and there they established a community they named Marycrest.

My mother's twin sister, Aunt Bea, and her son Bernie lived a few blocks from us in the Bronx. When my mother was pregnant yet again, Bea and Bernie moved with us to Marycrest so that Bea could help my parents with their growing brood. Bea's husband, my uncle Bernie Clark, had been killed in a plane crash on his way to the war in the Pacific when Bernie was three months old; he died before ever seeing his son.

My family's only prior brush with mobsters was through Aunt Bea's in-laws. Uncle Bernie had a sister, Catherine Clark, who was a Ziegfeld Follies dancer. As I was to tell my most infamous patient years later, Catherine caught the eye of Marty Krompier, an associate of the infamous gangster Dutch Schultz, and sometime in the 1930s, as my parents remembered, Catherine and Marty were married. Krompier was said to be the brains of the Dutch Schultz gang, much as Meyer Lansky was the brains of the mafia, and like Lansky, he was

Jewish. Krompier also "owned" prizefighters, but because of his criminal record he had to use front men. He was very friendly with Jack Dempsey, although Dempsey was not among the fighters he managed. My father remembered visiting the Krompiers with my mother in 1941 and seeing a picture of Dempsey inscribed, "To my friend Marty the Sheik, my best always, Jack."

Marty, who never smoked or drank, was a flashy dresser, always dapper. He collected jade and there was jade bric-a-brac all over their house. Krompier was with Dutch Schultz the day Schultz was gunned down; he received multiple gunshot wounds himself, but survived. According to family lore, this was because he was a health food and exercise fanatic, which at the time was rather uncommon. At Uncle Bernie's wake, Marty Krompier slipped Aunt Bea a 100-dollar bill, quite a lot money in those days.

⚜

Our house in Marycrest was far from finished when we moved there. An oil-fired generator supplied minimal electric power, enough to light a few lamps and pump water from the artesian well to the faucets, but not enough to run the refrigerator. A large tank of propane gas sat outside to provide fuel for the cooking stove. The toilet was hooked up to a septic tank, which periodically backed up and had to be pumped out. There was no central heating, just a coal-burning pot-bellied stove in the living room.

In December, a second family, the Willocks, moved to Marycrest. Their house was located about fifty yards from ours, across the dirt road into the community from Sickletown Road, itself a narrow (but paved) country lane. The half-mile dirt access road was often impassable that winter, so a week before my mother's due date, she moved in with friends in the nearby town of Tappan so that she could reach the hospital in time. When she gave birth to yet another daughter, I was bitterly disappointed. I longed for a little brother.

Ed and Dorothy Willock had six children at that time. Dorothy was a plain woman with straight brown hair, a prognathous jaw, and a strong Boston accent. She was the only one of the Marycrest wives to have attended college, but this brush with higher education did little to prepare her for the ceaseless bearing and rearing of children in dire poverty. Ed Willock was an intense, edgy man, a disciple of the radical Catholic pacifist Dorothy Day, the founder of the Catholic Worker movement.

The Willock children were already a wild bunch, shocking the timid, well-behaved Hudson daughters with curse words, screaming fights, and a blithe disregard of their parents' infrequent attempts to impose order. Dorothy Willock explained her disinclination to discipline her children by saying, "I don't want to break their spirit." She looked down on my mother's incessant battle against dirt and disorder. To Dorothy, a clean house implied a lack of devotion to God, and a certain spiritual sloppiness.

Of all the Marycrest families, we were closest to the Dermodys. Uncle Jacky, as we called him, had been my father's best friend since they were teenagers. He epitomized the word "hypomanic" long before I heard it spoken or understood its meaning. He delighted in debating arcane points of Catholic dogma with my father, and many a night I fell asleep listening to their contrapuntal voices wafting up from the living room. My sister Mary remembers that one of their interminable discussions revolved around the question of whether or not the new invention, television, was "intrinsically evil"—a position held by Carol Jackson, a co-publisher with Ed Willock of the Catholic magazine, *Integrity*.

For children from the Bronx, Rockland County was a primeval wonderland, and Marycrest was a forested sanctuary where we romped and played. Over the next few years, more families built homes and moved to Marycrest. Each family had five or more children, and the parents set about fulfilling their community's raison d'être: to create saints. Catholicism permeated every aspect of our lives. We celebrated our saints' feast days as well as our birthdays. Every Catholic child had to be named after a saint in order to be baptized, and every Catholic baby had to be baptized in order to attain heaven.

We were raised to be saints, preferably martyrs. If you died for your faith, no matter how sinful a life you had led, you went straight to Heaven without having to do penance for your sins in purgatory. Nothing was more important than obeying the laws of the Church. My father's favorite saying was, "Rally 'round your priests blindly." We were taught that the thirteenth century, the "Century of Saints and Scholars" was the zenith of civilization and that everything had been downhill since then. We were woefully ignorant of the outside world, cocooned in our left-wing Catholic commune, taught in school by nuns—celibate women who were "brides of Christ."

Gradually, Marycrest became well known in Catholic circles. Many visitors came to see how this latest attempt to create a utopia was faring. Dorothy Day was a frequent visitor, and on April 24, 1952 she gave a talk at our house that attracted people from all over Rockland County. My mother was pregnant with my brother Edwin—in fact she would give birth the next day. Her major memory of the talk is that there were seats for everyone but her.

Young seminarians and Maryknoll missionary nuns home from stints abroad, where they preached Catholicism to the "heathens" of exotic lands like the Belgian Congo, also visited Marycrest. They made a deep impression on me. We were taught that good Catholic women should either marry another Catholic and have as many children as God sent or become nuns, taking vows of poverty, chastity, and obedience. An independent life as a single woman, even one leading a blameless existence, was frowned upon.

When I asked how babies were made, my mother explained that when you got married, if God loved you and you obeyed his commandments, you were blessed with children. I decided that God must love my parents and the other Marycrest parents a very great deal indeed. However, I was not blind to the suffering these constant pregnancies inflicted. I could see the distortion of my mother's body and how often she appeared exhausted or in pain. Her workday ended when she dropped into bed at night; vacations were a thing of the past. Her days were a round of cooking, cleaning, changing stinky diapers, doing laundry, battling dirt, ironing clothes, wiping snotty noses, feeding babies, and scrubbing floors on her hands and knees. If not quite *Angela's Ashes*, our home life was still a very unappealing prospect for my future.

I decided I would become a nun when I grew up. What I really wanted to be was a man, but I knew that was impossible. Men had a much better deal. They didn't get pregnant. None of the scut work was their responsibility—they could leave and go to some job that got them out of the house. Their word was law. Boys got to be altar boys, helping the priest during Mass, and when they grew up they could be priests. Of course I wanted to be a man. Who wouldn't?

When I announced my intention to be a nun, my mother would say, "Yeah, the Order of Perpetual Recreation," or "the Order of Two Heads on One Pillow," but I was quite certain that being a nun was preferable to getting married. Nuns in those days lived in convents and wore habits that left only their faces—from eyebrows to chin— and hands exposed. They were mysterious and forbidding creatures. Some were patient and kind, but others were frankly sadistic.

A turning point in my life occurred in 1952. Shortly before my brother Edwin was born, a simmering conflict between my father and Aunt Bea came to a head. The unspoken substrate of their antipathy was their rivalry for my mother's love. Contributing to the fraught atmosphere in our home was the jealousy I felt for my Aunt Bea's son, cousin Bernie. Tensions between my father and aunt accelerated, and eventually, Bea and Bernie moved out. Within a few months, Aunt Bea would meet and marry her second husband, Joe Greaney, a widower with two daughters.

Bea's leaving meant that the responsibility for being mother's helper fell squarely on my shoulders. When my mother went to the hospital to have the baby who would become my first surviving brother, I stayed home from school and took care of the younger children. At eight years of age, I could cook meals, bake cakes, do the laundry, hang the wash, change the diapers, and mind my younger siblings with no adult in attendance. With Bea gone, the carefree years of my early childhood were over. I had responsibilities heaped on my shoulders, which I resented and tried to evade.

My reluctance provoked anger and punishment from my father, who was working long hours himself to support his large family. In addition to his job as a freight solicitor, which now necessitated him traveling throughout the state of New York, he spent the weekends either helping build the other Marycrest houses or typing patent applications for Chas Neill, an early Marycrest benefactor and local attorney. And he began drinking more and more. He had started keeping a journal at the age of eighteen, which he called *Thy Days Are Numbered*, a title that neatly encapsulated his preoccupation with time and death. Each entry was preceded by the number of days he'd been alive. His journal reveals that he began drinking to excess as a teenager.

In adulthood, as his family grew, as there were more and more mouths to feed, more and more bills to pay, his drinking accelerated. He excused this by saying that he had to drink because his job entailed taking out shipping agents and entertaining them. All alcoholics give you reasons why they drink too much. In his cups, my father castigated me for my failing to be more helpful with household chores: "You're such an ingrate. Your mother needs your help and you're always shirking."

Although he was never physically violent, he would work himself up into a rage and rail at me for what seemed like hours on end. I suffered these bouts in silence, but later would often burst into tears of anguish and humiliation. To this day, my palms get sweaty, my pulse races, and I cringe in the presence of a drunken man. My father went from drinking mainly at parties to getting, and staying, drunk for days at a time. The handsome, vital father whom I adored as a little girl was becoming a stranger to me—one I came increasingly to fear and from whom I increasingly wanted to escape.

In my memories of those years, my mother is always pregnant, always cooking or cleaning or feeding a baby. She had a great store of expressions that I only later realized were Irish, handed down from her own mother. She described her brother-in-law Frankie as looking "as Irish as Paddy's pig." If we complained about an ache or a pain, she would say, "You always have an annie or an elbow," or "it'll be better before you're twice married." When we asked what was for dinner, which we invariably did, she would respond, "Bee's knees and crow's kidneys, and monkey knuckles for dessert." She referred to anyone who was big and clumsy as an "omadon," and when frightened, she exclaimed, "Jesus, Mary, and Joseph!" even when I priggishly informed her that this was blasphemy. She accused us of being "thick as thieves" and warned us that "empty barrels make the most noise." If she thought someone was cheap or stingy, she said, "He wouldn't give his ghee to the crows." I know now that she was heroic, but as a child I wanted nothing more than to have a life as far removed from hers as it was possible to imagine.

Although I was bossy and overbearing, I was also fiercely protective of my siblings. I could pick out their cries from those of any other Marycrest child and came running out of the house, fists flying, if I heard one of them sobbing. I had in full measure what Mary Cantwell describes in her memoir, *Scenes from a Small Town Childhood*, as "that passion to protect which sooner or later is the curse of the oldest child." In retrospect, this fierce protective instinct was, perhaps, nowhere more apparent than in the years I was Raymond Patriarca's physician.

By the time I was in the eighth grade, I was aware of a darkness pervading my parents' marriage. Their quarrels were muted, occurring late at night when they thought us asleep and unable to hear, but on occasion I was awakened by raised voices from their bedroom, unable to distinguish meaning but tortured by the certainty that dangerous currents were swirling about the ship that was our family, threatening to drag us down into some calamitous abyss. Later I realized that these arguments arose from my mother's fear of another pregnancy. The only form of birth control allowed Catholics was the rhythm method, also called "Vatican roulette,"—the confining of sexual intercourse to the times in a woman's cycle when she was infertile. Even to practice the rhythm method, Catholic couples had to have a good reason and dispensation from their parish priest. Giving birth to ten children in ten years was not considered, a priori, an adequate reason. Catholic women were expected to defer to their husband's decisions in all things and to submit to the will of God without question, no matter how many children they were "blessed" with as a result.

I desperately wanted to escape from my increasingly chaotic home. I was able to win a scholarship to a Catholic girls' boarding school, Our Lady of the Blessed Sacrament Academy (also called Broadlea) in Goshen, NY. Before going away to boarding school, I was ignorant of all things sexual. I did not understand the reason for the strained relations between my parents, or their frequent retreats into emotionally charged silences, during which they ceased to communicate directly but sent messages to each other through me or my sister Mary. I only knew that my mother was engaged in a mysterious struggle with my father, whose cause was unfathomable to me but whose emotional fallout was poisoning the very air I breathed. My father was drinking more and more heavily. His friends called him Al, and as we got older, we took to referring to him as "Al Cohol."

I arrived in Goshen in September 1957 looking more like a ten-year old than a thirteen- year-old. I was inches shorter and a year younger than all of my classmates, having skipped a grade in grammar school. (This occurred when we were learning about homonyms. The teacher asked for examples and my response was "world and whirled." The next day I was taken out of the third grade and put into the fourth.) I had never traveled farther from home than rare trips to Worcester, Massachusetts to visit my father's sister Aunt Evelyn and her family. My classmates came mostly from the Northeast but a few were from South America, daughters of wealthy Venezuelans, Colombians, Cubans, and Mexicans who sent their children to boarding school in the United States so that they would become fluent in English. They arrived knowing only Spanish and seemed impossibly beautiful and exotic. Their olive complexions were never marred by the blemishes that spotted the faces of the American girls. They dressed with elegance and flair, and they had pierced ears with real gold earrings. I longed to own one of the black lace mantillas they wore on their heads to chapel, wanting to look as sultry and brimming with mystery as they did.

All of our teachers were nuns. One told us pointedly that our parents had sent us to them because "they want you to be taught by someone who has never descended to the level of animals." I was unsure exactly what she meant by this comment, but knowing how much my mother suffered and toiled to bear and raise her children, I was resentful and felt insulted on her behalf.

Each night I lay awake wondering what was happening at home. How was my mother faring without me to help her with the little ones? Who was comforting them when they fell or had an earache? Who was flying to their defense in the endless round of children's squabbles? How much was my father drinking, and who was now the target of his drunken anger? Gradually, these concerns receded as I made friends and was absorbed into the hothouse atmosphere of an isolated all-girls school.

My first and longest lasting friend was Mary Liz Keogh, who was to have a profound effect on my life. She was a sophomore, but like me had skipped a grade and was younger than her classmates. Also like me, she was physically immature and brainy. There the resemblance ended. She had kinky strawberry-blond hair, close-set eyes, a pug nose, and the fair Irish complexion that never tans but turns an angry red on exposure to the sun. She came from a wealthy family and was brash, irreverent, and foul-mouthed. Her uncle Eugene Keogh was a Congressman from Brooklyn, the author of legislation that resulted in the Keogh retirement plans. Her father was a judge on the New York State Supreme Court. She answered back, she talked in chapel, she was irrepressible.

I wanted nothing more than to be like her. No more being teacher's pet for me. I took my first timid steps into waywardness, amassing demerits for transgressions such as passing notes in class, neglecting to wear stockings, or handing in assignments late. I found I could make people laugh, and I set myself the task of becoming popular. By the time sophomore year rolled around, I had been elected Vice President of the class and was a member of the dominant clique. More important to me, that summer between freshman and sophomore years saw the onset of my periods, a milestone I had begun to despair of despite my decidedly ambiguous feelings about becoming a woman.

By the start of my sophomore year of high school, I had undergone a complete metamorphosis from the biddable, obedient teacher's pet

I'd been in grammar school. I was now a cut-up, a wise-cracker, one of the leaders of a coterie of popular girls who were looked up to by the more sedate misses. Being defiant was exciting, scary, and thrilling all at the same time. I was bursting out of a cocoon; I was trying my wings. It was something I HAD to do. I had been imprisoned by Catholic strictures, inhibited by fear of sin and going to Hell, but I knew that I had to grow beyond those fears or be forever enslaved. If I didn't, I would wind up with the kind of life that my mother and the other Marycrest women suffered.

I was growing out of my gawky, geeky stage. My hair was no longer cut short just below my ears but reached almost to my shoulders. Each year of high school, I grew an inch and gained ten pounds. My breasts, although still so small as to be a source of despair and embarrassment, were no longer just buds, and I could finally wear a bra. My nickname, bestowed by two Venezuelan classmates, was *Espinita*, short for *espinita pescado* (spiny fish) because they said that my breasts were so tiny and pointy that they reminded them of the spines on a spiny fish. I dared to hope that someday I might even be pretty, and thoughts of entering the convent and becoming a nun faded away. I continued to excel in the classroom, getting the highest grades in the class. I soaked up learning greedily and read voraciously.

Despite my stabs at rebellion, at heart I remained a good Catholic girl, chaste, devout, and certain that my faith was the one, true faith. I spent hours in prayer earnestly entreating God to reveal His plans for me. I still went to Mass and tried to commit only venial sins—the less serious sins that just got you time in purgatory, not an eternity in Hell. I was trying to work out a way to be a good Catholic but not end up married with ten children—and it was becoming apparent to me that nuns didn't have a better deal. They just inhabited a different prison. I had to come up with a way to be Catholic and free. That was oxymoronic, but at the time I wasn't ready to admit that.

When I was ten, a television program about the teeming microscopic life in a puddle of water piqued my interest in science. I read about Marie Curie, the first woman to win the Nobel Prize for physics, and she became my role model. I decided that I, too, would become a nuclear physicist, and signed my diary "M. Curie."

When Mary Liz was a senior, she made a shocking announcement: "I've decided to become a doctor."

"Really?" I asked, "Isn't that almost impossible for a woman?"

"I know it's not easy, but I'm going to do it," she assured me—falsely, as it turned out.

My ambition to be a nuclear physicist seemed less unrealistic. It was common knowledge that it was very difficult for women to gain acceptance to medical schools, that women made up less than ten percent of the student body, and that admission standards were higher for female applicants than for male. Astonishingly, we never questioned this. But Mary Liz was determined and made an important first step by being accepted into the Class of 1964 at Barnard College, the women's undergraduate college of Columbia University in New York City. Barnard was one of the "Seven Sisters," the female equivalent of the Ivy League. Its curriculum was rigorous, its student body noted for brains and achievement (which were perceived as unfeminine qualities).

During my senior year of high school, I suffered a bout of pneumonia and that was the direct cause of the fateful decision I made at the tender age of sixteen. Like the proverbial bolt out of the blue, I was seized with the desire to study medicine. If Mary Liz could decide to be a doctor, so could I. I would still be a scientist of sorts, but I would also be a healer, a comforter. People would look up to me, and I would make my father proud. As difficult as our relationship was, I still wanted him to love me and take pride in me. There were times I hated and feared my father, but there were other times when I longed for him to gather me in his arms and tell me how proud of me he was, how much he loved and appreciated me. He never did, but that didn't stop me from trying to make it happen.

My father reserved his greatest admiration for priests and doctors. I knew I didn't have a prayer of becoming a priest—that radical notion had not occurred to women in those pre-Women's Liberation days—but it *was* possible for a woman to be a doctor. It was one of the few wise choices I made as a young woman.

By the time I graduated high school, I was a very different person from the frightened prepubescent girl I was when I arrived there. I had changed in ways both trivial and profound. Physically I had become a woman, although like most young women—particularly those growing up flat-chested in the America of that time—I was dissatisfied with my appearance. I had noticed boys noticing me and was taking note of them in return. I had not experienced lust or even desire, but I was aware and interested in men in a way I had never been before. I was no longer bound for the convent but was still intent on avoiding the fate of my mother, the domestic drudgery and endless childbearing. If this meant I would never marry, then so be it. I still believed in the Catholic teaching that extramarital sex and using artificial methods of birth control were mortal sins. It was inconceivable to me that I would ever rebel against the dictates of the Church. I was secure, even smug, in my faith. But a bedrock stubbornness, a fundamental resolve to be my own person, was crystallizing out of all the amorphous fears and desires I struggled to contain.

❧

I'd applied to several Catholic women's colleges but now decided that my chances of getting admitted to medical school would be greater if I went to one of the Seven Sisters schools. I chose Barnard so I could be reunited with Mary Liz, who had been accepted there. My father, however, was insistent that I attend a Catholic college and refused to sign the Barnard application. All my entreaties were to no avail. Finally, I had the brilliant idea to appeal to my parent's friend, Father Duffy, who was then the chaplain of the Newman Club, the Catholic student's club at Columbia University. He agreed to intercede for me and convinced my father that I would not *necessarily* become a Communist if I went to Barnard. My father relented, and a few months later I received a letter of acceptance into the Class of 1965. I had won a New York State Regents Scholarship, and Barnard granted me additional scholarship money since my parents were unable to afford the tuition.

My freshman year at Barnard was fast approaching, an event I both longed for and dreaded. I intuited just how sheltered a life I had led and just how dissimilar my upbringing was from the norm. For one thing, I did not know one person who was not Catholic. I knew no Protestants, no Jews, no atheists. In Catholic school, we were taught that all non-Catholics were to be pitied and feared: pitied because they were not members of the one true faith, and feared because they would try to lead us astray. Only constant vigilance insured that the purity of our faith would survive exposure to the sinful world outside the bastion of Catholic institutions. This was why my father was so opposed to my attending a secular college.

In addition, over the summer between high school and college, I had briefly dated a fellow member of the Catholic Youth Organization. He was the President of the CYO, and like me, a devout, faithful child of the Church. I was thrilled when this handsome, admired college man asked me out on a date. It was the first time I'd been asked out by someone to whom I was attracted.

One night in the back of a car, after the friends we were with had wandered off to give us some time alone, he turned to me, took me in his arms, and kissed me. My body was instantly suffused with a warmth that radiated from that dangerous, forbidden area between my legs to envelop my whole being. I went weak with desire and would have fallen if I'd been standing. Trembling and panting, I broke off the embrace as the ravening beast of sexual appetite clamped me in its jaws for the first time. Here was something I had never envisioned: that I would be so sorely tempted to transgress the Church's dictates on chastity; that I might, in the end, be no different from those girls who "got in trouble" and disgraced themselves and their families; that I might, if I were not careful, wreck my dream of becoming a doctor on the shoals of Sex.

Physically and emotionally I had crossed a fateful Rubicon, and there would be no turning back. Over the next several years, I waged a rear-guard action against my sexual urges. It exacted a huge emotional toll, and ultimately, I lost the war. And so, as the date for my matriculation at Barnard approached, I prayed fervently that I would be able to resist all the temptations and blandishments that college life would lob my way. At the same time, I looked forward to dances, fraternity parties, football games, and the chance to meet new friends and study with new professors.

4 · The Learning Years

Change is the end result of all true learning.
—Leo Buscaglia

During freshman year at Barnard, I discovered that drinking blunted the free-floating anxiety I felt, which coalesced most often around the antipodes of sex and study. Alcohol simultaneously dulled my nascent libido and stimulated me to display a sham sexiness. Before long, my roommate Tupi Shute, a blond-haired, blue-eyed Tennessean, and I had more dates and invitations to fraternity parties than we could handle and still maintain good grades. We evolved a buddy system. We took turns drinking at parties, with the sober one making sure that the drunk roommate got back to our dorm safe and before curfew. I ruthlessly repressed any consciousness that I was aping the behavior in my father that had caused me so much pain and embarrassment.

My freshman courses included Chemistry, Psychology, Spanish, and English. The academic courses were more challenging than any I had taken in high school, requiring many hours of study. Five nights a week, I went to the library directly after supper and studied until ten or eleven. On Friday and Saturday nights, Tupi and I went out on dates or to parties. I made sure that anyone who asked me out knew that I was a pre-med student and had no intentions of getting "serious" with anyone until I finished medical school. I worried that my grades would not be good enough. I knew that even with good grades, women faced discrimination in medical school admissions— the kind of discrimination that today would be unthinkable, not to mention illegal. The Women's Movement was still several years in the future.

Only the very top female applicants won admission to medical school, and then only if they convinced the admissions committee that they were not going to drop out to marry and have children. Having announced to all and sundry that I was going to be a doctor, I felt enormous pressure to achieve this goal. The thought that I might not kept me awake nights. By the time each weekend rolled around, I was a cauldron bubbling with repressed sexual urges and fear of failure. My response to this was to drink more and more.

It was during my freshman year at Barnard that I first experienced alcoholic blackouts, drinking so much that afterwards I could not remember what I had said or done, or how I had gotten back to the dorm.

The constant tension between Catholic dictates on sex and my growing libido was a torment. It never occurred to me to assuage my libido with masturbation. In fact, I assumed that masturbation was something only men did, and I believed it was a mortal sin leading to eternal damnation, mental illness, and stunted moral growth. I languished in a cauldron of sexual frustration, allied with guilt and despair. If I could not have sex outside marriage, and I could not get married until after I completed medical school and internship—some ten years in the future—how would I survive? I began to envy those classmates who were not saddled with Catholic scruples and guilt. Their only worries were not getting a reputation for being "fast" and avoiding pregnancy. My Catholic girlfriends and I had a tougher row to hoe and used to joke that we should write a dating manual entitled, "What to do till the priest arrives." Years later, after surviving custody disputes in four different states and various costly love affairs, I swore that I was going to write a dating how-to book to be called: "What to Do Till Your Libido Dies: How to Get Laid Without Getting Screwed."

Despite the weekends spent partying and drinking, I finished my freshman year with a 3.37 grade-point average and decided to try to gain acceptance to medical school after my junior year. This was possible by choosing a program called Professional Option, which allowed a junior to apply a year early to medical school. If she was accepted, Barnard counted the first year of medical school as the senior year of college. This would save time and a considerable amount of money.

That summer, I rented an apartment with two Barnard classmates on 107th Street off Broadway. We all had summer jobs and spent little time at the apartment, except to sleep. I worked as a secretary for Diesel Construction Company, which was then building the Americana Hotel in midtown Manhattan. I was dating a Columbia University sophomore, and when he broke up with me, I turned to alcohol for comfort. One night, alone in the apartment which by now had a serious roach infestation, I drank myself insensible, everything I could lay my hands on, and when the booze was gone, the better part of a bottle of cough medicine with codeine. The resulting hangover was agony, but did not dissuade me from getting drunk again the next night. I met some friends at the West End Bar and proceeded to drink myself into oblivion.

I was awakened by screams. Somewhere nearby a woman was screaming, and then I realized that the woman was me. Just as this realization hit me, a mouth, open and slobbering, clamped down on mine, shutting off the noise I had been making and I became aware of something else, something far more frightening than even those screams. I was naked from the waist down, my legs were splayed apart and what felt like a battering ram was relentlessly pounding at me, seeking entrance. I recognized my assailant. He was a recently graduated senior, a football player, one of my ex-boyfriend's fraternity brothers. Horror overwhelmed me, and I blacked out again. When I awoke in the morning I was alone on a pull-out couch. I stumbled into the bathroom of an apartment that I had no recollection of entering. I looked in the mirror. There were no marks on my haggard face. When

I urinated and wiped myself, I was sore and felt bruised, but there did not appear to be any bleeding. I wracked my brain trying to remember more of what had happened, but it was hopeless.

Had I been raped? I knew that there had been at least an attempt, but had it been successful? Did I need to worry that I could be pregnant? Well, yes, of course, I did. I dressed hurriedly and left the apartment, making my way through the early morning streets of the Upper West Side in a daze, heartsick, terrified, ashamed, hungover, and guilt ridden. The term "date rape" had not yet been coined. By drinking to the point where I was, to all intents and purposes, "out of my mind," I was "asking for it." I felt that I had only myself to blame, and the thought of going to the police didn't enter my head. I stumbled through the day like a sleepwalker.

Incredibly, I began drinking again that evening, being careful this time not to get to the point where I would have a blackout, stoking up the courage to go back to the apartment and find out what had happened. My attacker was not there, but when I told his roommate that I thought I might have been raped the night before, he unfolded the sofa bed, pulled back the blanket, pointed to the sheet—which wasn't stained with blood—and said, "If you were a virgin when you came here, you were a virgin when you left." Wretched and mortified, I walked home, none the wiser. I had no one to turn to.

I fantasized a future in which I was an outcast, an unwed mother, subsisting with the child of a rape on welfare, cut off forever from my dream of becoming a white-coated, respected physician. I didn't consider abortion, which as a Catholic I considered beyond the pale—and besides, I would have had no idea how to go about obtaining one in those days of back alley, illegal operations. And yet, I knew that if I were pregnant I could never give up this child, who had not asked to be conceived, to be raised by strangers. In 1962, the stigma of out-of-wedlock motherhood was horrific, but I knew I would suffer that ostracism rather than give up a child of my body.

Finally, about a week later, in despair while I waited to see if I was pregnant, I went to confession in a church far away from the campus. I was afraid I might be recognized if I went to the church where I attended Sunday Mass.

The priest had a foreign accent. I poured out the story of what had happened and asked for forgiveness. He was a benevolent, compassionate soul, who gently told me that I must resolve to stop drinking. He assured me that whether or not sexual intercourse had occurred, I was morally still a virgin, because I had not consented to what had been done to me. I took great comfort from his words and started to heal. When my period started, two weeks later, I offered ecstatic prayers of thanksgiving. I stopped drinking completely. Now when I went to the West End Bar and a man offered to buy me a beer, I'd say, "No thanks, but I'd love some French fries. They cost the same." In fact, by that time, between loss of appetite from depression, drinking to excess, and poverty, I was suffering from malnutrition. I was thinner than ever and had bleeding gums. When school started and I could eat my fill in the dining hall, I piled my plate high with as many vegetables as it would hold

I swore off alcohol completely and saved every penny I could, since Barnard had cut my scholarship despite my good grades. I looked forward to the start of sophomore year, no longer anxious about my ability to handle the academic load.

During the summer between my freshman and sophomore years at Barnard, my freshman year roommate Tupi and her boyfriend Al Butts, a member of the football team, had shocked the Columbia community by getting married. The cynics on campus were convinced that Tupi was pregnant, but when four or five months had gone by and there was no baby in the offing, the rumors died down.

Tupi and I attended every Columbia football game, home and away, that fall. I began dating a sophomore fullback, Ed Malmstrom, a shy, small-town boy from Kane, Pennsylvania. He had a noticeable gap between his front teeth, one of which was chipped from a football injury. This caused him to have a slight lisp that was incongruous with the rest of his rugged appearance. He lifted weights and had a beautiful, chiseled physique. Tremendously strong, he was able to bench-press 250 pounds. His blonde hair was close-cropped. He had a sweet smile and an aw-shucks demeanor. He pined for the hills and forests of western Pennsylvania and talked of little else. He had an almost casual attitude to football. In fact, he had not been recruited as a football player. He was spotted by the coaches one day while he was working out in a track uniform and was invited to join the gridiron squad on the spot.

I was not in love, or infatuated, but I liked him tremendously and enjoyed his company. He was a lackadaisical Protestant and would try to push our physical relationship farther than I wanted to let it go, but in an almost joking way, and he always acquiesced good-naturedly to the limits I set. I never let him know how tempted I was to let nature takes its course. That whole year we dated, I felt an unspoken sadness that I would never know what it felt like to be possessed physically by such a gentle, beautiful boy.

Sophomore year at Barnard was a happy time. The weeks passed quickly with classes by day and study at the library in the evenings, except for Friday and Saturday nights, when I spent time with Ed at fraternity parties or college dances. I was thrilled that fall when there was an article in the *New York Times* about Archie Roberts, the sophomore quarterback, which included a picture of Ed. In the photo, Archie is delivering a newspaper to Ed who is depicted in his undershirt at the door to his room. The caption reads, "At New Hall where he lives, Roberts deliver a paper to Eddie Malmstrom of Kane, Pa., also on the squad. Although a sophomore, Roberts is Light Blue's recognized leader." The article was headlined: "Archie Roberts: Columbia's Answer to Frank Merriwell." The sub headline read: "Ace 2d-year Back Amazes Everyone by His Qualities." The article, by Howard Tuckner, went on to say:

> *Arthur James (Archie) Roberts has blue eyes, wakes up at 6:45 A.M. to deliver newspapers, never misses midnight sessions of the dormitory council, loves dogs, attends Mass faithfully, never cuts class. He is respectful to elders, holds doors open for homely co-eds, has his own radio program, gets good marks, works with retarded children, telephones his mother regularly, shines his own shoes. And he never tells anybody that he is perhaps the greatest quarterback Columbia has ever had. There are*

those who believe that Archie Roberts does not exist, that he is merely a paste-board figure from a Wheaties box. Others are ready to swear that he wears a halo, is 99 44/100 per cent pure and that on football Saturdays he floats up Broadway and lands in Baker Field. But those who know him say he is the nicest, sweetest, corniest guy who ever wore a pair of white bucks.

Archie was much as described by the press, a polite, affable, very handsome young man. I found him rather insipid. He and Ed were members of Alpha Chi Rho, one of the Columbia fraternities, and the one with the highest percentage of football "jocks." Archie was still dating his high school girlfriend, but shortly after the start of sophomore year, they broke up.

My marks for sophomore year were all A's or B's and I wrote off to medical schools in the New York area requesting applications to the Class of 1968. Ed left that summer to visit his parents and fulfill his obligation to the Navy. He was in the Naval Reserve Officers Training Program and had to attend several weeks of training at sea. We parted with the understanding that we would each be free to date other people. I was unable to find an apartment I could afford, so I was staying at Ed's fraternity, Alpha Chi Rho. This was not so unusual. The apartment building that housed the fraternity still had two tenants from the days when it was just another brownstone on Morningside Heights. One was a twenty-five-year old woman and the other was an elderly man. I obtained part-time baby-sitting jobs and enrolled in the summer session at Columbia, taking two chemistry courses, a quantitative analysis lecture and lab, and Calculus II. I needed these credits to complete my major requirements before going to medical school if I was accepted.

Archie Roberts was also living at Alpha Chi Rho in the summer of 1963, while he worked and played shortstop in a summer baseball league in New Jersey. Away from the pressures of classes and varsity sports, he seemed a more relaxed, likable person and we began spending more and more time together. We discussed our desire to become physicians and exchanged stories about our upbringings. Archie had one older sister, Mary Carol, who was married to her high school sweetheart, Ronnie LaMagdelaine. Archie's mother had stayed home to raise her children, but when Archie went off to Deerfield Academy for a postgraduate year after high school, his mother went back to school to become a licensed practical nurse. She and Archie's father had been high school sweethearts. A stout woman with tightly curled white hair, she smoked incessantly. Her weight and cigarettes were a source of constant irritation to Archie and his father, but they were unable to persuade her to change. Archie's father was a short, handsome man with chiseled features, a bald head, and a compact, muscular body. Archie revered his father, to whom he turned for advice about matters large and small. He was frankly envious of me because of my many siblings; he had always wanted to have younger sisters and brothers. By mid-June, we were dating.

Soon I was allowing Archie intimate caresses that I had denied to any other boyfriend. After necking and petting for hours, we would fall into an exhausted sleep on a narrow cot in my bedroom. Gradually I came to the realization that the shuddering release I sometimes felt at the end of these sessions was an orgasm. Incredibly, this happened a half a dozen times before I was able to put a name to it. The illicit but exquisite pleasure sent my guilt quotient skyrocketing. Archie was not as troubled by guilt as I was. He seemed confident that anything shy of actual intercourse would be readily forgiven. But I was wracked with remorse, and on the Sundays when I had not gone to confession to be absolved of my sins and could not receive Communion, I knelt and prayed in misery, convinced that I was in danger of losing my immortal soul.

Before long, it was common knowledge that Archie and I were dating, and it became important that I move out of the fraternity to avoid scandal. I found an apartment just down the street from Alpha Chi Rho, and we continued to see each other every spare moment and slept most nights together, always stopping short of intercourse. In addition to our common religion and desire to become doctors, there was something else that made Archie tremendously attractive to me as a possible mate. He was a teetotaler. I had vowed to myself countless times that I would never, never find myself married to an alcoholic, so Archie's abstinence from liquor enhanced his appeal.

Unfortunately, Archie's parents and coaches were not at all happy that he now had a girlfriend right on the scene, over whom they had no control. His parents in particular warned him constantly about the dangers of getting too "involved" in a relationship when he still had so many years of schooling to complete. They were also disapproving of my career plans. They felt he would be better served by a wife who stayed home, kept house, and raised his children. The more they tried to drive a wedge between us, the more we clung together.

When football season started, the time Archie and I could spend together was drastically curtailed. At the beginning of September, the squad reported to football camp in Litchfield, Connecticut for two weeks of pre-season practice. Girlfriends and even the rare wife were distinctly unwelcome. Just before he left, Archie gave me his fraternity pin, which meant that we were "engaged to be engaged." I suffered through this time, sending impassioned letters to Archie every day. Finally, the squad returned, and school resumed. Tupi's husband, Al Butts, was the captain of the football squad. As we had the prior year, she and I attended every game.

By now my entire identity was bound up in being Archie Roberts' girlfriend. I no longer feared being pitied, or thought unfeminine, because I was Archie's "girl." This must mean that I was pretty, and popular, and looked up to—all the things I had longed to be but doubted I would ever achieve as a geeky, plain girl from Marycrest. My younger siblings and even my parents were thrilled by my new status. My brothers Eddie and Mattie were now eleven and ten, old enough to be sports fans and to boast to their friends that their big sister was the girlfriend of the famous Archie Roberts.

A few months after the start of the school year, I was turning into the Barnard gates when a student rushed out of the library shouting that President Kennedy had been shot in Dallas. It was Friday afternoon, November 22, 1963. I hurried into the dorms where there was already a cluster of people around the television set in Hewitt Hall. When the news commentators announced the death of the President, I broke down in sobs, unable to believe that the young, handsome Kennedy was dead. That night, Archie and I arranged to stay at a friend's apartment, spending hours in impassioned embraces, struggling to beat back the grim specter of violent death. I kept remembering the night of Kennedy's election, which I'd spent on the couch in my family's living room recovering from pneumonia while my father and several of the other Marycrest men drank themselves silly and cheered, ecstatic that the country had its first Catholic President. Now he was dead, and the world was suddenly a darker place; in fact, it would seem in retrospect that all the upheaval and turmoil of the ensuing years had their origin in that one stark act of violence. Wrapped in each other's arms, we finally fell into an exhausted sleep, from which I awoke at 6:00 in the throes of a nightmare in which Archie had been shot to death.

That autumn, I went on several medical school interviews. I borrowed a camel's hair suit from a classmate who was much shorter than I. This showed off my legs to great advantage, but I acted serious and demure with male interviewers. They posed questions that are now illegal, such as "Are you married?" and "Do you plan to have children?" I was not a conscious feminist, so although I dimly resented these questions, I accepted as a matter of course that they would be asked and that I would have to answer. I felt I was walking a tightrope between appearing to be too feminine or too masculine, either of which would alienate the interviewer and prejudice him against me. I tried to appear attractive but not "too" attractive. The whole process felt demeaning.

After the Christmas break, I received a letter of acceptance from New York University School of Medicine. I was overjoyed that my long-time dream of becoming a doctor was a giant step closer to reality. Earlier that month, I was notified that I'd won a New York State Regents scholarship to attend medical school. Three Barnard students, two of whom were seniors, won scholarships—the first time that Barnard women had done so since 1959. The Barnard student newspaper noted that it was very unusual for a junior to win the award.

By the summer after our junior year of college, I was convinced that the only way our relationship could survive my scruples about our abortive lovemaking and the opposition of Archie's parents and coaches was to marry. Marriage would trump the forces trying to tear us apart. I began to work on Archie, to wear down his resistance.

"Archie, I can't take the guilt anymore. If you really loved me, you'd marry me."

"We can't marry now. We both have too many more years in school. We couldn't afford to have a baby. My parents would be furious if we got married before finishing medical school."

We had this argument over and over again.

The first birth control pill had just become available. I consulted a gynecologist who had no religious objections to prescribing oral contraceptives and went on the contraceptive pill Enovid. And I continued to wear down Archie's resistance, begging him to prove his love for me by marrying. I told him that I couldn't take the constant guilt over our petting to orgasm, that I was afraid that we would "go all the way," that the stress of having to deal with his parent's attempts to part us were all too much for me to bear. With the specter of pregnancy averted by the pill, marriage seemed the only answer to my fears about losing Archie, or about slipping into an illicit relationship that I knew would destroy my peace of mind.

Finally, Archie agreed that we would at least get a marriage license. We made the trip downtown to City Hall and stood on line with other couples seeking to legitimize their unions. I was one of the few women there who was not obviously pregnant.

When we told Archie's parents that we were getting married, they were outraged. After hours spent in fruitless wrangling, they told him that if he went through with this marriage they would disown him and have nothing further to do with him. We were not to be dissuaded.

The morning of the wedding, August 8, 1964, dawned bright and hot. Archie was flying in from Chicago, where he'd been sent by Wide World of Sports to help televise a pre-season NFL game. Roone Arledge, a Columbia alumnus and later president of ABC Sports, had gotten Archie the job. Pat Sheehan, Archie's best man, was meeting him at the airport and driving him to our parish church in Pearl River. At the appointed hour, I stood with my father at the back of the nave as the organist struck up the Wedding March. I was suddenly overcome with the solemnity of the occasion, wondering in a panic if I was making a dreadful mistake. My father hissed under his breath, "Don't look so serious," and I pasted a spurious smile on my face as we marched down the aisle. Archie looked impossibly handsome as he stood awaiting me. I fastened my eyes on him, brimming with love and yearning, ignoring the imps of doubt that gnawed in the recesses of my mind. Within a few minutes, our family friend Father Duffy left the altar, seized with a sudden illness. Father Wallace, a curate at St. Margaret's, stepped in to celebrate the Nuptial Mass and lead us in reciting our vows. He made a curious slip of the tongue, asking Archie if he would take me "for richer or better." I joked later that if I got poorer or worse, I'd be in trouble.

As we were walking down the aisle after exchanging our vows, we saw Archie's mother and sister sitting in the last pew, but they left immediately afterwards and didn't come to the reception. His father was nowhere in evidence.

Back at the house where the reception was held, we received the congratulations of our friends and relatives. For our honeymoon, we rented a car and drove first to Saratoga and then to Montreal. The Montreal Alouettes of the Canadian Football League were interested in having Archie play football for them and held out the hope that he could combine this with medical school at McGill University. It was late in the afternoon when Archie and I left for our wedding trip. By now, I was exhausted and suffering from a blinding headache. We got to Saratoga a few hours later and found a motel, the Coronet, that had rustic cabins for rent. We went out for a steak dinner to a restaurant called Mother Goldsmith's and then returned to the motel.

Archie immediately went into the bathroom attached to our room. I hurriedly changed into a nightgown and climbed into bed. The daylight slowly receded, and it became quite chilly. After what seemed like an interminable wait, Archie came out of the bathroom and into bed. By now it was dark, and I was shivering from a combination of nerves and cold. After fourteen months of longing to be possessed sexually by the man I adored, on my wedding night I felt completely devoid of desire. My libido, which had been boiling over for three years, was suddenly as placid as an alpine lake, deprived of the guilt which had bubbled just under the surface. We began to embrace and now that our caresses were no longer sinful, they lost the blistering ardor of our courtship's manqué lovemaking. To make matters worse, we were both virgins and not entirely sure of how to go about what we'd married to be able to do. For what seemed like hours we fumbled and failed to achieve the desired goal.

Finally, completely flummoxed as to what exactly was wrong, I gazed beseechingly up at Archie and asked, "What should I do now?" Rearing his head back, he flashed me a look that teetered on the knife-edge between chagrin and consternation. "You're asking ME?" he responded. At this we both started to giggle helplessly, and not long after we managed to shed our virginity. My overwhelming reaction was one of disbelief that THIS was what people made such a fuss about. I felt discomfort rather than pain, and none of the sublime pleasure that I'd been led to believe was in the offing. I told myself that it was just a question of inexperience, that things would get better.

⤳⤳

In the beginning of September, Archie left for football camp and I began my freshman year at New York University's School of Medicine. Located on the East River at 34th Street, the complex comprised the medical school proper, with its classrooms and laboratories, University Hospital, the private hospital affiliated with the school, and Bellevue, a sprawling labyrinthine public hospital through whose portals passed some of the most downtrodden, afflicted, and pathetic citizens of the city. There were prison and psychiatric wards and a morgue here, and one of the first tests freshmen had to survive was a visit to the Medical Examiner's autopsy room. Quaking inside but determined not to disgrace myself by fainting or displaying any other evidence that I wasn't as tough as my male classmates, I followed the instructor leading a small group of us into the bowels of Bellevue. We passed a company of prisoners shackled together, shuffling along between their guards, their vacant eyes scoured of hope.

The morgue was a large, gray room containing rows of metal tables, set up next to sinks for the washing away of blood and waste. All of the bodies were naked, in various stages of that last medical intrusion, the autopsy. I managed not to faint or vomit; the process of desensitization, which all medical students must go through, had begun.

The other rite of passage was freshman anatomy, in which we were split into groups of four (two to each side of the body) and given a cadaver to dissect. For unknown reasons cadaveric dissection always started with the axilla, the underarm. The corpse we were assigned had been hanging in a vat of formaldehyde for over two years before we were privileged to begin slicing it apart. The stench of a few dozen pickled corpses is utterly indescribable, made bearable only by breathing through the mouth. By the end of a session of anatomy lab, this would cause our mouths to be numb, altering the taste of food and imparting an interesting aroma to our breath. The corpses were stiff and unwieldy, and we contrived systems of ropes and pulleys to get at the axilla and other areas of the body as they came under our scrutiny. Attached by a wire to his great toe was a piece of paper with our cadaver's name: Thomas Barros. Mr. Barros had collapsed on the streets of the city and no one came forward to claim his remains.

Our initial trepidation at being cheek-by-jowl with long-dead bodies soon gave way to indifference, and before long we were eating sandwiches and drinking sodas as we dissected away, although this was highly unsanitary and against the rules. Until then, I had believed unquestioningly in the Catholic dogma of the resurrection of the body and life everlasting, but anatomy lab infected me with the germ of doubt. There was something so very *dead* about our cadavers, and the reality of death and its finality were brought home to me with shocking intensity. A fault line appeared in the foundation of my faith, which subsequent events would enlarge and amplify until the entire edifice came crashing down. For now, as I had since the age of two, I attended Sunday mass and prayed for the salvation of my soul and those of all my loved ones.

I entered a very different world on the weekends. I visited Archie at Camp Columbia, where the team was preparing for what would be his last college season. The opening game, against Colgate, was on September 26, 1964, at home at Baker Field. For the previous two seasons, Archie had finished ninth in the nation in passing. *Playboy Magazine* picked him as the quarterback for their annual pre-season All-American team, and Archie's picture appeared in *Playboy* along with other college football greats, including Dick Butkus and Jim Grisham. Archie had been Columbia's leading scorer for each of the previous two years. He also punted, returned punts and kick-offs, and played defensive back. Hardly a day went by without an article about him in the New York newspapers, and hopes were high that Columbia would have its best season since 1961, when it shared the Ivy League Championship with Harvard.

Despite these hopes, Columbia had its worst season in years, finishing the football season with 2 wins, 6 losses, and one tie. Yet this record notwithstanding, the subject of Archie's future was very much on our minds. We were living on scholarships and student loans; there was never enough money. The NFL and AFL (then a relatively new "upstart" league) drafts were about to take place. Professional baseball teams were also calling, offering Archie contracts to play baseball. The Montreal Alouettes flew us up to Toronto for the championship game of the Canadian Football League, and we got to sit in Prime Minister Lester Pearson's box. It was a heady time, and we convinced ourselves that somehow, we could have it all. Archie would combine medical school and a career as a professional athlete. It was just a question of picking the best offer.

In the event, Archie was not picked in the NFL draft. This was a surprise, but we attributed it to the teams being leery of his desire to combine pro football with medical school. He was drafted by the Jets in the AFL, after two other quarterbacks, John Huarte, the Heisman trophy winner from Notre Dame, and Joe Willie Namath from Alabama. Archie had been accepted by Columbia's medical school, the College of Physicians and Surgeons, and although not drafted by the Giants, they indicated an interest in signing him if he was willing to postpone starting medical school for two years. But for the time being, since he wanted to play college baseball in the spring, Archie could not sign any professional contract.

I was commuting by subway and bus from the upper West Side to the lower East Side five days a week to attend classes. Often, we had so little money that I had to collect empty soda bottles from around the apartment and return them for the nickel deposit, to get enough money for subway tokens, fifteen cents in those days. I was becoming run down and exhausted. I was often nauseous and depressed. More alarmingly, I was bleeding an inordinate amount, with no apparent pattern. Rather than regulating my periods, the pill seemed to have made them irregular and unpredictable. Finally, I went to the doctor. After examining me, he told me that I had developed an ovarian cyst and would have to go off the pill. On the way home I gazed out the windows of the bus in despair, convinced that I had cancer. But even this seemed less alarming than having to stop taking the oral contraceptives and risk becoming pregnant. The doctor gave me detailed instructions on the rhythm method, which prohibited intercourse from the 9th to the 21st day of the menstrual cycle. But since my periods were so irregular, I had little faith that he could identify the "safe" time of my cycle. He offered to fit me for a diaphragm but I was not yet ready to take a step that would be in clear violation of the Church's prohibitions on birth control. I told Archie who assured me that he would have no problems with adhering to the rhythm method.

One day in February 1965, Archie's parents, who'd gradually come to accept our marriage, called to say that they were coming for a visit. I still felt in competition with them for Archie's love. Their visits made me anxious: they fundamentally disapproved of my ambition to be a doctor, sure that I would shortchange Archie and any children we had. Utterly lacking in any sexual desire myself at that point, the night before their visit, I drew him into my arms using the trump card of my body and his desire for it to increase my hold over him, or so I imagined. It was, according to the doctor, the safe time of my cycle. I was not so sure, but in my compulsion to come first in Archie's heart I risked a pregnancy I was in no way prepared for.

Four weeks later, a pregnancy test confirmed that I was pregnant.

No prisoner ever heard her sentence pronounced with more horror. Rage, panic, and despair took possession of me. The fate of my mother and the other Marycrest wives, enslaved by their fertility, ground down by their annual pregnancies, drained by the ceaseless demands of their offspring, projected itself like a horror movie on the screen of my imagination.

Archie reacted to the news that we were expecting a child with elation, immediately pronouncing his desire for a son. His reaction only compounded my despair since I had to hide my true feelings in the face of his pride and excitement at becoming a father. I thought constantly about having an abortion, but there were major obstacles to getting one in those pre-Roe v. Wade days. The first was money—abortion was illegal and therefore expensive, and I had no money. I had no idea how to go about obtaining one even if I had the money, and knew that I would be risking my life putting myself in the hands of a potentially unskilled butcher. I feared for my life, but I had stopped caring about my immortal soul. It was at this point that I started to doubt I even had one. My Catholic scruples were overwhelmed by my horror at finding myself pregnant. But the final and most telling reason I did not choose abortion was that I feared the loss of Archie's love. That was something I could not survive, that was something I had to prevent, even if it meant risking my medical career.

My whole identity was tied up in being "Archie Roberts' wife." I had no sense of my value as a person aside from that. I was raised in an alcoholic family where my father heaped scorn on my head. I had been homely and nerdy and flat-chested. I had deep-seated anxiety about my attractiveness as a woman. Having Archie's love validated me as nothing else had. I felt that if I lost his love, I would have nothing—no identity, no reason to go on living.

We told our parents the news. Mine were delighted to learn that they were going to be grandparents but asked what I would do about medical school. "I'm going to continue, no matter what," I assured them, and myself. Archie's parents took it for granted that I would have to drop out, and I did not argue with them. But although I had no idea how I was going to manage, I was determined that, pregnant or not, I would continue my studies and graduate from medical school.

The question of Archie's future was taking on even more significance. The newspapers printed many articles speculating whether Archie would choose professional football or baseball and how, or if, he could combine sports with medicine. Archie's decision about how best to combine professional football with medical school was made easier by an unusual offer. He was approached by Art Modell, the owner of the Cleveland Browns in the NFL. Modell had become friendly with several of the doctors at Western Reserve University's medical school after Ernie Davis, a Heisman Trophy winner who had been drafted by the Browns, fell ill with leukemia. Davis died before his professional football career could begin. Dr. Austin Weisberger, the Chief of Medicine and the hematologist who had been Davis' physician, and Dr. Jack Caughey, the Director of Admissions, along with Art Modell, crafted a proposal that offered Archie the best opportunity to combine football and medicine.

That spring, we traveled to Cleveland, where on May 21, 1965, Archie signed what was said to be the most unusual contract in professional football history. Under its terms, the Cleveland Browns would pay him $7,000 a year during the next two years, which was the amount estimated to cover both of our tuitions and living expenses. During the first two years of school, Archie would attend the pre-season camp and games, but be on the reserve or "taxi squad" during the regular season, so that he could concentrate on his studies. During the third and fourth years, if he made the team, Archie would be able to use his elective time to play football on the regular squad and would be paid $14,000 per year. Several articles quoted Art Modell as saying: "In four years, at least I'll have a team doctor." It was this unique solution to Archie's dilemma that allowed me to tell people that I was the only woman ever to attend medical school on a football scholarship.

After graduation from Columbia and Barnard, we packed our meager belongings into a new Chevrolet Nova, bought with some of the money the Browns had paid Archie. We drove to Cleveland and moved into a one-bedroom apartment at the Commodore Hotel on Euclid Avenue. Several members of the Cleveland Browns and

Cleveland Indians baseball team lived there during their respective seasons. Archie had taught me how to drive before we left New York, and I hurriedly took and passed my test for a driver's license. The hotel was an easy walk to the medical school campus where I began a research project. Students were required to write a thesis and perform original research in order to receive the MD degree, and I chose a project involving rats and reproductive hormones. I met with the Director of Admissions, Dr. Caughey, and told him that I was having a baby, due in November. He wanted me to repeat freshman year, but I refused, pointing out that I had obtained good grades in all my courses, and promising that I would only take a week off from classes after I gave birth.

Archie had to leave almost immediately for the Browns' football camp located some forty miles away on the campus of Hiram College. It was a lonely time. I knew very few people and was still trying to come to terms with my pregnancy.

On a hot summer Sunday, I went to Mass at the local church. The sun was streaming through the stained-glass windows, and I was enveloped in the smell of incense. I had loved the Church as a child. I'd been proud to be a Catholic, convinced that my faith alone was the one, true faith. There is a comfort in being a true believer. There are no questions. All the big questions have been answered for you. There is a seductiveness in surrendering your will, your being, to a higher power. But I knew that in order to continue being a good Catholic, I would have to obey the Church's dictates on birth control. I would have to face the likelihood of endless pregnancies, of never achieving my yearned for medical degree. And I just couldn't do it. Something in me said, "NO, NO, and a thousand times NO!"

I knew I had to leave the Church. I left it with pain and regret, but irrevocably. Kneeling alone at Mass, I addressed the Deity: "All right, God, I will bear this child and try to be a good mother. But I will never, never let this happen to me again until I want it to happen. And no matter what, I will be a doctor."

I had slipped the mooring of my childhood faith. The finality of death as I had experienced it in the anatomy laboratory at NYU, in tandem with my unplanned pregnancy, laid the groundwork for my divorce from Catholicism. In later years, I would come to believe that compelling a woman to be pregnant against her will is a form of rape and involuntary servitude. I believe this still. Like rape, it brands the soul with a scar that nothing can eradicate. But as Nietzsche wrote: "What doesn't kill us makes us stronger." A tough proto-feminist was germinating inside the still-dutiful wife and soon-to-be mother that I was that summer of 1965.

⋉⋊

I gave birth to my first child on November 17, 1965. When a nurse brought me my firstborn, whom we had decided to name Dorothea (soon shortened to Dory) after my mother, I gazed down into a perfectly round, beautiful little face, which stared back at me with a solemn expression. Suddenly, with an intensity that left me reeling, I was assailed by wave after wave of the purest emotion, and that emotion was an overpowering love. I felt helplessly tossed about by surges of molten sensation. My emotional dependency on Archie fell away like a discarded cloak. In my mind's eye, I saw a giant king of beasts pad into the room, and I knew that to protect my child, I would place her carefully out of harm's way and, like Hercules with the Nemean lion, would throttle him with my bare hands.

I drank her beauty in with my eyes. She had none of the deformity of skull so common in newborns from the journey through the birth canal. Her fingers and toes were perfect little pink digits, each of which I examined minutely. The fontanel, the soft spot on the top of the head, throbbed with the beat of the artery coursing through it like a muffled drum heralding the successful launch of my DNA into the next generation. Completely entranced, I put her to my breasts, not yet filled with milk, so that she could drink the antibody-rich colostrum that would protect her from disease. As she suckled for the first time, my uterus contracted painfully, but with the powerful anesthetic of mother-love, the pain was easy to ignore.

I was a very different creature from the jejune girl who had entered the hospital a few days before. I had crossed an emotional threshold, and there would be no going back. Maybe the heart can hold only so much, and no more, of love. Maybe all mothers take some of the love they have for their husbands and transfer it to their children. I only know what happened to me. I would never again put Archie before all others. And the night before I was discharged from the hospital, when he leaned over and whispered, "If the next one's not a boy, don't bother coming home," I was struck dumb with a sick anger, hoping he was joking, but fearing that he was not. The slow, inexorable decline of our marriage had commenced.

I took a week off from classes, then returned to school. My sister Donna came out to Cleveland to babysit for Dory. In junior year, Archie was traded to the Miami Dolphins, and we moved to Florida for three months, where I did my obstetrics and gynecology rotation at Jackson Memorial Hospital and where I witnessed travesties against women that set me on the path towards radical feminism.

One night, we admitted a woman who had had an illegal abortion, as all abortions were in those days, with extremely rare exceptions. A foot of black, gangrenous bowel was hanging out of her vagina, mute testimony both to her desperation and to the ignorance and brutality of whoever had butchered her. With a hysterectomy and bowel resection, she survived—barely.

But the episode that was most egregious occurred with a patient whom I was never to see, only learn about. One day, I overheard two obstetric residents discussing a consultation that had been received on a pregnant patient who had been admitted to a medical floor. An alcoholic, she suffered from cirrhosis of the liver and was already the mother of several children. To make matters worse, she had rheumatic heart disease and one of her deformed heart valves was infected and severely leaky. The medical doctors had consulted the gynecology service requesting that their patient be given a therapeutic abortion. They were certain that the stress of pregnancy would exacerbate her heart condition, perhaps fatally. The obstetric residents, both Catholic, were discussing how to make sure this patient's case was presented to one of the Catholic attending doctors, so that the therapeutic abortion would be denied.

Incensed, I reported what I had heard to Dr. Dorothy Hicks, the only female attending OB-GYN. I suspected (correctly) that she would agree that an abortion was indicated. We were unable to find out the name of the patient, and months later, after I had returned to Cleveland, Dr. Hicks wrote to tell me that the patient had been readmitted in intractable heart failure late in her pregnancy and had died. To this day, I regret not looking for her until I found her. Had I been able to obtain for her the abortion she needed, I might have saved her life. Instead I left her in the hands of callous doctors who put their religious beliefs before her desperate need. In the fullness of time, all of these experiences, and more, gave birth to the anger and passion I would unleash in my work to legalize abortion.

>°<

After that last season, Archie decided to quit professional football and finish medical school. I finished my remaining clinical clerkships and in 1968 received my medical degree. As we recited the Hippocratic Oath and received our diplomas, I repeated the words with a full heart, vowing never to break the covenant to which it bound me. I *would* put my patients' interests ahead of my own. I *would* do no harm. I felt consecrated. I believed I was sealing a pact the tenets of which I could not violate without doing damage to the core of my being. Before the oath I was a lay person; after it I was a member of a priesthood of sorts, a group set aside and distinguished by a passionate commitment to curing and caring.

As we stood *en masse* to sing "America the Beautiful," my throat closed with an extremity of joy at reaching the goal I had pursued for eight years. Against great odds, in the face of prejudice against women, and despite the demands of motherhood, I had become a doctor. In my naiveté, I thought that once I had reached this goal, I would be forever content, and never desire anything else, ever again, with the same yearning. I could not foresee that adhering to this oath would exact an exorbitant price.

5 · The Radicalization of a Catholic Girl

The truth will set you free, but first it will piss you off.
—Gloria Steinem

For my first rotation as an intern, I was assigned to the male medical service, a sixteen-bed, open ward with a four-bed intensive care unit attached and one or two isolation rooms for patients with communicable diseases. My partner was a slight, blond Harvard graduate named Dick Adair. On that first morning of our internship, it was unclear which of us was more terrified. We tried valiantly to hide it.

Our resident, Dr. Franklin Browne, welcomed us and introduced us to the nurses. We then started morning "work rounds," going from bed to bed, listening to him relate the patient's history, examining the patient, and deciding what tests or treatments should be performed that day. These were so-called "charity" patients: poor, mostly black, inner-city residents without private insurance or doctors.

I was on call that first night, and never made it to my on-call room.

The male house staff had their own dormitory, Robb House, within the hospital complex, but the female house staff had to use the nearby dormitory of the nursing school. The schedule of thirty-six hours on call, twelve hours off, quickly had me in a stupor of exhaustion. (In those days, there were no laws limiting the hours that house staff could work each week.) At home, I wanted only to sleep, and became even more resentful of Archie's refusal to help with the housework. "That's women's work," he repeated, when I asked him to pitch in. I had no argument with which to counteract this. In those days, housework was, indeed, a woman's work, and he thought that I should be glad that he was "allowing" me to pursue a career.

The upside of the long hours on the wards was that we absorbed vast amounts of material quickly. Despite the arduous on-call schedule, I discovered during my internship that I loved taking care of sick people. I was endlessly fascinated by the patients, their stories, and their diseases, and I was humbled by the faith they showed in me and in their other neophyte doctors.

It might seem unthinkable that we would choose this time to conceive our second child—but we did. I'd had an IUD inserted after Dory was born, but now I had it I removed and began taking my temperature so that I would know when I was ovulating. Archie and I were on rotations that allowed us only one night a week off-call together. On the appointed day in November, I paged him and told him the time was ripe. We arranged to meet on our lunch hour in his dorm room on the fifth floor of Robb House. There we had hurried intercourse, and our son was conceived that day.

The internship year sometimes flew by with the speed of light and sometimes moved at a glacial pace. My last rotation was on the private service, which was a little easier than the wards with night call only every third night. I looked forward to beginning my residency in Internal Medicine. I was sure that I wanted to subspecialize but had not yet chosen a subspecialty. That was something the residency would help me decide. And when, a few years later, I decided on cardiology, I had no inkling of all the consequences that would flow from that decision.

Archie was accepted into the surgical program at Yale University, and I looked forward to being closer to my family. My baby was due about six weeks after the internship was scheduled to end, and because I would now have two young children to care for and a husband beginning the grueling surgical training program, I met with the Dean and the Chief of Medicine at Yale, who were sympathetic and arranged a schedule that did not require me to take night call. This was a very unusual concession, but I wasn't about to look a gift horse in the mouth. Archie's fame no doubt had a lot to do with their being so accommodating, but I was just grateful that my life would be made a little easier.

On my last night on call as an intern, I had six admissions and never got to bed. Archie had already left for New Haven, driving a rented van with our furniture. My sister Donna came out to Cleveland to help me with Dory during the drive east. I had to go first to Bethesda, Maryland for an interview at the National Institutes of Health. The Vietnam War was now in full swing, and all male doctors were being drafted into the service, with very few exceptions. In fact, all eighteen-year-old men had to register for the draft, and those with low draft numbers had an excellent chance of being sent to fight in Vietnam. One of the ways for interns to avoid Vietnam was to win a draft-deferred position in the Public Health Service. These were coveted jobs with many more applicants than places. The fortunate few who obtained them were referred to disparagingly as "Yellow Berets" to distinguish them from the Green Berets, whose exploits in the jungles of Southeast Asia were depicted in a John Wayne movie. In those days, the Armed Services excluded women with children under the age of eighteen, so that even if I wanted to accompany Archie into the Army, I would be unable to do so.

Archie and I both applied to the National Heart and Lung Institute. I had not yet chosen a subspecialty, but Archie was determined to go into cardiac surgery, and the cardiac surgical program at the NIH was world-renowned.

Sporting a hugely pregnant belly, I arrived for my interview at the NIH. I found out that there were positions available that did not come with a draft deferment, and the interviewers advised me to apply for one of these. This made sense to me, since I was in no danger of being sent to Vietnam, whereas a male physician who did not get a draft-deferred position was still eligible to be called up. I applied for and was approved for a non-draft-deferred position at the National Heart, Lung, and Blood Institute. Archie was accepted into the cardiac surgical program for the two years starting in 1971, which meant that he was no longer eligible for the draft.

In July of 1969, we moved into a garden apartment on Treat Street in West Haven, Connecticut. During those last weeks of my second pregnancy, I waited anxiously for the birth, longing for a son. Finally, on August 9th, the day after our fifth wedding anniversary, my labor pains started, and a neighbor drove me to Yale-New Haven Hospital (Archie was on call and unable to come home to get me). After one or two painful contractions, the anesthesiologist gave me an epidural block, and I spent the rest of my labor in comfort, reading *The New England Journal of Medicine*.

When the obstetrician presented me with a squalling, chubby baby boy, I was enraptured with relief and joy. Like the birth of my brother Edwin, seventeen years previously, it has lodged in my memory as one of the most blissful moments of my life. He weighed 8 pounds, 8 ounces, and we named him Arthur Hudson Roberts, but called him Archie. My husband was quietly delighted to have a son. He sent me a dozen red roses.

Baby Archie had sparse, light hair and the solemn cobalt-blue eyes of a neonate. I called him the Mad Mouse of Treat Street because of the angry howls he uttered when hungry. Rushing in to nurse him, I guided my bursting nipple to the side of his mouth. In an absolute frenzy of desire, he whipped his head from side to side, rooting frantically to find the teat, screaming in frustration, until at last he clamped it between his gums and commenced to nurse voraciously, a look of utter tranquility now affixed to his face. From the earliest days of his life, Archie and I bonded with that special intensity of mothers and sons. I adored him, and our relationship even during his teen years was eerily conflict-free. Once, when he was about four years old, I scolded him for some forgotten misdemeanor. His eyes filled with tears and his lower lip quivered. "You shouldn't talk mean to your little boy," he whispered in a tremulous falsetto. I was struck to the quick, crestfallen, and never "talked mean" to him again. As the years went by he grew, in the biblical words, "in wisdom and age and grace," and his love has nourished and sustained me through many trials and travails.

After Labor Day, I began my medical residency, dropping the children off each morning with a babysitter before going to the West Haven Veteran's Administration Hospital, where I was rotating through various medical subspecialties: gastroenterology, infectious diseases, renal diseases, and endocrinology. "Big Archie," as we now called him to distinguish him from our son, was on call every other night. His weekends on call required him to be at the hospital from Friday morning until Monday night, and I began to spend these weekends visiting my family, who had moved from Marycrest to the nearby town of Pearl River.

My siblings, the little children I had fed and protected, cosseted, and chastised, were growing into adulthood. The next oldest, my sister Mary, had graduated from Hunter College in New York City. She was working at Parke Bernet Galleries but had already decided to move to Paris, which she did the next April. She was evolving into a political activist and later joined a Trotskyist organization in France. Donna, her earlier shyness overcome, was now an organizer for Cesar Chavez's United Farm Workers, spreading the news of the grape and lettuce boycotts. Chavez used the boycotts to pressure growers into paying living wages to migrant farm workers. Donna's transformation began when she moved away from home to help me take care of Dory in Cleveland. We all, to one extent or another, blossomed when we escaped from our alcoholic home. Kaye was living in Columbus, Ohio, where she had moved in with friends after dropping out of the Fashion Institute of Technology. She would soon return to Pearl River. Regina lived at home and attended a local community college. Rosa, Edwin, Matthew, Vicky, and Mark were attending the local public schools.

My parents were no longer the strict disciplinarians of my younger days. They were burnt out. They just didn't have the energy any more. The world was changing, and they changed along with it. My mother and many other Catholic women parted company with the Church over the issue of birth control. My father told his children that they could decide to go to Mass or not when they reached the age of eighteen. One by one, they stopped going.

It was a summer crammed with memorable and disparate events. Men landed on the moon for the first time. In upstate New York, a concert seized the public imagination and came to symbolize an era. The television news coverage of Woodstock had a profound effect on me. It brought home with stunning force that while I had been slaving away becoming a doctor and having babies, the world I grew up in — an ordered, reverent, obedient world — had died and was being replaced by something pagan and wild and free, which my heart both feared and yearned for. The stirrings of discontent I had been squelching about my marriage, about the inequities faced by women in medicine and in the wider world, were bubbling up to the surface, demanding to be faced and dealt with.

I was working five days a week at the hospital, but the fact that I did not have to take night call caused the other residents to resent me. I found it hard to make friends. I missed the camaraderie I'd enjoyed with my fellow interns in Cleveland. Waking hours outside the hospital were taken up with childcare and housecleaning, cooking and study. Archie somehow found time out of his busy schedule to work with the Yale freshman football team and play basketball. Between his on-call schedule and extracurricular activities, we saw little of each other, and I was aware of a deepening dissatisfaction with my marriage. I found myself becoming sexually attracted to other men — but for my own husband, my libido continued to be AWOL.

My sister Kaye moved home from living in Columbus, Ohio in the fall of 1969. She turned twenty-one that December and had already fallen in love with Johnny Hansen, our brother Matt's best friend. Johnny was an eighteen-year-old boy whose father, a carpenter, had moved to Pearl River from Norway. On February 7, 1970 they went through a hippie wedding ceremony that had no legal standing but consisted of readings from Kibran's *The Prophet* and the exchange of homemade vows. Dory was the flower girl, but neither the bride's nor the groom's parents were in attendance. Johnny's parents had refused him permission to marry, and he couldn't marry legally without their consent. My father, outraged at their failure to be married in the Church (never mind that it wasn't an option), disowned Kaye and banned her from the house.

Johnny had a cheerful, insouciant manner, with a grin as wide as all outdoors, honey-colored curls, a Norwegian accent, and a propensity to touch the breasts of any girl who came within range of his hands in a manner so innocent and playful that few took offense. Kaye never outgrew her childhood beauty. Her skin was unmarred, and her blonde curls fell almost to her waist. Within a week of their marriage, she was pregnant. She resembled nothing so much as a Botticelli painting of the Virgin Mary as she waited that summer for her baby to be born.

A few days after my father's 50th birthday, which fell on September 13th, the phone rang with news that Johnny, who'd been working as a carpenter, had crashed his pickup truck on a rain-slicked mountain road in Fishkill, New York. He was in the operating room at a hospital in Poughkeepsie with massive brain damage and was not expected to live. I piled the children into the car and drove from New Haven to Pearl River. Kaye was spending the night at our parents' house, unable to face her empty apartment in Nyack. In the face of the tragedy, my father relented and welcomed her home. By the time I arrived, the doctor had already called to report that Johnny was dead.

I told the children that Aunt Kaye's husband had been killed, but they were too young to have any real understanding. Archie was thirteen months old, and Dory was four going on five. Kaye, seven months pregnant, fell weeping into my arms—like Aunt Bea a generation before, fated to bring a fatherless child into the world. We slept not at all that night; just lay on the bed crying, recalling how we had shared a bed as children, ignorant of the crushing sorrow that Fate had in store for us.

Johnny's wake was a grim affair, with a eulogy in broken English by Johnny's boss Ralph, who was also from Norway and had an unpronounceable last name. We buried him in a plot in the Nyack cemetery. His headstone reads, *Our Beloved Johnny, 12/31/51–9/18/70*. On Monday morning, I accompanied Kaye to the welfare office in Nyack, where she applied for aid. Johnny had left no money, there was no life insurance, and she was unlikely to be hired for a job in the final weeks of pregnancy. I returned to New Haven with the children, a fresh and raw grief now added to my growing discontent.

Two months to the day after his death, Johnny's daughter was born in Nyack Hospital. Kaye had attended natural childbirth classes and refused any anesthetic. I drove down again from New Haven and was allowed to accompany her during her labor and delivery. My first niece was named Liv—Norwegian for life—and from the beginning, her face was a tiny version of her father's.

Back at work, I could no longer hide from the realization that I was severely depressed. It was almost more than I could manage to get out of bed each morning. During my second year of residency at Yale, I was doing a postdoctoral fellowship in renal disease, which I'd initially chosen as a subspecialty. But caring for patients bound to their dialysis machines who were as depressed, or more, than I was myself was increasingly unbearable.

During that year, Dr. Richard Gorlin, a noted cardiologist at Harvard, gave a Grand Rounds lecture at Yale describing the research he had done with his father, a hydraulic engineer, which led to the ability to mathematically determine the area of a heart valve. Dr. Gorlin became famous for his research and was head of the division of cardiology at the Peter Bent Brigham Hospital in Boston, one of the Harvard teaching hospitals. I was fascinated by his lecture and decided on the spot that I wanted to study with him after the two years that we were committed to spend at the NIH in Bethesda. I had finally settled on a different subspecialty of medicine—cardiology, the study of heart disease.

That fall, I dragged myself through the days in a fog of discontent. I'd achieved my ambition to be a doctor but was filled with inchoate yearnings for romance and adventure. I wanted to be liberated from the domestic treadmill that my life outside of medicine had become. Archie threw himself into his surgical training with the same single-minded intensity with which he had played sports: When he wasn't at the hospital working he was sleeping or studying or playing basketball. We had less and less to talk about, and my loneliness grew. I would sneak away from the hospital and spend hours sitting on the shore, gazing out at Long Island Sound, certain that I would never again know joy, or adventure, or sexual passion. Now that I had decided I wanted to be a cardiologist, I was able to resign my renal fellowship and was accepted into the cardiology program at Yale-New Haven Hospital.

About this time, I also began to read some of the articles and books coming out about the women's movement. I considered myself a "liberated" woman; after all, I had a career. I was a physician, not "just" a housewife economically dependent on her husband. But the more I read, the more the scales fell from my eyes. I realized that I had been discriminated against by medical school admissions committees who had quotas for women, limiting the number of women to about 10% of any class, restricting their admission to just a few select individuals and keeping the rest out, no matter how qualified they were. I was discriminated against when I was told that I should quit medical school when Dory was born, yet her father was not told the same thing. I was discriminated against by laws that made me a criminal if I became pregnant and had an abortion. I had been an obedient mare plodding along with blinders limiting my vision—if not quite the broodmare my mother had been—but now these blinders were stripped away, and I saw clearly how even I had been discriminated against and held back.

I devoured Kate Millett's *Sexual Politics*, Shulamith Firestone's *The Dialectic of Sex*, and Robin Morgan's *Sisterhood is Powerful*. Millett's brilliant explication of the raw misogyny in the works of Henry Miller, D. H. Lawrence, and Norman Mailer left me particularly shaken and enraged.

To see, spelled out in black and white, the myriad ways women throughout history had been relegated to the status of broodmares and domestic drudges ignited a fury in me that was frightening in its intensity. The anger I had been turning inward, where it mutated into melancholia, I now turned outward. I renewed my demands to Archie that he take some responsibility for domestic chores and childcare, but to no avail. These tasks were still, and always would be in his eyes, "women's work." My resentment at his refusal to share domestic chores resembled a festering infection, always on the verge of popping like an abscess.

Archie was not thrilled with my new-found radicalism. He made no bones about his dislike of my political beliefs and his resentment at my leaving him to mind the children while I worked extra hours. The woman I was becoming was a far cry from the devout Catholic girl he'd married. I longed to become even more involved in radical politics. I didn't want my daughter to face the same discrimination I had. I didn't want her ever to experience the nightmare of an unwanted pregnancy. I didn't want my sensitive little son to grow up to become cannon fodder. What I wanted was to find like-minded women and work with them to change the world.

I was moonlighting at the Yale University Student Health Service to make the extra money we needed to pay back student loans. Most of the students who came to the Health Service had minor illnesses like colds, sore throats, or muscle sprains. But some of the coeds came with gynecologic complaints. When this happened, the staff were delighted to have a female resident working there, because it freed up a nurse who would otherwise have to be present whenever a female student needed a pelvic examination.

While working at the Yale Student Health Service, I met several female law students. They told me that they were about to file a class-action suit against the Connecticut abortion law. Slowly but inexorably, the call for abortion law reform was starting to crescendo around the country. New York State passed a liberal abortion law in 1970, and the District of Columbia soon followed.

I was invited to an organizational meeting called by the female lawyers who were planning the class-action suit, which they called

Women vs. Connecticut. The meeting was held in a library reading room on the Yale University campus. The room featured rich, hand-carved wood paneling, overstuffed chairs, and portraits of patriarchal Yale men of the previous century who would have gazed askance at the proceedings, had they been alive. The room reeked of male power, privilege, and prestige. The hundred or so women who gathered there were all in their teens, twenties, or thirties. One by one, women rose and spoke of overturning laws that denied them the right to decide what transpired in their own bodies. They discussed legal arguments and political strategy, and were poised, confident, and knowledge-able.

I was enthralled. I had never before seen women meeting in force, secure in the rightness of their cause, unafraid to brave what would surely be storms of opposition. At the end of the meeting, I timidly approached one of the lawyers, identified myself as a physician, and volunteered to help in any way I could. On the spot, I was made the Medical Coordinator for Women vs. Connecticut, and my career as a feminist began. I did not know that it would catapult me into the media spotlight, bring me to the attention of the FBI, lead me into the anti-war movement, deal the death-blow to my marriage, and come close to costing me my children. I only knew that my doldrums had lifted, and that adventure, and passion, had re-entered my life.

Soon I was being invited to speak on abortion and our class-ac-tion suit all over the state. I spoke at teach-ins about abortion to stu-dent groups, church groups, wherever the organizers sent me. The Connecticut legislature was holding hearings on a proposed bill that would make the Connecticut abortion law marginally more liberal. There was intense interest in the hearings, and the organizers of the suit asked me to speak on behalf of Women vs. Connecticut. So many people attended the hearings that they were moved out of the legisla-ture in Hartford and into a nearby auditorium. Busloads of Catholic school children were brought in to observe the proceedings, and the audience was heavily weighted with those who were adamantly op-posed to any liberalization of the law. *In for a penny, in for a pound*, I decided, and wrote a speech I knew would enrage the fetus fetishists.

It began:

> A popular medical dictionary defines disease as 'literally a lack of ease' and venereal disease as 'one usually acquired through sexual intercourse.' It is apparent, therefore, that unwanted pregnancy is THE most common venereal disease. It is associated with immense physical, mental, social, and economic suffering. In seeking to be cured of this disease, women, throughout history, have risked pain, mutilation, and death, in numbers that stagger the imagination. Today, when the cure for this disease is statistically safer than carrying that pregnancy to term, abortions are still widely withheld by antiquated laws and religious tenets not shared by the majority of people.

I spoke of the horrors of back-alley abortions and castigated the "senile, celibate Cardinals and sniveling, scared politicians" who had the "colossal arrogance to uphold laws whose consequences they will never have to suffer," ending with a demand that abortion laws be not reformed, but repealed.

By the end of the second sentence, my speech was interrupted by thunderous boos, hisses, and cries of: "Shame on you." My two-minute oration was interrupted five times by audience outbursts, and I was shaking with fright by the time I finished. A phalanx of security guards shepherded me out of the auditorium while people shook their fists and hurled curses at my head.

On a spring day in 1971, Women vs. Connecticut had its day in court. Eight hundred fifty-eight women plaintiffs were in agreement that the Connecticut abortion law violated our rights and should be declared unconstitutional. Many of us who had worked on the case (the correct designation of which was *Abele v. Markle*) were on hand to lend moral support to the lawyers as they presented our arguments to the judge. All of the plaintiffs' lawyers were women.

Three male lawyers represented the state. In a sneering, condescending tone, one of the state's lawyers remarked to the judge: "Frankly, Your Honor, I find it hard to believe that 200 [sic] women can agree on *anything*." This comment won an understanding smile from the judge but gasps of outrage from those of us who had come to fight, incredulous that we were not being taken seriously. My face flushed with anger, and I knew that I was in this fight for the duration; neither ridicule, nor denial, nor defeat could make me abandon the struggle.

Our lawsuit was dismissed, but we appealed the dismissal. At one meeting, as we discussed strategy, we decided that opposing abortion laws on a state-by-state basis was not an effective way to proceed. We knew that the Supreme Court would be hearing arguments against the Georgia and Texas abortion statutes in the fall of 1971. We sent letters to every feminist organization we could find, proposing a national coalition to mobilize support for overthrowing anti-abortion laws nationwide—which the Supreme Court decision had the potential of doing. Rulings are not made in a vacuum, and we felt that even nine male Supreme Court justices might be swayed by large numbers of women demanding the right to control their own bodies.

The response to our letter calling for a national coalition was far greater than we had expected.

In July 1971, in response to that call, over a thousand women met in New York City, representing 253 organizations from 29 states. I was one of the keynote speakers, along with Nancy Stearns, a lawyer with the Center for Constitutional Rights. We formed the Women's National Abortion Action Coalition, WONAAC, dedicated to the repeal of abortion and contraception laws. We decided to hold mass demonstrations in Washington, D.C. and San Francisco on November 20th and began the process of setting up local WONAAC offices all over the country.

By this time, Archie, the children, and I had moved to Bethesda, Maryland. Archie began his stint as a "Yellow Beret." I started my job in the Lipid Metabolism Branch of the NIH. Dory was almost six and had finished kindergarten in New Haven. She was bright, feisty, bossy, and beautiful. Young Archie was going on two, as blond as Dory was dark, a lively but well-behaved little boy who volunteered to all visitors, "Daddy is my fodder." We moved into a two-bedroom garden apartment near the NIH.

The Lipid Metabolism Branch was established to fund and coor-

dinate research into cholesterol and heart disease. It was headed by
Dr. Robert Levy, who with Dr. Donald Frederickson, had performed
ground-breaking research into the diseases associated with high lev-
els of blood fats. In addition to Dr. Levy and myself, the other physicians working in the program office were Dr. Barry Greenberg, who
like me had not yet completed his postgraduate training, and Dr. Basil
Rifkind, who was then in his late thirties. Our job entailed travel all
over the country and even to Canada to set up a network of Lipid
Research Clinics to study the relationship of cholesterol and heart disease. We knew our travel schedule several months in advance, and
this allowed WONAAC to set up meetings, teach-ins, or press conferences with me as a featured speaker in the cities to which I was
traveling at government expense. After working hours, I threw myself
into preparations for the November demonstration. I gave speeches
to student groups, women's clubs, church groups, and I appeared on
local television shows.

I repeatedly told Archie, to his dismay and incomprehension, that
I wanted more than anything else to work for the feminist revolution
and the total transformation of society as we knew it. He wanted the
basis of our marriage to remain unchanged, but I was coming to view
marriage as a patriarchal class institution that oppressed women—
one that legitimized rape and prostitution. Our marriage had become,
in words Mary McCarthy used in another context, "a jungle of incom-
patibilities."

When I told him, "I want nothing more than a total feminist revolution," he responded, "You're nuts. You're completely insane."

On November 20, we were about 5,000 strong as we marched in
D.C. Five of my six sisters (Mary, at the time a committed Trotskyist,
was living in Paris), my mother, Dory, and young Archie all marched
with me, although Archie was carried more than he walked. My
mother was in great spirits, and at one point turned to me and said,
"Father Duffy should see me now!" Another woman marching ahead
of me had embroidered on the seat of her jeans, "Free your mind and
your ass will follow."

Finally, we reached the speakers' stand, built up on scaffolding to look out over the crowd. The New Haven Women's Liberation Rock Band played feminist songs. In my speech, I railed against the laws that denied women the right to control their own bodies. I castigated President Nixon, who prattled about the "sanctity of life" while he napalmed Vietnamese children. I quoted Margaret Sanger, who said: "No woman can call herself free until she can choose whether she will or will not become a mother." Of course, I was preaching to the choir, and the audience was on my side. I was elated and euphoric. That night, the local and national television news reported on the demonstration, and it was written up in the newspapers the next day.

Twenty-five years later, in 1996, HBO presented a made-for-television movie about abortion and its impact, in different decades, on the lives of three women. It was entitled *If These Walls Could Talk*, and the women were played by Demi Moore, Sissie Spacek, and Cher. The opening credits are run over film clips from actual demonstrations, including WONAAC's of November 20, 1971. I am shown, and heard, crying in an impassioned voice: "We will no longer tolerate laws that degrade, mutilate, and murder women!"

The publicity from this demonstration generated even more invitations for me to speak, and the next months went by in a blur of work and travel, both medical and political. Wherever I traveled for my government job, the WONAAC staff arranged for me to speak at the local university or women's group in the evening after my medical work for the day was over. And I began to speak at anti-war demonstrations as a representative of the women's movement.

By the spring of 1972, despite my involvement in political causes, I was blundering in a thicket of fear, anger, and frustration. I was miserable and wanted to escape from my marriage, but I quailed at the thought of what a divorce would entail. In 1972, it was not nearly as easy to get a divorce as it is now. "No-fault" divorce was only available in places like Mexico, Haiti, and Nevada, and both parties had to agree to the divorce for that to happen. In Maryland, where we were residents, a couple had to be legally separated for eighteen months before they could be divorced. We would not even *be* in Maryland in eighteen months. And I was afraid of what pound of flesh my husband would extract if I broke free of the marriage. I knew on some level that the only way I could get Archie to agree to a divorce was to have an affair, but I knew it would enrage Archie and I feared—rightly, as it turned out—what he would do in retaliation. I had evolved from a girl-woman desperate to be married in 1964, to a feminist woman who felt that to be married was an embarrassment, an indication that I was a man's chattel, a sign that I had bowed to the power of the patriarchy. I longed to escape, but Archie refused to consider an amicable divorce, despite my entreaties.

On March 9, 1972 the *Washington Daily News* published an article about me. Written by Judy Flanders, it chronicled not only my work volunteering at an abortion clinic but also my activities in WONAAC. It featured a photograph of me wearing a hippie-style blouse. The article describes me as, "The eldest daughter of a Catholic family of 10 children ... a charming young woman who looks barely out of her teens; she goes off to work in a pea-jacket and slacks, her long black hair covered with a rakish knit cap."

The article reported that I worked at the National Institutes of Health. It mentioned my husband, Dr. Archie Roberts, and recounted that the "former All-American quarterback ... put himself and his wife thru medical school playing pro football for the Cleveland Browns." It told of the experiences I had as a medical student in Miami that helped impel me into the abortion law repeal movement. It went on to say that:

> *Dr. Roberts' convictions are strong enough to give the Pope pause. She believes 'senile celibate cardinals are the last people who should be upholding abortion laws that murder women. Trying to inflict these beliefs on others is not only immoral, it is unconstitutional... If men could become pregnant, abortion would become a sacrament,' she says, quoting New York attorney Flo Kennedy. 'No man ever had his guts ripped out by a back-alley abortionist. It is a colossal arrogance to uphold laws whose consequences one will never have to face.*

It was about this same time that I had my first visit from the FBI.

An agent came to my office at the NIH and questioned me about my activities and associates in the women's and anti-war movements. He asked outright if we were trying to "overthrow the government" and questioned our loyalty as citizens. I assured him that we weren't breaking any laws and weren't plotting to topple the government.

In April of 1972, I traveled to New York City to speak at a mass anti-war demonstration, which was attended by an estimated 100,000 people. The line of marchers was twenty-seven blocks long. It was a rainy day, and a few dozen people clustered under umbrellas on the speaker's platform. I was agog to see John Lennon and Yoko Ono standing nearby, along with the famous anti-war priests, the Berrigan brothers, and baseball player Jim Bouton. Lennon and Ono seemed shy and tiny as they huddled under their umbrella. He urged people to "stay in the streets" and led the crowd in singing "Give Peace a Chance." I was asked to speak as a representative of the women's movement, and gave an address which began:

> *Millions of women in this country oppose the Indochinese War, and for many different reasons. One of the reasons feminists like myself oppose the war is that we don't like pimps. And the men in Congress, the men in the Pentagon, and that despicable man in the White House who are waging this war are nothing but* pimps! *They are taking our lives, our labor, our money, and our honor and they are prostituting them for the sake of a corrupt Saigon dictatorship that isn't worth one cent of our money or one drop of blood, American or Vietnamese.*

It was the first time I had spoken before so huge a throng. Daniel Ellsberg, the defendant in the Pentagon Papers case also spoke, as did John Kerry—then a decorated Vietnam veteran, not yet a Senator or Secretary of State.

More than a generation later, it is difficult to convey how passionately we felt about the war and how deeply it divided the nation. I had come to see the war as another instance of the insanity that flowed from the patriarchal system—but by now I had another, more personal reason to be involved in anti-war activities. His name was Cappy Kidd.

Cappy was a member of the Socialist Workers Party. He was six years younger than I, and in addition to his political activities, worked as a carpenter. A minor deformity of his foot saved him from the draft. Tall, rugged, with almost shoulder-length, light brown hair and a mustache, I was instantly attracted to him, not only by his looks but also by his demeanor. Trotskyist men bent over backward to be non-sexist, in speech and in action. Cappy was originally from the South, where his divorced parents still lived. We became lovers in the spring of 1972, shortly after my anti-war speech in New York. I suppose it was a feather in his cap to be the lover of a well-known feminist. We came in for a lot of teasing, and he was accused of "horizontal recruitment," but I never joined the Socialist Workers Party. I remained a "healthy independent." I was not in love, but making love to someone I actually liked and admired, whose politics agreed with my own, was a balm to my spirit.

By then I had come to accept the fact that only a radical step on my part, such as carrying on an extramarital affair, would propel Archie into agreeing to divorce. And so, the next time, in the heat of one of our endless arguments about my political involvement and general inadequacy as a wife, when Archie asked me if I was having an affair, I responded, "Yes." His face took on the stunned look of a slaughter-house steer at the moment it's pole-axed. After a few seconds of silence while he processed this information, he demanded to know who it was. I told him that it was a man I had met in the anti-war movement but did not tell him Cappy's name. "You have to stop, you're my wife," he said.

"I'm not going to stop. I can do what I want with my body. I'm not your property," I replied, and we proceeded in this vein for some time, resolving nothing.

I suggested we divorce, asking him to move out and leave the children with me, but he refused: "I won't divorce you, because then you would have everything you want."

Towards the end of May, I consulted a lawyer, resolved to get a divorce on the grounds of irreconcilable differences. It was then that I learned that the state of Maryland required an eighteen-month separation before such a divorce could be granted, and by that time I would have moved away from Maryland to continue my training as a cardiology fellow with Dr. Richard Gorlin at the Peter Bent Brigham Hospital in Boston. Archie was still waiting to find out where he had been accepted into a cardiac surgery residency, having decided not to return to Yale. I was no longer willing to follow him wherever he went, especially if it meant giving up my fellowship in Boston.

On the last day of May, relieved to have taken the first step to end our marriage, I came home from work and cooked us all dinner for the first time in weeks. Afterward, Archie took the children and said he was going out for ice cream. I had no inkling of the bombshell that was about to shatter the last illusions I held about my husband, about justice, and about the lengths I would go to keep my children. An hour after he left, Archie telephoned from the airport to say that he was taking Dory and little Archie to stay with his parents in Massachusetts. He hung up when I demanded to know why and when they would return.

A spider of foreboding held me fast in its web. Dread and a keen longing to hold the children in my arms kept sleep at bay through an endless night. The next morning, the doorbell rang, and I ran to answer it with crazy joy, convinced I would find the three of them standing on the doorstep. A stranger shuffled his feet in the doorway: It was a process server holding a sheaf of court documents. These innocuous-looking pages signaled the beginning of a nightmare. He scurried away as soon as the papers were in my hands. They were an order to show cause and a bill of complaint for divorce "a vinculo matrimonii," on the grounds of adultery. In the papers, I was accused of having a sexual affair with at least one man, of refusing sexual acts with my husband, of stopping my wifely duties to take care of washing, cooking, and caring for the home, of expressing my dislike and opposition to religion, and of openly working for the goal of revolution against the United States. It asked that full custody be awarded to Archie because I was an unfit mother and demanded and that I be enjoined from interfering with his care of the children.

Based on this bill of complaint and without any prior notification or questioning of me, the judge signed an Order to Show Cause awarding Archie temporary custody and ordering that the investigative office of the Court undertake an investigation of the "care, custody, and control of the minor children." The same document set a hearing date six weeks later, on July 14, 1972. Dory was six and a half years old and young Archie was a few months shy of his third birthday. I was allowed to visit them every other weekend, in Holyoke, Massachusetts, but they would stay with their paternal grandparents until the hearing.

If I had any misapprehensions about how marriage oppressed women, they were irrevocably shattered by the evidence set forth in the Bill of Complaint. In enumerating the ways in which I had failed as a wife, it delineated clearly what was expected of women in marriage and what they must deliver if they wished to continue as the mothers of their children. I called Dr. Levy, gave him an expurgated version of what had happened, and told him that I would be unable to work for at least a few weeks. He readily granted me leave, and I moved out of our apartment and in with Movement friends in the District of Columbia, spending most of my waking hours huddled on a mattress crying. My parents were horrified, but my father took Archie's part, writing me to advise that I "ask Archie's forgiveness and tell him you are interested only in a good marriage and medicine, nothing else." I didn't bother to reply.

I was notified that a court-appointed investigator wanted to interview me. I hoped that the investigator would be a woman and would have some sympathy for me. In the event, the investigator was a man, and in the space of just a few moments, it was clear that he was the worst possible man I could have drawn. He asked me to tell him of the contentious issues in our marriage.

I related to him that Archie and I both worked as doctors, but that I was expected to do all the housework and be responsible for all of the childcare, and that we argued because Archie refused to help with any of these chores.

"Well the solution to that is very simple," he said. "You should have quit your job and stayed home with your children." He questioned me about my political beliefs, which he clearly found repugnant. "Don't you know that if women could get abortions, they'd be promiscuous?" he asked. Finally, he delivered the coup de grâce. "You know," he said, "if half the things your husband says about you are true, then you're clearly an unfit mother. On the other hand, if half the things he says about you are true, he's an unfit father for putting up with you, and I'm going to recommend to the Court that the children be taken away from both of you and put in foster care."

The thought of Dory and Archie being wrested away from *both* of us was unbearable. My mind scurried around like a cornered rat frantically seeking escape from a predicament that seemed to grow more fraught with each day that passed. I was sick with longing for the children. It was a bruising lump that lodged in my chest, taking away my appetite. I spent more and more time curled up in bed in a fetal position.

I knew I had to get my children back or die.

My lawyer advised me to play the good suburban housewife, but that was impossible. My political activities were a matter of public record; they had been chronicled in the newspapers and on television. Certain she was mistaken, I consulted another attorney. What he said was not encouraging.

Rufus King, III was the descendant of a signer of the Declaration of Independence. A tall, thin, etiolated WASP, he was handsome, with chiseled features and a head full of prematurely gray curls. He'd been recommended by Carol Burris, a friend who'd founded the Feminist Lobby. Unbeknownst to me, Archie had been having me followed by a private investigator for a few weeks before filing for divorce. He'd hired the detective as soon as I told him that I was sleeping with another man. The detective would testify that I had spent the night at Cappy's apartment. That alone was prima facie evidence that I'd committed adultery. He didn't need lurid photos of us in the act.

In Maryland, in 1972, a woman who committed adultery was considered to be an "unfit mother." Nothing else needed to be proven against her. If she kept a spotless house, dressed and fed her children impeccably, and steered clear of radical politics, it didn't matter. If she slept with a man not her husband, she was an unfit mother. It goes without saying that the same did not hold true for fathers. Rufus told me, "Look, if you go to trial in Maryland, you are going to lose. You can appeal it, but it will take at least four years, it will cost you over ten thousand dollars, and during that time, he will have the children. That's one choice. Your second choice is to take the children the next time you are in Holyoke, and disappear. I'd suggest you go somewhere out of the country and don't plan on coming back until the children are grown. You have a third choice. Reconcile with your husband. Call him up and tell him you've reconsidered, that you want to stay married. Tell him whatever you have to, do whatever you have to do, to get him to drop the suit."

Heartsick and defeated, I realized that I would have to go to Archie and beg him to take me back. At first, Archie refused to meet with me. I found out later if a man sues his wife for divorce on the grounds of adultery but subsequently allows her to return, or even if he just has sex with her, this amounts to "condonation" of her actions and precludes him charging her with adultery. Eventually we met, and, sobbing with anguish, I told him that I would do anything if he would bring the children back from Holyoke and give me another chance. He was suspicious, but eventually I convinced him that we owed it to the children to try to make our marriage "work."

He set four conditions for agreeing to drop his divorce and custody suit. First, I had to agree to stop seeing Cappy. Second, I had to give up all my political activities in the women's and anti-war movements. Third, I had to give up my fellowship at the Peter Bent Brigham Hospital and go with Archie wherever he went to complete his surgical training. And fourth, I had to agree to have another child. Knowing I had no choice, I acquiesced to all these conditions, and he brought the children home. I did get Archie to agree that I would not have to write to Dr. Gorlin declining the cardiology fellowship he'd offered me until it was certain that Archie himself would not be joining a residency program in Boston.

I had railed against the oppression of women, I had agitated for change, but faced with losing my children, I bowed to the superior force of the law. I learned in the most traumatic, personal way just how egregiously the law was stacked against women. It was a lesson I never forgot: a lesson that kindled in me an even stronger predilection for the underdog and a deep and abiding distrust of the judicial system—a distrust that would be front and center about a decade later, when I took on my most infamous patient.

Emotionally, I was hollowed out, shriveled, maimed in some vital core of my being, utterly bereft of joy or its possibility, an automaton plodding hopelessly through the days. I felt like a bird with a broken wing, hobbled, at the mercy of a man who would wrench my children away if I didn't conform to his image of what a wife should be. In my heart, I loathed him and all he stood for.

I'd had to break off all contact with the people I was closest to, my friends in the Movement. I had no friends at that time who weren't in the Movement. I was isolated, lonely, and miserable. Any depressions I suffered previously paled before the all-embracing desolation I now endured.

I came directly home from work each evening, cooked meals, did all the housework without complaint, attended to all the errands that small children generate, had sex with my husband. I did all these things on automatic pilot, like a Stepford wife, trying to hide my misery. I abided by the rules Archie set down, but what he could not compel was my happiness.

Eventually, he agreed with me that we should see a marriage counselor. He realized that despite getting what he thought he wanted, neither one of us was happy. We had little in common and nothing to talk about. We were strangers sharing a household. I was never going to revert to the simple, acquiescent girl he'd married. Maybe he thought that a therapist would make me see the error of my ways. I wasn't sure what I hoped for, but could think of no other way forward except seeking professional help. Little of these sessions remain in my memory, but I remember being honest about my abhorrence of marriage as an institution. Within a few weeks, Archie seemed to accept that our marriage was untenable—that even though he had gotten what he thought he wanted, I would never be anything other than a reluctant participant in the charade our relationship had become.

Whatever remained of trust, affection, or hopefulness had been skewered on the stiletto of that bill of complaint. Undoubtedly, for him my sexual infidelity played the same role.

We decided that we would split custody of the children and that they would stay with Archie the first year, moving to Boston with me the following summer. I would have visitation three weeknights each week, and the children would stay with me every other weekend. I would move out, and Archie would stay in the apartment with the children and keep the car. I agreed to this because I would still be living in the same area and could see the children often. Archie insisted on having them the first year because he knew that the following year he would be back in residency training. It would be much harder to find someone to care for them when he was working six days a week and every other night. In the back of my mind, I knew that this alternating custody would never work, especially as the children got older. I thought I would have a better chance of getting full custody when I lived in Massachusetts, which I knew was a more liberal state than Maryland.

For the divorce itself, Archie elected to go to Haiti. I signed the necessary documents saying that I consented to the divorce, and that there were no property or custody issues. Archie flew off to Haiti and divorced me. It was July 24th, 1972, my twenty-eighth birthday. We had been married just two weeks shy of eight years.

Archie hired a live-in babysitter named Anne Dulishan. It was clear that she had no control at all over Dory, who was deeply traumatized by the divorce and misbehaving in a rather flagrant fashion. I can never look at Dory's school picture from that year without a sense of heartbreak and shattering guilt. Her little shoulders are very slightly but perceptibly hunched, a timid smile bends her mouth, but her eyes have a cringing, pleading look, as if she is expecting another catastrophe at any moment but is putting up a good front nonetheless. For his part, Archie began a determined search for a new wife as soon as he returned from Haiti, spending little time with the children. Anne Dulishan was not someone I wanted taking care of my children, but I could not convince Archie to fire her. She stayed with the children until they moved with me to Boston in the summer of 1973. Within three months of our leaving, Anne committed suicide.

In September 1972, *The Washington Post*'s Meryle Secrest wrote an article about me that appeared in that paper and, sent out by their wire service, in papers all over the country. Under the headline, "The Radicalizing of a Catholic Girl" was a photograph of me in surgical scrubs and gloves, taken at the Pre-Term abortion clinic where I worked part-time as a volunteer physician. It queried, "How did a shy, serious Catholic girl become so fierce an advocate of a woman's right to reject her traditional role of wife and mother, by even the most radical means? First there was the idealism of her parents, who moved into the Catholic community of Marycrest in 1948 [sic] with others who were 'trying to get away from the corrupting values of the city and back to the land'... Next there is the role Barbara played as surrogate mother, since her mother had a child every year..."

It took note of the fact that I was recently divorced, "in part because of their diverging views about her role. She says that he still thought in terms of a wife and mother; she wanted an equitable division of responsibility for the children and housework between them. She is a conscientious mother and warmly fond of her children, the bright-eyed Dory and the flaccid, logical Archie." The article says that I am "angrily convinced that the Supreme Court will let women down when it sits this fall on the constitutionality of all abortion laws." (Luckily, I was wrong.) It ended by quoting me: "The only way to change things is to do it ourselves. We can't depend on the men. They've had it too good."

The article produced reams of letters about equally divided between those who considered me a mass murderer ("No wonder your husband left you," wrote one woman) and those who thanked me for working for women's rights, often accompanied by hair-raising stories of what they had endured to obtain illegal abortions.

I resumed my political work with WONAAC, which was now receiving more support from NOW and other mainstream feminists because of the growing mobilization of anti-abortion forces. WONAAC filed an *amicus curiae*, or "friend of the court," brief to *Roe v. Wade* when it was argued in front of the Supreme Court that fall and continued to sponsor speak-outs, debates, and demonstrations. Three nights a week and every other weekend, I spent time with Dory and Archie, trying hard not to spoil them, and usually failing.

Cappy was off campaigning for the Socialist Worker's Party, and our affair fizzled out. I took up with a colleague at the NIH, Dr. Greg Brown. He was another Yellow Beret, working off his service commitment to the government by doing research on atherosclerosis at the NIH. When I first saw him during my first year there, I remember gaping at him because he was so handsome. Of medium height, with dark brown hair and eyes, he had a square face with even features—except for his nose, which had been broken playing rugby in college. He had a rugged, athletic build and stayed in shape by running. He had an engineering degree from MIT and both an MD and PhD from Johns Hopkins University.

Greg introduced me to sailing, which became a passion I have never outgrown. He was the first man I had ever met whom I suspected was a lot smarter than I was, but he was convinced that I knew more clinical medicine than he did. I pined for him when I was traveling or when, as could happen, he spent days on end in his laboratory or at the Clinical Center, where he was involved in both basic and clinical research. He was an adamant supporter of abortion rights, but otherwise was far more conservative politically than I was.

There is a movie from that time, *The Way We Were,* starring Robert Redford and Barbra Streisand, that had eerie parallels to our affair. In it, the two protagonists fall in love and have a child, but the relationship is doomed because of their political differences. I could never watch that movie without crying, and as much as I wished otherwise, I knew that Greg and I would part. The only question was when.

Amidst the clinical research, volunteering at the Pre-Term abortion clinic, and spending as much time with Dory and Archie as I could, I continued my political activities, appearing frequently on local television shows and once on the David Susskind show. In October, ABC-TV televised a debate on abortion at NYU's Law School in which Elaine Amendola, an attorney for Women vs. Connecticut, and I took on Father Lynaugh, the Catholic chaplain at Columbia University, and Dr. Carl Klinges, a gynecologist at St. Vincent's Hospital where I had been born. Later that month, I spoke for women's right to abortion at the University of California at Berkeley, and in November I debated abortion foes again, this time in Detroit. In January, I traveled to New York for events held by *Ms. Magazine* to honor "Found Women," a group selected because they had made a difference in women's lives. I was named as one of this first group and went to New York for the round of parties and press conferences that announced the new feature.

Another mass anti-war demonstration was planned for the grounds of the Washington Monument on the day of Nixon's second-term inauguration, January 20, 1973. I was invited to speak as a representative of the women's movement. The crowd was again estimated at 100,000 people, and facing a barrage of microphones and cameras, I spoke out against the continuing bloodshed in Southeast Asia. This proved to be the last of the mass anti-war demonstrations. On January 23, Nixon announced that Henry Kissinger and the North Vietnamese negotiator Le Duc Tho had signed an agreement "to end the war and bring peace with honor in Vietnam and South Asia." Within sixty days, the remaining 23,700 U.S. troops would be withdrawn. However, fighting continued between North and South Vietnam until April of 1975, when the North Vietnamese entered Saigon as the last American embassy officials and their terrified South Vietnamese allies were helicoptered to safety. With the signing of the peace accord, the anti-war movement withered away, at least as a mass movement.

The day before Nixon's announcement of the signing of the peace accords, the Supreme Court handed down its decision in *Roe v. Wade*, the case that attorney Sarah Weddington had argued the previous fall and that we in WONAAC had supported with an *amicus curiae* brief. At 10 a.m. on January 22, 1973, by a vote of seven to two, the justices ruled the Texas anti-abortion statutes unconstitutional because they violated the right to privacy.

Now, in one fell swoop, these laws that had brought death to thousands of women and unspeakable suffering to countless others, were struck down. Elation, jubilation, euphoria, relief, vindication—all these words describe my reaction to the news but fall far short of capturing the tumultuous emotion I felt. I had spent countless hours, as had thousands of other women, demonstrating, speaking, debating, writing, traveling, and arguing. Women won a victory that would improve their lives immeasurably. Fifty-three years, four months, and twenty-seven days after women won the right to vote, we won the right to abortion. Abortion had gone from being unmentionable in polite company to a constitutionally protected right, in the space of a few years. In one week, the raison d'être of two movements that had involved hundreds of thousands of people was abruptly no more. Abortion was legal, and the soldiers were coming home.

Having been forged in the cauldron of the anti-war and women's movements, I would be left with a deep distrust of authority, the courage to court controversy, and a willingness to stand up for the underdog. These characteristics would be my key weapons in the years I strove to keep my most notorious patient out of prison.

6 · THE WINDING ROAD TO RHODE ISLAND

Two roads diverged in a wood, and I—I took the one less traveled by,
And that has made all the difference.
—Robert Frost

I met Ned Bresnahan, who would become the father of my youngest child, when he answered an ad for a live-in babysitter I placed in the *Boston Phoenix*. As a first-year cardiology fellow at the (then) Peter Bent Brigham Hospital, I would have to take night and weekend call, so a live-in babysitter seemed the best option. At the time, Ned was a twenty-one-year-old part-time student at Boston University. He was six feet two inches tall and weighed about one hundred ninety pounds. He had a shock of blue-black hair and a very handsome, photogenic face. My father often said of him, "That Ned's not handsome, he's BEAUTIFUL." And he was. Dory took an instant liking to Ned, which was fortunate because she was shortly to be dealt another blow.

Not long after he moved to New York City to finish his surgical training at Cornell University's medical center, my ex-husband was introduced to Nancy Seymour Perryman, a divorced mother of two young sons. After dating for a few months, Archie and Nancy married on February 23, 1974 and moved into an apartment on the Upper East Side near the hospital. I felt a sense of relief. I knew instinctively that Nancy would not be all that keen on having my two children on a full-time basis if it came to another custody battle, and I thought that if Archie was happy with his home life, he would be less likely to fight me when I asked for full custody. Nancy had two sons, Jay and Scott, who were then five and three years old. She became pregnant almost immediately after the marriage and discovered that she was carrying twins. I had never been happy with our alternating custody arrangement and asked Archie to modify our agreement so that the children would live with me except during the summers and alternate school vacations. He refused. I retained a lawyer in Boston and applied to the Family Court there for full custody. Archie could no longer claim that I was an unfit mother, having let me move with the children to Boston.

Two weeks before the date set for trial, Archie withdrew his suit and agreed to allow me to have full custody. He was granted visitation every other weekend and every summer, from two weeks after school let out until a week before school started.

Little Archie was now four, an adorable little blond boy who appeared unscathed by the turmoil of the previous two years. Dory was another matter. She remained angry with me over the divorce and missed her father bitterly. She was furious at him for remarrying; she wanted to remain his number-one girl. But at least Dory and Archie got to spend alternate weekends with their father and his new family. I would put them on the shuttle flight to New York every other Friday and meet their return flight every other Sunday.

The cardiology fellowship was challenging but enjoyable. About once a month, I would either fly to Bethesda to visit Greg Brown, or he would come to Boston. However, in 1974, he would be moving to Seattle to do his own cardiology fellowship, and I knew our relationship would not survive the thousands of miles between us. On June

8, Greg flew to Boston for what was to be our last weekend together before his move to Seattle. He'd been invited to present his research findings at the prestigious Gordon Conference in New Hampshire the following week, and we were spending the weekend with his college classmate on Martha's Vineyard. It was my first trip to the island, but my depression over Greg's imminent departure blinded me to its beauty. On Sunday evening, I drove him to the conference and returned to Boston, my sadness once again a physical ache centered in my chest and throat. I would not see him again before he left for Seattle. We made no plans to meet again.

My new baby-sitter Ned proved to be a wonderful distraction. He also made himself useful around the house, cleaning and offering to cook dinner. We often sat up late, talking about our lives, our hopes and dreams, our pet peeves. Ned was the second child born to his parents; his older sister had been severely brain damaged at birth (the result of the obstetrician's incompetence) and eventually had to be put in an institution. Ned, who was born two years after his sister, got little of his father's attention but was his mother's darling. Mary Cashman Bresnahan came from a well-off family who considered themselves "lace curtain" Irish. They looked down on her working-class husband who was called "Handsome Eddie" for his dashing good looks. Ned grew up despising his father.

After her husband's death, when Ned was twelve, comfortably off with the proceeds of his life insurance, Ned and his mother grew even closer. She took him out to dinner every night of the week. She chose a different restaurant each night afraid people would think her a bad mother if they knew she didn't cook for her son. Ned swore that the only food in their refrigerator was a bottle of maraschino cherries.

What I found much more fascinating than the story of his upbringing was Ned's confession to me that he was gay; he had been to bed with a woman, but he was predominately attracted to men, and the more macho the better. He would later tell me why he had no trouble having sex with me: "Barbara, my dear, you are more macho than any man I have ever been with. That's why I find you so sexy."

He had known that he was gay from early childhood. He longed to have a daughter, but doubted he would be able to find a woman who could accept him as he really was. He did not feel capable of hiding his true nature. What he really wanted, he told me, was to stay home, take care of children, and be supported. He envied women who were married to wealthy men and could fritter away their days at the hairdressers, the country clubs, the department stores. He didn't think it was fair that this lifestyle was approved for women but not for men.

By this time, I realized that what every doctor needed, myself included, was a wife, or at least someone who was willing to perform the myriad duties of a wife. Our needs seemed to dovetail perfectly. We drew up mock contracts in which he promised to take care of the children, cook and clean and have sex with me, and I promised to give him an allowance, money for household expenses, and sexual freedom outside the home.

The day we decided that we would seal this pact by becoming lovers, and even before we consummated our "non-marriage of convenience with sex-role reversal," as I took to calling it, Dory sensed a change in our relationship. We brought the children out to dinner with us that night, June 28, 1974, at a local Italian restaurant. Dory kept giving us questioning looks and finally erupted at Ned, "You're not my mother's boyfriend, Dr. Greg Brown is." Ned was always able to placate Dory, and he agreed with her, taking the path of least resistance. A week later, she and Archie left to spend July and August with their father and his new family in New York. Ned and I were left alone to begin a fun-filled summer.

Ned became an avid lover, as proud of his prowess with a woman as I was vain of my ability to turn on a gay man. In my heart of hearts, I was always the flat-chested, freckle-faced, nerdy pre-teen who never expected to be desired. Having Ned as a lover shored up my still-shaky self-esteem. Our needs dovetailed wonderfully: mine for a house-husband, and Ned's for someone willing to support his unconventional lifestyle. At the end of the fellowship, despite his misgivings about moving to rural Pennsylvania, Ned decided to come with us as I started my first job out of training, on the full-time faculty of Pennsylvania State University's Medical School, in Hershey.

I found a split-level house in a new development, and at the end of June 1975 we packed up the furniture, plants, pets, and children and moved to Hershey. Many of my new fellow faculty members lived in the same neighborhood. One day, little Archie came home from playing with one of the neighbor's children and said to us, as if it was the most outlandish thing he had ever heard, "Mommy and Ned, do you know what Dougie told me? He said that MOMMIES stay home and DADDIES go out to work every day!" We told him that this indeed was a common practice, but it was news to him.

In July that year, Aunt Bea and Uncle Joe rented a beach house in Long Beach, New Jersey for two weeks and invited us all to visit. For a long time, I'd had been considering getting pregnant and this weekend, for some reason, made me yearn even more for another child. I think that part of this desire was strictly biologic; that old, dogged determination of DNA to reproduce itself. When I'd been pregnant with young Archie, it never occurred to me that he would be my last child. I wanted to have another infant in my arms, I wanted to nourish another baby with my own milk, I wanted to savor the inimitable aroma of a newborn's scalp and feel perfect pearly limbs caressing my hands in the bath water. But part of my desire was political. I wanted to make a statement. I wanted to thumb my nose at the institution of marriage. I wanted to tell women, you *can* have a baby without getting married, without becoming an outcast, without suffering the fate of Hester Prynne in Hawthorne's classic, *The Scarlet Letter*.

Ned needed no encouragement; his heart was still set on a daughter of his own, and we began to discuss having a baby. I told him that I had no intention of getting married, which he accepted, at least then. By February, 1976, I was pregnant. Ned was beside himself with joy at his impending fatherhood. I broke the news to my parents and told them that we were not going to marry. At this my father became furious, and I was banned from the parental home.

At first, I was not bothered by the fact that Ned, once I was pregnant, lost all interest in having sex with me. But as my first trimester depression and nausea cleared, my libido reasserted itself. Ned continued to shun me. Finally, I said, "Ned, I'm not going to harass you about sex because I couldn't stand it when Archie did that to me, but I'm curious, why are we no longer having sex?" He looked down his nose at me and replied in an affected hoity-toity accent, "Men of my class don't fuck pregnant women." (Pronouncing class as "closs.") "Oh," I replied, "what closs is that?" He refused to elaborate. I told him, "If I wanted to be celibate I would enter a convent, but at thirty-two, I am not ready to give up my sex life."

Just as he was free to sleep with whomever he wished, I would also take lovers, but I wanted us to continue to live together and raise the children. In theory, he agreed that this was only fair, but he began a campaign to try to convince me to marry him. He was quite irate that I would not make an "honest man" of him. "You don't love me. If you loved me, you'd marry me. What are you afraid of?"

Aside from my political objections to marriage, I was beginning to realize the extent of Ned's emotional problems. He was drinking more and more and smoking marijuana on a daily basis. He felt stifled and lonely in Hershey, where his sexuality had to be hidden, and he had no gay friends. He pined for the bright lights and night-life of a big city. He wanted us to move to New York or Los Angeles. "I can only be happy, and be myself, in a big city. Why can't we ever do what I want?"

This led to almost daily arguments, as I couldn't imagine living in either place.

As for marriage, I'd made it clear to him from the beginning that marriage was against my principles as a feminist, and that I would not marry him. He wanted the financial security of marriage, but what he said was, "I don't want my daughter to be born a bastard."

On October 31, at 3:15 am, Meagan came into the world. Ned had his longed-for daughter, and I dared to hope that he would moderate his drinking and drugging and be the kind of father that she and the other children needed.

When Meagan was a few months old, we were paid a visit by Gloria Steinem. We'd remained in touch in the years since I had been chosen as one of *Ms. Magazine*'s "Found Women." I picked her up at the airport in Harrisburg to take her to a nearby speaking engagement, and on the way, we stopped at the house in Hershey so I could show off my new daughter. She took one look at Meagan and joked, "Oh, babies from Central Casting, I see." Ned beamed with pride at this compliment, and we enjoyed an all-too-brief truce in our escalating war.

Although Ned slept with whomever he pleased, and our own sex life was moribund, he became insanely jealous whenever I slept with another man. By now, he'd run through all the money he'd inherited when his mother died in 1973 and was living on what I paid him to stay home and be a "house-husband." He was extravagant and utterly unable to live within a budget. He warned me not to even think of breaking up with him. "If you ever leave me, I'll hound you and make you miserable for the rest of your life." Our non-marriage of convenience with sex-role reversal was not working for either of us. Ned was going through mood swings that were becoming unmanageable and frightening. I worried about the effect his emotional state would have on the children, but my main concern was not to cause another major disruption in their life. I clung to the hope that things would get better.

By this time, I'd also become disillusioned with academic medicine and decided to look around for another job. Several friends from my years at the NIH, and a medical school classmate, Dan Lederer, had moved to Providence, Rhode Island, to become faculty members at Brown University's new medical school. I was offered a full-time, salaried position at the Miriam Hospital, one of the Brown teaching hospitals, but ultimately decided that I wanted to go into private practice. For one thing, I could make more money if I built up a successful practice than I could by remaining a salaried academician.

The part of academic medicine I enjoyed most was teaching, and that I could do as a private practitioner. I was tired of moving. I wanted to settle down in one place and stay there until I retired. Since 1969, I'd moved every other year, moves of hundreds of miles with children and pets in tow. After several trips to Providence I made up my mind to go into private practice there. There were no other female cardiologists in the state, and I thought this could work to my advantage, at least with female patients. I also feared, correctly as it turned out, that there would be male doctors who'd never refer their patients to a female physician as long as one of their male colleagues was available.

Rhode Island was within a few hour's drive of Rockland County, where most of my family still lived. Moreover, with my connections at Brown, I was assured of getting hospital privileges without difficulty. In fact, the only drawback was that Ned was less than delighted at the thought of moving back to his native state. He still pined for New York or California, but since I was the breadwinner, I got to make the decision. It is ironic that I would consider such reasoning sexist in a man, but that did not deter me.

In May, a month before we moved, I appeared on David Hartman's *Good Morning America* television show, debating abortion once more with another fetus fetishist. I refused to use the term "pro-life" to describe these people. As later events showed, abortion opponents would rack up an appalling record of carnage, murdering innocent clinic staffers and physicians with bombs and guns. My appearance on national television delighted Ned, and for a while he moderated his drinking, but before long our fights erupted again. We fought over his drinking and drug use, over our respective sex lives, and over his profligate spending habits.

I was consumed with anxiety and trepidation about the move to Rhode Island. I had no idea how one went about setting up a private practice, and I had three children and a "house-husband" to support. I wondered if patients would be prejudiced against me because I was a woman, although I had seen little of that in my previous positions. In academic medicine, patients are referred to the medical center and usually have little say over which physician they will see. In private practice, I would be depending on referrals from other doctors and on patients who could choose their own doctor. I tossed and turned for hours every night, unable to sleep as I fretted about whether I'd made the right decision. However, before six months had elapsed, my practice was doing well, helped along by referrals from an older cardiologist who no longer wanted to make hospital rounds and had me take care of his many patients who required hospitalization.

My relationship with Ned continued to be difficult. We both dated others, but Ned was consumed with jealousy whenever he learned about my forays with other men. One of these was an Italian-American from Cranston, a Providence suburb. Then twenty-six years old, Vinny and his partner owned a bar in Cranston, where I would occasionally go to have a drink. He told me that when he was younger he'd been a car thief, but now he had gone "legit." His brother-in-law "ran protection" at a local night club and was a "made man," according to Vinny. Like thousands of others at the time, I'd read *The Godfather* and seen the movie. I found them enthralling entertainment, and wondered what mobsters were really like.

It was through Vinny that I first heard the names Jack Cicilline, Nicky Bianco, Junior Patriarca, and Louis "Baby Shanks" Manocchio.* I'd already heard of Raymond Patriarca, who was familiar to anyone who read newspapers. Sensing my interest, Vinny loved to regale me with stories about Rhode Island's mobsters. To Vinny and his cronies, these guys were heroes, the neighborhood Robin Hoods, and they gossiped about them often. Eventually, Vinny sold his bar and started working construction, and our brief affair dwindled into friendship.

I returned to an old love, one that I had missed greatly during my two years in Hershey—sailing. During my time at the NIH, I had taken sailing lessons and had fallen in love with the sport. During my cardiology fellowship in Boston I'd bought a small sailboat, which I sailed on the weekends I was not working. In Rhode Island, I moved up from dinghies to bigger boats and began crewing on a thirty-four-foot sailboat that was raced on Narragansett Bay. There were regattas almost every weekend with parties afterwards.

*Retired State Police Captain Brian Andrews says that the correct term was "Baby Shacks" and that it described Louis' appearance when he was young and the success he had "shacking up" with the ladies. A policeman later made a typographical error on an arrest booking form and entered the alias "Baby Shanks" for "Baby Shacks."

Dory and young Archie went to Illinois to visit their father for the month of August. Big Archie had taken a job in the cardiac surgery department of Northwestern University. Ned was drinking heavily but refused either to move out or to seek help, blaming me for everything that was wrong in his life. His litany of recriminations was endless, and I escaped, or tried to, into work and play. My heart was soothed by the rhythm of the waves, by the sight of flocks of bird-like yachts beating to windward, by the mournful cry of foghorns, and by the sun's pirouetting frolic with the water. I felt a crisis was looming, but I could not envision when or what form it would take.

7 · The Stage Is Set

All the world's a stage, and all the men and women merely players...
—William Shakespeare

I met George Gregory during a sailboat race. At the time, he was working for C & C Yachts. C & C offered George's services as an adviser after the boat I was crewing on had a dismal showing in the first race of the season. George had sailed all his life; his mother, a superb sailor, had continued to race sailboats while she was pregnant. Originally from Ohio, he'd recently moved to Rhode Island from Toronto where he had been a member of the Canadian Olympic Sail Team. He raced in a dinghy called the Finn, which was even more of a sailing hot rod than the International 14, the boat my former lover Greg Brown raced. The Finn was a one-person boat, and Finn sailors had to be strong and muscular to control this stallion among dinghies. In fact, George could have modeled for Praxiteles. The muscles in his body strained at their covering of flesh, and his strength was prodigious. He was six years younger than I, with thinning blond hair and a perpetual tan. He lived, ate, slept and dreamed of sailing. He was a regular member of the crew, and we bonded during several sailboat races.

On September 9th, 1978, we crewed on our first over-night race. The start was in Newport, in the midst of a howling nor'easter. We had a downwind start in heavy seas, boats jibing out of control, the starting line a confusion of screams, shouts and near collisions. One yacht was dismasted and had to drop out, others tore their spinnakers, but we survived and settled in for hours of cold, wet torment. (I came to believe that I raced sailboats to discharge any masochistic tendencies I had in a way that was compatible with my feminism. It was Mother Nature beating up on me, not some man.) Every time I went below to warm up, I became nauseous from the wallowing of the boat, and had to run back up on deck to keep from throwing up. Others were not so fortunate and hung wretchedly over the lifelines, vomiting until there was nothing left to come up. I huddled next to George for warmth when he wasn't on the foredeck wrestling with the spinnaker pole. At one point during that endless night, I commented that I would give anything for a nice, hot shower. "Do you want to come shower at my apartment when we finish?" George offered. "You bet I would," I replied—and we both knew I had agreed to more than a wash up.

We finished the race at 5:30 the next morning in last place. I followed George's Volkswagen van to his apartment, located just outside Newport in Middletown, but my heart sank when we walked in the door. He had left his black Labrador, Sam, alone for almost a whole day and a fetid pile of dog shit sat in the middle of the living room floor. Next to this were the remains of a sweater Sam had chewed to death. Seeing this George erupted in fury (he later told me it was a gift from a woman in Canada he'd been enamored of) and began chasing the dog around the room, screaming curses.

A partially dismantled boat engine coated in greasy oil was the apartment's only decoration. "Barbara" I thought to myself, "I don't believe the things you'll go through to get laid." I showered first, bouncing off the walls because my body had not yet adjusted to the stillness of being on land. After George showered, we climbed into his bed and managed to warm ourselves up quite nicely. Afterwards, we fell into an exhausted sleep, wakening late in the afternoon. We had dinner that evening at the Black Pearl, a popular Newport restaurant located on the harbor. After dinner I drove back to Providence. After that, things moved quickly.

Within a few weeks, I convinced Ned to move out by telling him that George was moving in. It was only the fact that I was moving another man into the house that made Ned realize he had no choice but to leave.

Ned and I met with a lawyer in late September 1978 to draw up a separation agreement, which we both signed and swore to abide by. Ned affirmed that we were not married under the Rhode Island common law, and we each gave up any title or interest in the property of the other "by reason of cohabitation." The exception was that I agreed to give Ned $5,000 and title to the Volvo station wagon I'd bought the previous fall. The money was to tide him over until he could find a job, and the car was to allow him the mobility to search for one. We agreed that we would have joint custody of Meagan, but that physical possession would remain with me. We worked out a visitation schedule, which allowed him to have Meagan for overnight visits every weekend and for much of the summer. We both pledged not to remove her from the state without written consent of the other, or a court order. In return, he waived any claim to "future support, maintenance, care, or liability of any kind" from me and agreed to move out of the house.

I signed the papers with relief, hopeful that our agreement would allow our daughter to grow up having a relationship with both her parents. Meagan was not yet two, a beautiful, brown-haired child with a winning disposition. She had started walking at nine months and was beginning to talk. She showed no outward signs of trauma from the war between her parents, and I was hopeful that Ned would abide by the terms of our agreement and start to rebuild his life.

This hope was short-lived. Despite the agreement, he began a concerted campaign of harassment. Whenever he came to pick up Meagan, he demanded more money. He called my ex-husband with lurid tales of drunken orgies and drug dealers using my house as a base of operations, all products of his fevered imagination. He called my parents and several of my sisters and brothers with similar stories.

Hoping that he could placate Ned, George agreed to meet with him. "She's a slut and a whore," Ned told him, "and she'll break your heart like she broke mine."

He called the police in the middle of the night, pretending to be my husband, and told them someone was trying to break into the house. They came banging on the door, ruining our night's sleep. He wrote suggestive, sexual comments on the walls of men's rooms in bars, giving my home phone number. This led to middle-of-the-night phone calls from strangers.

After somehow finding out George's parent's telephone number, he called them in Ohio. He identified himself as my husband and told them that I had thrown him out of our home and installed their son in his place, that my ex-husband was suing me for custody of my two older children, that their son George had signed a written agreement to be financially liable for the support of the children, that my house was under observation by agents of the FBI and the Drug Enforcement Administration, and that my arrest, and that of their son, on charges of drug dealing, was imminent.

The inventiveness of Ned's imagination was truly breathtaking. In a panic, they called George at work and beseeched him to fly home to Cleveland immediately. I telephoned them myself after learning from George what Ned had done and tried as best I could to convince them that everything they had been told was false. They were somewhat placated, but asked that we fly out to Ohio for a visit, which we did the following weekend. Meeting me in person reassured them that I was not a Siren luring their son to doom. But my travail had only just begun.

After a physical altercation when Ned came to pick up Meagan for a visit, and I refused to give him more money, I called my lawyer at the time, Jim Mullen, and on October 11, 1978 he filed a petition with the Family Court asking for a restraining order against Ned, suspension of his visitation, and recognition of me as sole custodian of Meagan. On October 17, Ned, through his lawyer, filed a cross petition in which he averred that I was "an unfit person to have the care, custody and control" of Meagan, and asked that he be awarded custody.

On November 2, a Family Court judge, Angelo Rossi, issued a restraining order against Ned's harassing or molesting me, granted me full custody of Meagan, and ordered supervised visitation for Ned at my residence in the presence of one or more adults of my choosing. Ned's cross-petition was denied, but Ned persisted in his efforts and in December upped the ante by suing me for common-law divorce on grounds of irreconcilable differences, adultery, and "gross misbehavior in that she openly and notoriously lives and cohabits with a man not her husband." He also sought custody of Meagan on the grounds that I had "neglected the child's emotional and physical needs" and kept her in "an unsanitary and emotionally unstable environment." And finally, he asked the court to award him a "sum certain out of the earnings and estate of the Respondent for the support of the minor child; ordering an equitable division of the real and personal property of the parties."

A four-year battle, which before its resolution would involve almost every judge then hearing cases in family court, multiple lawyers, the Department of Children, Youth and Families, psychiatrists, psychologists, the *Providence Journal*, the Mafia, arrests, physical violence, and countless hours of heartache, had begun.

I'm convinced Ned's primary motive was revenge; the second was monetary gain. He firmly believed that I should support him for the rest of his life because I'd given birth to his child. I have no doubt the breakup was devastating to him. We were all the family he had left. His parents and sister were dead, and he wasn't close to his cousins, aunts, or uncles. I believe that he cared for me and the children, but his addiction to drugs and alcohol was worsening. I remember reading a wise statement once: "Alcoholics don't have relationships. They have hostages." The children were hostages in our drama, a lever he thought he could use to force me to continue supporting him.

On Saturday night, February 7, 1979, while I was working up a patient in the emergency room, I was paged by the hospital operator for a phone call from Ned. He'd called the house and was livid that the children were home with George while I was at the hospital. "I don't want that gigolo taking care of Meagan," he screamed into the phone. When I hung up, he kept calling and having me paged. I ignored these subsequent calls when the operator told me it was the same man. I was frightened because Ned sounded out of control, and I suspected he was either drunk or high on drugs. I was afraid he would confront me in the hospital in front of nurses and other physicians and cause a scene. I was also terrified that he would physically assault me, as he had tried to do in the past.

Then George phoned to say that Ned was repeatedly calling the house. When I went to leave the hospital, I was accosted by Ned and his friend Janice, who jumped out at me from between cars in the parking lot and tried to grab me. Janice was a friend from Ned's childhood. Frightened, I ran back into the hospital and asked the security guard to escort me. He wrote a report of the incident to the head of hospital security.

After leaving the Miriam Hospital, balked of their desire to confront me, they drove to my house. Realizing that Ned was drunk, and on the warpath, George was frantic with worry and left the younger children with Dory while he drove to the hospital to make sure I was alright. I'd already left the hospital, but as he was driving back to the house he realized that Ned and Janice were in the car in front of him. Just before they all arrived at our home on Laurel Avenue, Ned recognized George's car and stopped, blocking the street. He and Janice left their car and advanced toward George, demanding to talk to him. He rolled down his window and Janice reached in and hit him in the face, knocking his glasses off. At this point George jumped out of the car, but they ran away, got into their car, and drove off. Six days later, the police came to the house and arrested George for assault. He was released on personal recognizance, but by now even the mention of Ned was enough to enrage him. Ned's goal to drive a wedge between us was having its intended effect, but there seemed little we could do to stop his rampage, other than seek resolution through the Family Court.

※

On Labor Day weekend in 1979, George and I took the children to Block Island. We traveled by ferry. Block Island is a small, pork-chop-shaped island about twelve miles off the coast. We'd visited there earlier in the summer and fallen in love with its bucolic hills, Victorian homes, water-lily choked ponds, and empty beaches. I resolved to buy my own sailboat so that we could go to Block Island on our own, and I chose a J-30, a new design that resembled a large dinghy but slept six people comfortably. It had a small galley, a head (bathroom), an icebox, and a navigation station. I named her *Boadicea* after the Celtic warrior queen who led a revolt against Rome in A.D. 69, leveling the towns that later became Colchester, St. Albans, and London before being defeated by the Roman legions. Since I'd been rebelling against Rome for much of my life, I thought it fitting to name my boat after an earlier rebel. George was delighted to have a boat to captain, and I hoped it would serve to distract him from Ned's campaign of harassment.

In spite of all the turmoil in my private life, my practice was growing. I had office hours three days a week, reserving the other two days for teaching and performing heart catheterizations in the hospital, so I needed only a part-time secretary.

One other person entered my life as the '70s drew to a close, and my friendship with him would be the proximate cause of all the turmoil the decade of the '80s would bring. He was a cardiac surgeon, and his name was Robert Indeglia.

I have no recollection of my first meeting with Bob Indeglia, but he was the second local physician to refer me large numbers of patients. Bob remembers seeing me for the first time at one of the weekly cardiac catheterization conferences at which I was the only female attending physician in those days. I made it a point to make my opinions known. I was trying to set an example for the other women there who were nurses or residents or medical students.

At one of these meetings, I disagreed with one of the more bombastic older cardiologists who in stentorian tones was emphatically expounding a position that I was convinced was very mistaken—and I said so. "That woman has balls," Bob thought to himself, and asked one of the nurses who I was. "That's Dr. Roberts," she replied, "the new cardiologist in town." It was after this incident that he began to refer me patients.

Then in his early forties, he'd attended college at Johns Hopkins University, where he played lacrosse against Jim Brown, later to be an All-Star running back for the Cleveland Browns and a teammate of my ex-husband's. Bob Indeglia had a face that could have been lifted whole from a Renaissance painting of a Venetian doge—at least, one of the few handsome ones. In fact, *il Doge* was what I nicknamed him. Some marauding Norse raider in the last millennium had spilled the DNA for pale blue eyes into the Mediterranean gene pool, and Bob's baby blues were a startling contrast to his ebony hair. His nose meandered crookedly down his face, broken by a lacrosse stick, but this did nothing to detract from his good looks. He was flirtatious and charming, but more important, he was a brilliant and talented surgeon.

His father, Pasquale, was also a doctor, one of the first surgeons of Italian descent to practice in the state; "Dr. Pat," as he was called, was much loved by his patients. Bob's mother was a Cianciarulo, from a prominent Italian-American family on Federal Hill. Her father, Bob's grandfather, Benjamin Cianciarulo, was one of the first Italian-American lawyers in Rhode Island and was an early entry into the lists of attorneys who would defend the then-young criminal, Raymond Patriarca. Benjamin Cianciarulo was also elected to the state house of representatives and the state senate. The law firm he founded in 1915 is still in existence, directed by his great-grandson, Vincent Indeglia. Bob was raised in a huge Victorian pile on Broadway, then the street where the successful doctors, lawyers, and undertakers in the Italian-American community had their homes.

We became friends as well as colleagues, and in November 1979, at a political fund-raiser, he introduced me to his best friend, Jack Cicilline. Jack was a larger-than-life figure, a brilliant, flamboyant lawyer who was soon to acquire his most famous client.

Jack came from a family of modest means. His father had been employed by the state government and his mother stayed home to raise Jack, his two younger brothers, and a sister. Jack married Sabra Peskin, his high school sweetheart, when he was a freshman at Providence College, after they eloped. He worked part time in the mail room at the State House, and he and Sabra and their growing family, which would eventually number five children, lived rent-free in a South Providence tenement owned by Sabra's father, Irving Peskin. Irving also owned and managed a small grocery store, the Elmwood Spa, and was a bookmaker on the side. During Prohibition he'd been a bootlegger. When he opened his bookmaking operation in the early 1950s, he sought and received the blessing of Raymond Patriarca, already the acknowledged head of the New England mob.

After college, Jack attended Suffolk Law school at night, graduating in four years. As a law student, he clerked for Joseph Bevilacqua Sr., a prominent attorney with a large criminal law practice, and worked in Providence mayor Joe Doorley's office as the mayor's administrative assistant. Jack had political aspirations himself, but after an abortive run for state representative in 1968, he went into practice with Bevilacqua, then the Speaker of the Rhode Island House. Bevilacqua left the firm when he was appointed Chief Justice of the Rhode Island Supreme Court in 1976, by which time his sons Joe Jr. and John had joined Jack in the practice.

In 1979, Jack hired an alleged mobster, Nicky Bianco, as a paralegal soon after Bianco's release from prison on charges of income tax evasion. This caused considerable controversy with the Bevilacquas, and Jack left to start his own firm on Federal Hill, across the street from Raymond Patriarca's office on Atwells Avenue, the Hill's main thoroughfare. He rented the space from Raymond's son, Raymond Jr., whom he had known for several years. Jack had met Raymond Sr. in 1968 when he first joined the Bevilacqua firm. It was Jack's practice to leave his home each workday at about 6:30 a.m. and drive to the Hill, just as Raymond Sr. was driven up to his own office. Raymond's place of business was the National Cigarette Service, a small, nondescript storefront from which Raymond supplied cigarette vending machines to restaurants and stores throughout New England. Jack and Raymond struck up a casual acquaintance because, as Jack said, "We were the only ones up that early." At the time, Harvey Brower was Raymond's lawyer. The following year, Raymond was sentenced to prison in a murder conspiracy case. When he was released in 1975, he resumed his early morning routine on the Hill and renewed his friendship with Jack. By the time he had his next brush with the law, Harvey Brower was in prison himself, convicted for conspiring to help a client jump bail.

My friendship with Jack Cicilline was cemented when I became his father's cardiologist, in April of 1980. The elder Cicilline suffered a massive heart attack and was admitted to the South County Hospital, a small community hospital in southern Rhode Island that did not have a cardiac catheterization laboratory or an open-heart surgery program. Unfortunately, by the time Mr. Cicilline was transferred to the Miriam Hospital, the damage had been done, and there was nothing, other than manipulating his medicines, that we could offer.

During the weeks he spent as a patient in the Coronary Care Unit, I got to know all of the Cicillines and they got to know me, my boyfriend George, and the children. Jack's father never recovered from his heart attack, and died on May 26, 1980 after a six-week hospitalization. During the weeks of his final illness, Jack and I spent hours together, both in the hospital and outside, and I met many of his clients and friends. One of these was Raymond "Junior" Patriarca.

A year younger than I, Junior was the only child of Raymond Sr. and his first wife, Helen, who'd died of cancer in 1965. Junior was a distinctly unprepossessing man of medium height with a liverish complexion, receding dark-brown hair, and a manner that seesawed between truculence and timidity. His devotion to his father, however, was deep and unfeigned. He told me that he was very concerned about his father's health. Raymond Sr. had been diabetic since the 1940s, had had a heart attack in the 1960s, and had developed vascular disease in his legs. His current physician was Dr. Frank Merlino, but Junior wanted to get a second opinion about his father's cardiac condition and asked me if I would be willing to see his father as a patient. Perhaps naively, I had no qualms about agreeing to this; the aging crime boss had kept a low profile since being released from his last prison term. I arranged an office appointment, but before that could take place, Raymond Sr. was admitted to the Fatima Hospital with a gangrenous toe, which eventually had to be amputated. His office visit was put on hold until after he'd had a chance to recuperate from the operation. But that office visit was never to materialize; Raymond would be arrested and I would become his cardiologist on the same fateful day.

PART THREE

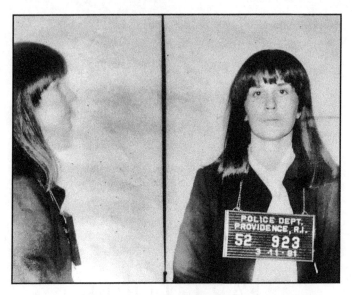

Above: Mug shot of Barbara Roberts, March 11, 1981.
Courtesy of Providence Police Department.

Below: Louis Manocchio mug shot, 1979.
Courtesy of the Providence Police Department.

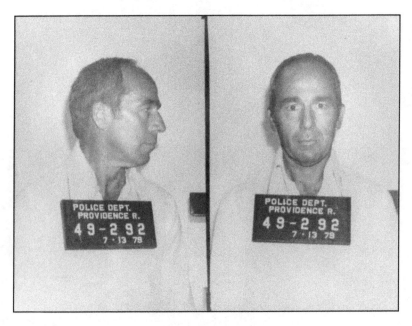

Dory, Louis Manocchio, and Barbara Roberts, 1982.

Louis Manocchio, Dory, and her husband,
Luis Reis, August 2018.

*Rita O'Toole Patriarca, Raymond, and their
daughter-in-law, Barbara Patriarca.
Courtesy of Raymond J. Patriarca.*

*Rita O'Toole Patriarca, Raymond, unknown woman, and
grandson, Christopher. Courtesy of Raymond J. Patriarca.*

Raymond L. S.
PATRIARCA
Entered into Eternal Rest
JULY 11, 1984
Providence, Rhode Island

Rest in Peace

3-0187
V. J, Berarducci & Sons

Funeral Mass Card of RLSP.
Courtesy of Raymond J. Patriarca.

Raymond and grandson, Christopher.
Courtesy of Raymond J. Patriarca.

8 · MUG SHOTS AND MAGAZINES

Notoriety and public confession in the literary form is a frazzler of the heart you were born with, believe me.
—Jack Kerouac

Raymond had been discharged from his first hospitalization in January 1981, and I had begun making house calls to check on him. He continued to have frequent bouts of angina, usually brought on by emotional stress. The forces of law and order were closing in for another go-round. Raymond Junior was subpoenaed to appear before a grand jury, which upset his father greatly. On the night of March 15, 1981, Junior's wife Barbara and son Christopher were stopped by the police after leaving Raymond Senior's house, where they had been visiting. They were not charged with speeding or any other violation, but when Raymond found out about it, he became extremely upset and developed severe angina, which did not respond to three nitroglycerines. I was called and immediately had him brought by Rescue to the hospital, where he was admitted to the Coronary Care Unit.

In a way, I was glad that the police had given me an excuse to hospitalize Raymond. Jack Cicilline had told me that he expected Raymond to be indicted by Massachusetts any day in conjunction with the murder of a man called Bobby Candos, and I wanted him in the hospital when that happened so I would be able to monitor him more closely. The next day, the *Providence Journal* reported this latest admission on the front page and said that: "Dr. Barbara Roberts, Patriarca's physician, declined early this morning to describe Patriarca's illness. Her answering service said she would not do so without Patriarca's consent..."

The paper neglected to mention that it would be a breach of medical ethics for me to discuss a patient's condition with *anyone* else, without his consent. I could always rely on their putting a negative spin on my actions. At least they were predictable, and my loathing for the newspaper grew.

Within hours of his admission to the hospital, Raymond was indicted by a grand jury in New Bedford, Massachusetts for "allegedly ordering the 1968 execution..." as the *Journal* reporter wrote on March 18. By now, an abnormally slow heart rate had made it necessary for me to implant a temporary pacemaker wire in Raymond's heart, a development that the *Journal* duly noted, reporting that "Patriarca was admitted to the hospital Sunday night, only 15 hours before he was indicted" and adding that "Attempts to reach both Cicilline and Dr. Roberts last night were unsuccessful. The UPI quoted Cicilline as saying that he did not know how the operation would affect scheduling of Patriarca's arraignment on charges of accessory before murder and murder conspiracy in the Candos case. 'I wouldn't know,' UPI quoted him as saying, 'until I talk to the doctor about the extent of hospitalization that is going to be required.'" In the end, Raymond didn't require a permanent pacemaker because his pulse did not again drop so dangerously low.

He continued to have attacks of angina, and these were easily provoked by discussions of the legal cases pending against him. Jack tried to have his arraignment on the latest charge postponed, but Massachusetts refused and insisted that Raymond be brought to the Superior Court in New Bedford. I approached Beth Mancini, the CCU nurse

I thought was the most competent, and asked if she would be willing to ride with me and Raymond in the ambulance and to assist me if he required CPR. She agreed and helped me put together a collection of all the intravenous medications we thought we might need in the event that he suffered a cardiac arrest. With an intravenous line placed in his arm, electrodes on his chest to monitor his electrocardiogram (EKG), oxygen running into his nose via a tube, blankets covering his wasted frame, and a towel draped over his head, enclosing the sides of his face like a nun's wimple, he was wheeled into an ambulance for the 45-minute ride from Providence to New Bedford. He'd awakened at 5:00 that morning with an episode of angina that responded to one nitroglycerine tablet. On the way to New Bedford, I sedated him with intravenous Valium, hoping to prevent a recurrence, and gave him an additional, prophylactic nitroglycerine just before we arrived at the court house.

The cortege leading and following the ambulance consisted of more than a dozen cars, stuffed with armed policemen, FBI agents, lawyers, and reporters. I remarked *sotto voce* to Beth, "You'd think he was Attila the Hun in his prime instead of a sick old man who can barely walk 10 feet without getting angina." As we pulled up to the courthouse in New Bedford, a crowd of hundreds of people lined the streets hoping to catch a glimpse of Raymond. We hurried past the television cameras. I was wearing a mauve suit, a white blouse with a small jabot, and I was carrying a doctor's bag filled with drugs I hoped not to have to use. The scene struck me as surreal.

In the courtroom I sat directly behind the stretcher, my eyes glued to the monitor screen where Raymond's EKG was displayed continuously. Jack and I listened to the prosecutor, Robert Kane, request that bail be set at one million dollars. "This man's role in that murder (Candos) was to issue a death warrant punctuated by the words 'Nail him,'" he said.

Not five minutes into the proceedings, I noticed that Raymond's EKG was showing clear-cut signs of ischemia, or insufficient blood supply to the heart muscle. I leaned over and, in a whisper, asked him if he was having any angina. He admitted that he was, so I motioned

Jack over and told him. Jack reported this to the judge, who allowed me to take Raymond into an adjoining room, where I gave him additional oxygen and nitroglycerine. After two of the tablets, his angina resolved. It recurred once more in the hour or so we waited for the arraignment to be over, but again it responded to nitroglycerine. On the way back to Providence, he developed hypoglycemia (low blood sugar) because his lunch had been delayed, but this was easily aborted with the orange juice we had also brought along, just in case.

Only one thing kept these proceeding off the front page of the *Providence Journal* the next day, March 31, 1981: President Reagan and his aide, James Brady, had been shot by John Hinckley. On page 3, The Second Front Page, were pictures of Jack, Raymond on the stretcher, me, the prosecutor and assorted other courtroom observers, a close-up of Raymond's towel-wrapped head, and another picture of Raymond being wheeled into the courthouse. A head shot of me, a very unflattering one, was placed in the midst of the text. The *Journal* noted that: "Earlier in the day, Patriarca waived extradition to Massachusetts from his hospital bed in proceedings that were barred to the press on orders from Dr. Roberts. The seriousness of Patriarca's condition has been the subject of sharp debate virtually since his arrest last December... There are those who, like Johnston Police Chief William P. Tocco Jr., say they suspect that Patriarca's most recent hospitalization two weeks ago was simply a ploy to enable him to delay a court appearance..."

In fact, at least among all the doctors who examined him, there was no controversy about the extent of Raymond's heart disease, its seriousness, or what the stress of a trial and incarceration could precipitate. During his first hospitalization in December, the state hired Dr. Albert Most, Chief of Cardiology at Rhode Island Hospital, and a professor of medicine at the Brown University School of Medicine to render an "independent" assessment of Raymond's cardiac status. Dr. Most was asked to see Raymond again during his admission in March. In the report he submitted to Henry Gemma, a prosecutor in the Attorney General's office, he noted that: "...since the stress of a trial could be deleterious to his health I would caution against exposing him to that stressful situation."

The Attorney General's Office reportedly refused to release a copy of Dr. Most's report to the press. It was finally mentioned in the newspaper several weeks after it was given to the Attorney General when Jack Cicilline submitted it, along with other doctors' reports, in support of a motion to postpone Raymond's trial on the Curcio murder charge. Had Dr. Most found that Raymond was faking his cardiac disease, I have no doubt his report would have been plastered all over the front page of the *Providence Journal* within hours of being submitted. The attempts of the *Journal* to cast doubt on my testimony did not go unnoticed.

Under the headline "A case of 'biased reporting," the *Journal* printed a letter that was written by one of my patients. In it, he said:

> *Being a patient of Dr. Barbara Roberts, I found a story hidden next to the daily temperature of Pittsburgh interesting. This little story stated that a state appointed cardiologist, Dr. Albert Most, had found Mr. Raymond Patriarca a 'bona fide coronary artery disease' case. Also, it states that a trial would put him in jeopardy and that this 70-plus-year-old man must soon undergo an operation to try to prevent a stroke. This man's legal entanglements aside, it seems the* Journal *has presented an unfair indictment of Dr. Roberts and Miriam Hospital. The* Journal's *long-time habit of slanting its stories was never more prevalent than in the series of front-page articles that questioned Dr. Roberts' medical judgment and Miriam's ethics. To suggest that Dr. Roberts' decisions were based on circumstances and personalities other than medical considerations has now been proven to be biased reporting and possibly sensationalism on the part of the editors. Because I am a patient of Dr. Roberts, I know first-hand that her decisions are based on medical realities and fact. To question her ethics in this questionable manner violates a doctor's basic quality—trust. In my opinion, this borders on slander. Further, I have been a patient at Miriam Hospital many times and can personally state that medical judgments there are based strictly on medical evidence and are not designed to accommodate anyone's whims. The* Journal *once again has neglected to present both sides of the story and*

now that Dr. Roberts and Miriam have been shown by the state's own doctor to have been prudent in their decisions, either a public airing of this exoneration or an apology should be forthcoming.

In reply, the *Journal* editors appended to this letter a statement saying that the story on Dr. Most's findings was carried by both the *Journal* and the *Evening Bulletin*. It claimed that "The other stories cited were straight-forward news accounts in which the *Journal-Bulletin* questioned neither the medical judgment of Dr. Roberts nor the ethics of Miriam Hospital."

❧

My custody battle with Ned was still pending. There were hearings on February 4 and 9, 1981, but each resulted only in continuances. A reporter for the *Providence Journal*, Martha Smith, was calling my office repeatedly asking to interview me for an article she was writing for the Sunday Magazine supplement. I was horrified to learn of this, knowing how likely it was to cause the children grief, and to cause even more gossip about my private life. I refused to meet with her for many weeks, while I called everyone I knew who I thought might have some influence with the *Journal*, but to no avail. The paper was going ahead with the article whether I co-operated or not. Ms. Smith interviewed Ned, my ex-husband Archie, Jack Cicilline, and even Kevin DeMarrais, a classmate of Archie's who was then the sports information director at Columbia. Finally, with great reluctance, but wanting her to hear my version of events, I met with her on February 27th at 3 Steeple Street, a small restaurant in downtown Providence. I refused to discuss either Ned or Raymond, but otherwise answered her questions honestly. Despite my trepidations about meeting with her, it proved to be a wise decision.

The weekend of March 8 and 9, Ned took Meagan for her scheduled visitation. He was living in a one-room apartment in an old Victorian house on Arlington Avenue, about a mile from our home. I had only seen the exterior of the building and wasn't even sure where his apartment was located, just that it was on one of the upper floors of the four-story house.

On Saturday night, Meagan called, and I could tell from her voice that something was bothering her. She told me that her father said she wasn't coming home to me the next day. I assured her that she would be coming home the next night, just as she always did on weekends she spent with her father. We talked for a few more minutes and then she hung up, sounding less anxious.

I was furious at Ned for manipulating her emotions this way. At four and a half, she was a beautiful, precocious child who immediately won the hearts of everyone she met. My mother often said, "It's not that child's first time around. She's been around a few times before." Meagan seemed to possess wisdom far beyond her years, as if she were indeed inhabited by an old soul that had survived many lifetimes. I adored her, as did her older siblings, and was determined to protect her as much as possible from the ugliness of the court battle. I lived in constant fear that Ned would kidnap her again, as he had once when she was an infant. At that time, he flew both of them to San Francisco and only returned after I paid him the expenses for the trip.

From personal experience I knew that he often drank to excess and used drugs. In fact, he smoked marijuana in Meagan's presence, something I never did. My style of parenting was to lead by example; I believed that actions spoke louder than words. I seldom drank alcohol and never smoked marijuana in the children's presence. Now that I was Raymond's physician, I never smoked marijuana at all, unsure when I might be followed by undercover police, or FBI agents. I also knew that Ned sometimes left Meagan with a seventeen-year-old male baby-sitter when he went out. Meagan said she didn't like this teenager but refused to tell me why. So I worried constantly when she was with her father during his court-ordered visitation, and I'm sure she sensed this, despite my efforts to hide my unease.

That Sunday morning, the shrill note of the telephone awakened us at 7:30. Even before I picked up the phone, I was seized with dread and a premonition of danger. Meagan's hysterical voice screamed, "Mommy, come get me; Mommy, come get me," before the telephone was slammed down. I was instantly awake, and frantic. I called her back, but the line was busy. George tried to calm me down as we both hurriedly dressed. The phone rang again, within minutes, with Meagan's terrified voice repeating the same plea.

Various scenarios played obsessively across the screen of my mind. Had her father taken an overdose? Had he brought someone home who was attacking them both? Whatever was going on, I needed to get her away from it and back to our home where I could protect her. I called Jack Cicilline, awakening him. He tried to calm my fears and said he would send Matty Guglielmetti, a friend of Junior's over to Ned's apartment to see what was going on and bring Meagan to me. "No, Jack," I replied, "I don't want that. I can just see the headlines if someone with mob connections gets involved. George and I will go and get her."

On the way out of the house, George grabbed a baseball bat, not knowing what we would find at Ned's apartment. We got into the car and drove the short distance to Ned's address. On the street all was quiet. There was no sound emanating from the house, which only increased my terror. Were we too late? Were they already dead, or gone? The back door to the building was locked, and no one responded to our knocks. We forced the door open and crept up the stairs. After Meagan's phone calls, the silence was eerie and chilling. On the second-floor landing was a suitcase I recognized as Ned's. I turned the knob of the door handle and was able to open the door a few inches before it was caught and held by a flimsy hook and eye latch, like the ones used to secure screen doors. I was able to see into the tiny room.

Ned cowered on the floor in the corner, hissing like a cornered cat. "The police are on their way," was all he said. A mattress took up most of the floor space and on it I could see the outline of a little crouched body, covered with soiled blankets. I was terrified that Meagan was dead and screamed her name. Putting our shoulders to the door, George and I burst open the lock and entered the room. With this, Meagan jumped up from the bed and held her arms out to me in mute appeal. I scooped her into my arms and we ran down the stairs, Ned in pursuit. Meagan kept pleading, "Take me home, Mommy, take me home." Ned followed us across the street to where the car was parked, but when we got there, George took the baseball bat from the back seat and started to advance towards him. At this Ned turned and fled while I screamed at George to leave him alone and get back in the car. Ned was never touched, but I knew what would happen next.

When we got home I told George to leave because I was sure that it was only a matter of time before the police arrived. I tried to comfort Meagan, who refused to divulge what had made her so upset that she placed those telephone calls. She clung to me like a limpet to a rock and wouldn't leave my arms. Dory, Archie, and I all hugged and kissed her and told her that nothing bad was going to happen, and gradually she became quiet. A police car pulled up to the house. I told Archie to take Meagan up to the third floor and not come down unless I told him to.

I called Jack and told him that the police were at my door. He instructed me to let them in and asked to speak to them. Jack explained that he was my lawyer and gave them some background information on the custody suit. The police wanted to know where George was, and I told them truthfully that I did not know, although I was fairly sure he had gone to Portsmouth where our boat was in dry dock for the winter. They also said that Ned wanted Meagan returned to him. I told them that I wouldn't allow that, and that Meagan would refuse to go. They insisted on seeing her themselves to make sure she was all right, so I brought her down from the third floor. She was now, once again, shaking with fear. They asked her if she wanted to go back to her father's, and she very emphatically told them, "No! No! I won't go there." At that the police left.

The next morning Jack, Meagan and I went to the Providence police station. A large gray building located conveniently close to Federal Hill, it had the usual miasma of police stations around the world, a witch's brew concocted of grime, stale coffee, cigarette smoke and the detritus of afflicted lives. We met with Major Wilson and Lt. Rocchio, who was assigned to investigate Ned's complaint. I told them the sordid, sad story of my relationship with Meagan's father. I recounted his warning that if I ever broke up with him, he would make my life miserable forever.

I told them what had happened the day before, up to the point where we arrived at the door to Ned's apartment building. At this they told me not to tell them anything else because I might say something that would incriminate myself. This was worrisome. How could it be incriminating to take a child from a situation that, for whatever reason, had terrified her? If I had not rescued her and some evil had befallen her, I had no doubt that I would have been accused of child neglect. It was a classic Catch-22, and I feared that worse was to come. I was not mistaken. I found out that Ned had repeatedly called the police since the incident on Sunday, demanding that George and I be arrested.

That Wednesday my Family Court attorney, John Bevilacqua and I were in court trying to get an order to suspend Ned's visitation rights. My beeper went off. It was Jack Cicilline's secretary, her voice quivering with the barely suppressed excitement of a passerby at the scene of a spectacular car wreck. "Dr. Roberts," she whispered, "wherever you are, Jack wants you to make yourself scarce until he can make some arrangements with the police. We just got a call that there's a warrant out for your arrest, and the police are looking for you." "Gail," I responded, "if they want me, I'm not that hard to find. I'm in Family Court with John Bevilacqua."

I gave John the news; he called the police and made arrangements to "surrender" me as soon as our Family Court business was completed. The police met us outside the courthouse. They told John that as a special favor to him, they would not handcuff me. It all seemed unreal, a dream dredged up from some ludicrous cranny of a lunatic's subconscious. I had been almost trampled by mounted policemen at anti-war demonstrations in the '70s, and had caught an occasional whiff of tear gas, but I had never even come close to being arrested. I was absolutely certain that if I were not Raymond Patriarca's physician, the person who had snatched him from the jaws of the law three months before, Ned would have been told to get lost and stop wasting the police's time. But I was fair game in the war between the Mafia and the law, and if my children got caught in the crossfire too, then so be it.

Much as Raymond had been, but without the rifles at the ready, I was put in the back seat of a police cruiser and driven to the police station. I was wearing the mink coat that Junior had given me a few months before, and the cop who took my mug shots and fingerprinted me told me, "Gee, you sure don't look like a criminal."

"I'm not. I'm the victim here," I replied.

He had an Irish brogue, and to distract me from the mortification I was feeling, I engaged him in conversation about Ireland. I told him about my brother-in-law, Jack Holland, whose first book had recently been published to great reviews. I told him about a trip to Ireland we'd taken in 1976 — anything to blot out the reality of what was occurring. I was reminded of what Adlai Stevenson said on losing the presidential election to Dwight David Eisenhower. "It hurts too much to laugh, and I'm too old to cry." I WOULD NOT cry, at least not where anyone could see me, but my heart was shriveled with desolation. I was charged with a felony, breaking and entering, daylight, occupied dwelling. It carried a five to seven-year prison term if I was convicted. George was later arrested on the same charge. I was taken to District Court, but since it was a felony, I was not allowed to enter a plea of not guilty. Pleas to felony charges had to take place in Superior Court, but John Bevilacqua secured my release on personal recognizance, since I had no prior criminal record.

Try as I might, I could find nothing amusing about being arrested. Jack told me that the identifying numbers under my mug shots were quickly known, and bookies did a banner business from gamblers wanting to play them that day. When the older children got home from school, I told them what had happened to prepare them for the publicity I was sure would follow. They were quietly sad, young Archie in particular, ever my defender, upset at this latest proof of the extent to which Ned would go to hurt me.

The next day, the *Providence Journal* carried reports in both the morning edition and the *Evening Bulletin* about my arrest. The latter, under the headline, "Doctor Released on Charge Linked to Girl's Custody" noted:

Dr. Barbara H. Roberts, one of Raymond L.S. Patriarca's physicians, surrendered this morning to police, who had a warrant for her arrest on a charge that she entered the home of her former boyfriend without his consent last Sunday. Dr. Roberts, 37 [sic], of 312 Laurel Ave., was arraigned in District Court and released on personal recognizance by Judge Paul P. Pederazani. Because the charge is a felony, she entered no plea. The charge stemmed from an incident in which Dr. Roberts reportedly went to the house to retrieve her four-year-old daughter, who has been the subject of a custody battle between her and her former boyfriend, Edward Bresnahan, 28 of 41 Arlington Ave.

Bresnahan told police that Dr. Roberts and George Gregory, also of 312 Laurel Ave., smashed in the door to his home and assaulted him after he refused to let them enter the house to get the child. Dr. Roberts' lawyer, John Bevilacqua, accompanied her when she surrendered. A warrant also had been issued for Gregory, and police were waiting for him to surrender early this afternoon. Police said neither Dr. Roberts nor Bresnahan had documents that would prove who had legal custody of the child.

On the same day that the *Journal* reported my arrest, the news was broadcast by a local television station on the evening news show.

In fact, as I later learned from Family Court documents Ned's version of the incident bore little relation to reality. He claimed that after we took Meagan from his apartment George had assaulted him with a tire iron. I was mortified to have my personal problems and arrest broadcast large. Much like women in earlier days, doctors are only supposed to get their names in the paper when they marry or die, unless they discover the cure for cancer or win the Nobel Prize. The *Journal* was out to depict me in the worst possible light.

When I went to the hospital, I could see people looking at me with pity, or barely concealed amusement. Some turned their backs pointedly as if they didn't want to be contaminated by my notoriety. It was excruciating. I could do nothing but hold my head up high and continue taking care of my children and my patients. The latter were incredibly loyal during this ordeal. Several told me how sorry they were to learn about my problems. Some brought presents of chocolate candy, or homemade pastries. I know of only one patient who transferred to another physician as a result of all the notoriety.

What was clear, however, was that some of the physicians who had started to refer me patients no longer did so. This was more than made up for by the new patients who began to refer themselves to me. Some probably just wanted to be vicariously involved in the unfolding drama; others quite frankly told me that they knew that Raymond could afford the best, and if he chose me, then that must mean that I was best cardiologist around. I did not care what their rationale was. I had a family to support and expenses to pay.

Meanwhile, my family and friends rallied round me to give me the emotional support I sorely needed. Janie McGroarty, a college friend with whom I had stayed in contact in the years since our graduation from Barnard, came for a visit with her daughter Anne Carol. Anne was three weeks younger than Meagan, and they had been friends from infancy. A few days later my mother and Aunt Bea came to spend a few days with us. I mentioned this to Raymond Sr. while making a house call that week. During their visit, we all went out to dinner to a restaurant on Federal Hill. The manager was Rudolph Sciarra's brother Anthony, another AOCF who looked the part — fat, gravelly voiced, with a pockmarked face that had a lot of miles on it. He hovered over the table most of the night, making sure we were happy, being rather obsequious. Every time he did leave us alone for a few minutes Aunt Bea cracked, "I'd sure like to see HIS Italian sausage!" My mother and I laughed out loud. The children were mystified. When the time came to pay the bill, Anthony said that we were guests of Mr. Patriarca.

In fact, for several years, there wasn't a restaurant on Federal Hill that would allow me to pay for a meal. It was both gratifying and embarrassing, amusing and exasperating. But there was nothing that I could do about it, short of not eating there.

☙❧

On Sunday, April 5, 1981, I discharged Raymond from his second hospitalization, which had begun in mid-March. Again, I did so without warning the nursing staff in advance. I didn't want reporters and photographers hovering about. I could not avoid the *Providence Journal* completely that day because the article that Martha Smith had interviewed me for in February appeared as the cover story in the *Sunday Magazine*. The title was "Who Is the Real Dr. Roberts?" and the magazine cover depicted watercolor drawings of my face, my ex-husband in his Columbia College football uniform running with a football, a microscope, Jack's face, and Raymond from the waist up, in a suit jacket and tie, cigar in his mouth. Inside, the subtitle read: "Barbara Roberts is a cardiologist, a profession not normally in the public spotlight. But then she admitted Raymond Patriarca to a hospital within hours of his arrest. And suddenly she was on center stage."

The article began: "Dr. Barbara Roberts is no stranger to publicity, but that does not mean she likes it." and continued:

> *Ever since she married college football superstar Archie Roberts in 1964, just before his All-American senior year at Columbia, Barbara Hudson Roberts has hovered on the edge of the limelight.*

It went on to chronicle the story of my marriage and the years in the women's movement. It mentioned that I had been going about my business "unobtrusively," practicing at the Miriam Hospital, teaching medical students, volunteering for the local chapter of the American Heart Association, raising my three children and sailing my boat for relaxation, before being "rediscovered" by the newspapers three months before.

> *Patriarca is big news around here and Dr. Roberts found that his notoriety rubbed off... Medical insiders say they were surprised to see Dr. Roberts named as Patriarca's doctor since his long-time physician is Dr. Frank Merlino. Curiosity about Barbara Roberts grew.*
>
> *Who is she? How did she become Patriarca's doctor?*
>
> *The story is, like its subject, complex — in many ways, fascinating. It's a story that Dr. Roberts doesn't volunteer; she is convinced that publicity will make her a pariah on the local medical scene. She depends on patient*

referrals from other doctors and is worried that image-conscious physicians will shun her.

It is also a story that inspires strong feelings in others. Shortly after this magazine story was finished, an anonymous male caller threatened the life of the reporter. Dr. Roberts, when told of the threat, interpreted it as an attempt to discredit her, to make her appear to have strong-arm connections....

(The call was never traced, but I have no doubt that it was made at Ned's behest, much as he had prompted the FBI tap on his phone by claiming that he was receiving threatening calls from mobsters on my behalf.)

The reporter quotes me as saying, " 'I really don't want to talk about Mr. Patriarca ' ...She puts it another way. 'I won't discuss him at all.' " Jack Cicilline then recounted the story of how I came to be called in as Raymond's doctor on the night of his arrest. The article tells about my Catholic upbringing as the oldest in a family of 10 children. About my college years and relationship with my ex-husband, the article quoted Kevin DeMarrais,

...now the sports information director at Columbia... He recalls that not everybody thought Archie and Barbara were a good match.

'Some people felt she used Archie,' he says. 'She was dating some other football players before she started going with Archie. Both she and Archie were devout Catholics. She just seemed to change as a person. It was a typical case of someone who got out on her own and rebelled against her whole background...'

Archie was now chairman of cardio-thoracic surgery at the University of Nevada in Las Vegas. (He would only remain in that position for about nine months, moving then to the University of Florida at Gainesville). He was quoted as saying: "Over the past several years I've only talked with Barbara on the telephone a few times." (This was true; his wife Nancy was the one I usually spoke to in order to arrange the children's visits.)

We don't see one another. At the present time I'm not sure what she's like. The marriage was an evolutionary period in our lives. The person she was when we got married was not, in some respects, the person she was when we broke up. We had very little to do with one another professionally. We went through training, med school and the residency, but as far as being 'real doctors' we had very little contact. I wouldn't be surprised if she's a very good doctor now. She's a bright girl.

The article went on to recount all the publicity I received during the anti-war years:

'I didn't seek it,' she says of the publicity... 'I did a lot of public speaking... I have no qualms about it. I believe in a woman's right to abortion. As far as taking an unpopular stand, if physicians don't want to refer patients to me because of my stand on abortion, that's their right. I firmly believe in a woman's right to have an abortion and so does the Supreme Court...'

It gave Ned's skewed version of our four years together, and breakup:

Bresnahan, who never finished school, has no marketable skills and does not work, says he relied on Dr. Roberts to support him. 'One day it just ended,' he says. 'Barbara threw me out. She cut me off without a cent. My whole world ended.' ...Bresnahan, who claims that he was once a paid companion of author Taylor Caldwell, says his health is frail and has deteriorated in recent years. 'I'm no prince,' he confesses in a rush of candor.

The article goes into great detail about our dueling assault charges and continues:

Bresnahan, like Patriarca, is a subject that is off limits with Barbara Roberts ... She isn't shy about discussing Meagan, who carries Bresnahan's name. 'Meagan is a delight,' says her mother. 'She's beautiful, bright, happy, a joy. Her older sister and brother adore her. She goes to Montessori nursery school and says she's going to be a dentist when she grows up.'

After discussing more about my practice and the reasons I came to Providence, the article concludes with:

> *In the summer, says Dr. Roberts, she races in just about every Narragansett Bay regatta. "That's what I want to be when I grow up," she grins, "a world-famous sailboat racer." Her sloop, moored in Bristol, is called the* Boadicea, *named for a Celtic tribal queen who led a revolt against Rome. "Appropriate, isn't it?" she says. "I guess I want to continue pretty much as I am," she adds, "taking care of patients and teaching. I feel it's important for me as a woman to be a role model for younger women. I love what I do. I guess I take my Hypocratic [sic] oath very seriously. I want to be the best doctor I can be.*

❧

Although I'd fought against having an article written about me, I realized it could have been a lot worse. I had no particular feelings about my ex-husband's comments. "She's a bright girl" sounded like him; he probably remembered how it irked me to hear women referred to as "girls." Young Archie didn't seem fazed by the article. At eleven, he thought it was "neat" that his mother was in the newspaper. Dory was upset to have our private life written about yet again. As I made rounds that morning at the hospital, I overheard two of the floor nurses gossiping about this latest publicity. "Did you read the article about Dr. Roberts in the paper this morning?" one said. "Nah," her colleague replied, "I'm gonna wait for the movie."

As the spring of 1981 wore on, I was feeling exhausted and burnt out. Just being a single mother requires inordinate stamina, and I had a few other things on my plate. I bounced between my office, the hospital, meetings at Jack's office, meetings in John Bevilacqua's office, testifying in court about Raymond's health, and visits to Family Court over the custody suit. By now I was a regular at Jack's office. Our meetings had to do with Raymond's health, his legal predicament, and what further steps the prosecutors might take to bring him to trial. In addition to Nicky Bianco, who was working there as a paralegal, I met Gerard Ouimette, an alleged gangster whose daughter was Jack's godchild. Bo-Bo Marapese, another mob associate, was frequently in attendance, and various others with colorful names like "the Saint," and "Crusher." Eddie Bucci was another connected gentleman who seemed to spend a lot of time hanging out in Jack's office.

Sometimes Jack had Eddie accompany me to pick Meagan up at school, if I was worried that Ned would show up and cause a scene, which he did with regularity. At times, Ned arrived at the Montessori school claiming he had visitation when he didn't; he became irate when the teacher refused to let him take Meagan. I needed a vacation but didn't want to take Dory and Archie away from their classes and extracurricular activities. Archie was appearing in *Inherit the Wind* at Trinity Square Repertory Theater.

I decided to take Meagan and go to Disney World, which Dory and Archie had visited with their father. George stayed with the older children while we were away. Meagan had never been to Disney World, but was jumping with glee at the thought of meeting Minnie, Mickey, and the rest of the Disney characters. As we got off the plane in Orlando the following Friday, Meagan looked around, taking in the palm trees, tropical flowers and bright sun and said, "So this is Florida," with a self-satisfied little nod, as if it was already living up to her expectations. We had a wonderful rest, just the two of us, and flew back to Rhode Island the following Tuesday.

Her visits to her father were always fraught with worry that he would not return her, and on more than one occasion he refused to bring her back to the house at the appointed time. On two occasions when this happened, I called the police. Twice they brought Meagan home from her father's, which amazed even the judge who finally presided over the custody trial. He would write: "How she ever got the involvement of the Providence police is beyond me." I was just grateful that they did respond. In this respect, being Raymond's doctor probably had a lot to do with their willingness to intervene. I continued to be concerned about Ned's drinking and drug use while Meagan was with him. She told me that her daddy smoked "pot" and that she didn't like the smell. I knew from the years we'd lived together that Ned drank to excess. Now that I had cast him out, there was no brake on him. I feared that under the influence of drugs or alcohol, he would get into a car accident or bring the wrong person home with him and that Meagan would be injured, if not killed.

There was other evidence that things were not going well for Ned. The East Providence police called me and asked if I knew his current address and telephone number. When I wanted to know why, they said they were looking for him for writing bad checks. The Social Security office called to "verify" Ned's employment, because they said, he had applied for benefits for Meagan. No progress was made in Family Court. There were endless postponements and cancellations of hearings. There wasn't any particular reason for these; it's just the way the judicial system works. A physician friend who was going through a divorce at the time told me, "Barbara, when you get involved with the courts, don't expect speed, justice, or logic. Because you won't get them." Only a criminal defendant has a constitutional right to a speedy trial.

One of these visits to Family Court stands out in my mind. It was a meeting in Judge Gallogly's chambers with our lawyers, Ned, and me. Judge Gallogly was then the Chief Judge of the Family Court, a stern man who was old-fashioned in his views but considered fair by the lawyers who tried cases before him. Toward the end of the meeting, in which Ned was trying to obtain money from me, and increased visitation, the judge turned to him and asked, "By the way, Mr. Bresnahan, where do you work?"

"I don't have a job, your Honor," Ned replied.

"You don't have a job?" Gallogly inquired, anger apparent in his voice and expression. "How do you survive then?"

"I'm on welfare," Ned informed him.

At this, the judge exploded. "You're on welfare? An able-bodied young man like you has no business being on welfare. You get a job. I don't care if it's pushing a broom in this courthouse, but you better have a job before you ever appear before me again."

It was hard for me to keep a poker face at the image of Ned pushing a janitor's broom — that was about as likely to happen as the sun rising in the west, but by the time the next court appearance came around, the case had been assigned to yet another judge, so Ned, still out of a job, did not have to face the wrath of Judge Gallogly.

My boyfriend George was now also unemployed. C & C Yachts had let him go, and he was spending his time moping around the house when he wasn't tinkering with *Boadicea*. It infuriated Ned that George sometimes picked Meagan up from the Montessori School. He was forever ranting about this to his lawyers. I asked Jack what I should tell Ned when he demanded to know who was picking Meg up at school. "Just tell him Eddie Bucci's picking her up, but that's only because Nicky's busy," he replied impishly, referring to Nicky Bianco, who was then alleged to be the "#2 man" in the New England Mob. This would have only fed Ned's increasing paranoia about my "mob connections."

One afternoon, in the midst of busy office hours, my secretary Donna came into my consulting room, very distressed. "Dr. Roberts," she said, "there's an FBI agent here, and he wants to talk to you. What should I do?"

"Send him in," I told her, "I don't think it will take long." I was both anxious and peeved. I was pretty sure the visit had to do with Ned; I knew what outlandish accusations he was capable of. And I was afraid that Ned, or the FBI, or both would try to "frame" me for some crime, the former to get custody of Meagan and the latter to discredit me and make it impossible for me to continue as Raymond's physician. With all the notoriety I'd gained, no other physician was likely to stick his neck out to keep Raymond from going to trial. And I was annoyed because I had an office full of patients who would now have to wait while I attempted to deflect this latest episode of harassment.

In fact, the agent spent close to 45 minutes there, at one point telling me, "You know, if anything bad happens to Bresnahan, you could be in serious trouble."

At this, I became furious, although I tried not to show it. "Look," I told him, "I first came to the attention of the FBI in the '70s because I'm completely OPPOSED to violence, of any kind. Not only that, I'm not stupid. Don't you think I know very well that if anything ever happened to Ned, even if I could prove that I was on the moon at the time, I'd be the prime suspect? How dare you imply that I would try to have him harmed." And in fact, I was sincere. I didn't want any harm to come to Ned. I just wanted him to accept the fact that our relationship was over and end his vendetta. It was having a pernicious effect on all of us.

That summer, I had the kitchen remodeled. When I bought the house, the kitchen was my least favorite room. It had ugly blue metal cabinets, crumbling yellow Formica counters, and drab blue-and-yellow plaid wallpaper. There was a small breakfast room off the kitchen that had pockmarked walls painted a gun-metal gray. Jane McGroarty, my Barnard College classmate, had become an architect, and I asked her to design a new kitchen for me. It was her first commission. The contractor assured me the work would be completed in six weeks. In the end, it took three months, and during much of that time we had to eat out in restaurants.

George and I had not been getting along. We argued about his lack of a job, which put me in the position of having to support him. After Ned, I'd sworn that I would not financially support a man again. I'd cosigned a car loan for him, and he was missing payments. George resented all the turmoil Ned caused and blamed me for it, as much as he blamed Ned.

One evening, as we drove home with the children from yet another restaurant meal, he began castigating young Archie for not helping more around the house. They got into a shouting match. George, who was driving, drew his arm back as if he were going to hit Archie. At this I threw a paper cup fill of iced soda in his face and he veered off the street, coming to a screeching halt in the driveway of a doctor I knew from the Miriam. George leapt from the car screaming curses at us as the physician watched, dumbfounded. I had acted without thinking, and thankfully we were driving slowly down a quiet residential street, not on the highway—but I never raised my hand to my children and would not tolerate anyone else doing so. As emotionally harmful as Ned was, he never, in his four years living with us, had struck any of the children.

I drove them the short distance home and sent them all upstairs while I waited for George to return. He arrived looking as if he was going to blow his stack at any moment. Magenta-faced, breathing noisily, he stormed into the house like a bull charging into an arena. Rushing by me into the kitchen, he flung a fan at me, missing narrowly. I screamed at him, "Don't you dare! Pack your bags and get out of here NOW!"

He sneered, "What if I don't? Are you going to have one of your Mafia friends beat me up?" Lying, but trying to frighten him, I replied, "You bet your ass I will," and that seemed to sober him up. He packed and left within the hour. About a week later, he called and asked me to meet him for a talk. He was broke, out of a job, and asked if he could stay on *Boadicea* until he got back on his feet financially. By this time, my anger had cooled; I felt sorry for him and agreed to let him stay on the boat. I also agreed to help him get a job. I called Tony, the contractor who'd remodeled my kitchen, and asked him to hire George, which he did as a favor to me.

At the time, Tony and his crew were remodeling the plating department (which was heavily guarded since it contained a lot of gold and silver) at the Catanzaro Jewelry company. The rest of this story I was not to hear until more than thirty years later. Unbeknownst to me, Jack Cicilline took it upon himself to pay George a visit at his job with Tony's crew to tell him not to bother me. He pulled up at Catanzaro's in a black Cadillac, where he was recognized by another Catanzaro employee, who reported this to the boss. The boss then assumed that Tony had mob connections and was "casing the joint" for a planned heist. Within a short period of time, security escorted Tony and his crew off the premises.

Losing the contract was devastating to Tony. He had grown up in Rhode Island and had dropped out of school in the 8th grade. He remembers that after this incident, he had no self-esteem and no money. He decided to reinvent himself and start over in a place where no one knew him. He moved to California and found an investor who staked him in a new construction company, which became very successful. He later started a national publication called Healing Retreats and

Spas and traveled the world as Founder and Editor in Chief. After retiring, he started an organic soup kitchen. As he wrote me when he recounted this recently, "I'm well-respected in a corner of the world I never knew existed 38 years ago. So, believe it or not, you were an integral part of my life. A life I truly love. Thanks for the memory."

><

When the cold weather arrived, George could no longer stay on the boat; he moved back to his home state of Ohio and lived with his parents. I lost track of his whereabouts after that.

The week after the breakup with George, I took my son Archie sailing on *Boadicea*, accompanied by Bob Indeglia's son, Paul, and Raymond's grandson Christopher Patriarca. I was the only adult with them, and although we never ventured outside Narragansett Bay, it was one of the more foolhardy things I did during those years. What made this trip foolhardy was that I was the only one aboard who really knew how to sail. If the weather got ugly, or if I dropped dead, those boys wouldn't know how to get the boat safely to our mooring or a dock. In the event, nothing untoward happened. We enjoyed the hours under sail; the weather was sunny, and the winds were the merest zephyrs. That night, we had dinner at a restaurant in Warren and slept over on the boat.

Later that summer, young Archie elected to go away to camp in New Hampshire with one of his school friends, and Dory went to visit her father, who was now living in Florida. Raymond Sr. and Rita moved to their summer home on Indian Lake in Narragansett, and I made my weekly house calls there. Like their home on Golini Drive in Johnston, it was a modest dwelling, almost hidden among the trees, with a large vegetable garden in the backyard. Bob Indeglia's son Paul sailed with us quite a bit that summer and often stayed at our house in Providence. I took him and Meagan along on one of my house calls, and watched Raymond walk hand-in-hand with Meagan to show her his tomato plants. All I could think of was the scene from *The Godfather* where Marlon Brando as Vito Corleone cavorts with his grandson in *his* garden before keeling over with a fatal heart attack. But the angel of death was not lurking in ambush among Raymond's tomato vines that day.

A few months later, I had to testify once more in Superior Court on Raymond's health, and what the impact a trial might have on him. The prosecutor was trying to pin me down on how long exactly I thought Raymond was going to live. The gist of her questioning was, "If this guy is as sick as you say he is, why is he not dead already?" I was refusing to be pinned down, and finally, in exasperation, answered, "Look, only God, in **HER** wisdom, knows when any one of us is going to die." The courtroom erupted into laughter, Jack pretended he was hiding under the defense table in embarrassment, and the judge continued to look out, stony-faced, at all of us. "I like that answer," the prosecutor, Susan McGuirl said, and shortly thereafter, she excused me from the witness stand.

9 · LOUIS

Forbidden pleasures alone are loved immoderately;
when lawful, they do not excite desire.
—Quintilian

On a Friday in mid-September, 1981, I performed a heart catheterization on an elderly patient who'd been referred by Bob Indeglia for consideration for aortic valve replacement. On the first injection of dye into the left coronary artery, we noted a very tight proximal blockage, one we called "the widowmaker," — and immediately thereafter, the patient went into cardiac arrest. For close to an hour, we tried to resuscitate him, but to no avail.

I was devastated. To have a patient die from an intervention you are performing is harrowing. I left the catheterization laboratory to inform his family in a fog of misery. As is usually the case, they were kind and understanding, which paradoxically increased my distress. When I'd finished talking to them, it was lunchtime, and I called Jack Cicilline. I related what had just happened and he said, "I was about to go out for lunch. Come up the Hill and have lunch with me."

We drove a short distance down Atwells Avenue, stopping at De-Pasquale Square. Decades before, it was lined with push-carts selling fruits, vegetables, and in winter, roasted chestnuts, but it was now host to small grocery stores, a poultry vendor, a pharmacy, and a restaurant called the Forum, which was one I hadn't been to before. A large fountain topped with a sculpture of a pinecone graced the courtyard in front of the Forum, plumes of water performing a glissando into progressively larger pools. A few people sat relaxing on the marble rim of the lowest pool, soaking up the residue of warmth that lingered like a friendly ghost in the plaza. Inside, the hand of a talented interior designer was evident. Warm, exposed beams set off the original brick walls; the tables held Italian tile insets, and a shelf on the back wall displayed an assortment of colorful Italian ceramic vases and urns. Under this shelf was a long banquette, upholstered in a rich maroon paisley material. To the right of the dining room was a small bar with a mirrored backstop and rows of crystal wine goblets hanging overhead.

A succulent aroma, redolent of garlic and olive oil, tomatoes and spices, permeated the air. A man I took to be the manager came over to greet us as soon as we were inside the door. He was of medium height and carried himself with an effortless but steely dignity. He was bald on the top of his head, with short-cropped gray hair, a tanned face, and a very slight but unplaceable accent. I guessed his age as somewhere in his fifties. There was an indefinable aura about him that I found compelling. Somehow the air around him had a different density; it refracted light at a sharper angle. "Jack!" he said, shaking Jack's hand and giving me a look of polite inquiry. "Welcome to the Forum."

"Hi, Louis," Jack replied. "Meet my friend, Dr. Barbara Roberts. Barbara, meet Louis Manocchio."

The name set off instant alarm bells in my mind. Was this, I wondered, THE Louis Manocchio, the one who had been "on the lam" for ten years and had only recently returned to Rhode Island? I wracked my brain for other details about him but could come up with nothing more. I had long since stopped buying the *Providence Journal* and read it only rarely.

"I'm very pleased to meet you," Louis said, extending his hand to shake mine, then leading us to a table by a window that fronted the square. I can't remember what we ate for lunch that day, and in truth, I had little appetite after the events of the morning. Louis was kept busy seeing to the normal bustle of a restaurant at lunchtime but visited our table frequently. I had the distinct impression that he knew who I was. He emanated a subtle authority that made his attentiveness seductive and flattering. When we had finished eating, he asked Jack if he could give me a tour of the restaurant, and Jack waved us off. He showed me the upstairs dining room and the kitchen. I had already visited the ladies' room with its walls of rich, burnt umber tiles, every eighth tile containing the delicate tracery of a flower. He introduced me to the waitstaff and urged me to open an account there, saying that he hoped I would return often.

My impression was that Louis was in some subtle but definite way both courting me and paying me homage. I could feel the tachycardic thrumming of my heart as he took my hand and made a slight bow over it as we left. Out in the square, I turned to Jack: "Is he the one they call 'Baby Shanks'?" I asked. "He's the one," Jack replied, "and I think you made a big impression." I gave an uncertain laugh, not at all sure this was something I should be pleased about, but I was intrigued. I felt a sexual attraction to Louis, which surprised me no end because I'd never before been attracted to a man so much older than I. Since my breakup with George that summer, I'd been celibate—but with hormones coursing through my veins like a chemical Charge of the Light Brigade, I yearned for sex, for the oblivion and surcease of orgasm. I longed to be stoppered and shaken, to lie under a man, pelvis to pelvis in the slow, grinding dance of lust. My taste in men was clearly atrocious, but over the ensuing days, I could not expunge Louis from my thoughts. Like a ditty half heard on the radio that replays incessantly in the darkened theater of the mind, the opening lines of an Edna St. Vincent Millay sonnet repeated themselves endlessly in my head:

> *I too beneath your moon, almighty Sex,*
> *Go forth at nightfall crying like a cat...*

I knew it would be insanity to become involved with Louis, despite what I had to admit to myself was an intense and probably mutual attraction. The credibility of my testimony on Raymond's health would be severely impaired, if not destroyed, if I became intimate with Louis and the relationship became known. I had no doubt that Ned would seize on my relationship with an alleged organized crime figure as further proof of my unfitness as a mother. I'd already lost referrals from some physicians because of my notoriety. I did not need the added complication of becoming known as a "mob mistress." I tried to put Louis out of my mind, with little success, drawn again and again to reliving that lunch, scratching obsessively at the mental itch his memory had become.

At the time, my three closest girlfriends were all nurses. Ginny Beggs and Patty Wilson were coronary care unit nurses at the Miriam Hospital. Rita Greene, whose brother had been married to Ginny, was a psychiatric nurse who worked at the Training School for Boys, the juvenile prison in Cranston. They had met as nursing students at the University of Rhode Island—URI or "you are high," as it was nicknamed. We were all single and looking for lovers, if not husbands. I told them about my lunch at the Forum. "I met this really attractive older man at the Forum Restaurant the other day," I said, "but I'm pretty sure he's connected. He invited me to come back, but I don't want to go alone. Would you come with me?"

They jumped at the chance. A week to the day after my first meal at the Forum, the four of us traipsed up to Federal Hill and entered the restaurant. Louis was there and exerted himself to be charming, winning them over immediately. He asked about their families, their jobs, their hobbies. He was very attentive. It was clear however, that I was singled out for his special attention. We were not presented with a bill.

"I would like to treat you lovely ladies to lunch," Louis replied when we asked for the check. His old-fashioned manners, which I might have found off-putting in a younger man, were endearing. My friends lapped up the attention he showered on us. "You'd be crazy not to go out with him," they assured me afterwards, "he's so sexy, and it's obvious he's crazy about you."

I continued to worry and fret. I wanted to see Louis again, I wanted to get to know him better, but I was terrified of allowing our friendship to blossom into a sexual affair, which would up the emotional ante and potentially complicate many more lives than our own. A week later, Patty and I again had lunch at the Forum. I invited Louis to go for a sail with me and Patty that Sunday on *Boadicea*, and he accepted with alacrity.

By now it was early October, and the trees wore their gaudy fall foliage like flaming capes as we sailed out of Bristol harbor, past the mansions on Poppasquash Point and the smaller homes on Hog Island. Louis brought champagne and panini, and we toasted each other with mimosas. He told me that he'd once owned an old Herreshoff sailboat, which he sailed for a number of years and then donated to the Museum of Yachting. Louis had bought it from an elderly Yankee, at a time when he was still a novice sailor. Louis recounted how he'd told the owner, in a hilarious malapropism, that he wanted to learn that "ecclesiastical navigation" (instead of celestial), and how the old man had looked at him as if he were some freakish lower life form. I was happy that he could laugh at himself, but a bit taken aback by his giving me advice on sailing. I was certain that I was the more experienced sailor, and in fact, our only arguments would take place when we sailed together.

Every year, the Columbus Day weekend is celebrated on Federal Hill with a three-day "festa." A parking lot is transformed into a carnival, with ferris wheel, carousel, booths where marksmanship will win you a garish doll or stuffed animal, candied apple and cotton candy vendors, and a fortune teller. Up and down Atwells Avenue, carts sell fried dough, sausage and peppers, meatballs, and other mouth-watering Italian foods. There is a parade and speeches from politicians. That Saturday, I took the children and a troop of Archie's friends with us to the celebration. I gave them spending money, and they went off to go on the rides while I had lunch with Louis at the Forum.

It was our first lunch without others, but the children burst through the doors every half hour or so to replenish their supply of money. We made idle small talk until I could stand it no longer and said, finally,

"Look, Louis, what do you want of me?" He reared back as if I had struck him physically, insulted. "What do I want from you? I don't want anything from you!"

"That's not what I asked," I replied. "I asked, what do you want OF me?"

His demeanor changed instantly, and a wry smile played around his lips. "What do I want OF you? Okay, I see the difference. Well, I'd like to get to know you better, I'd like to hold your hand and have you hold mine. I'd like you to have dinner with me here tonight. My lawyer, Marty Leppo, is coming down from Boston with his wife. Can you join us?"

It was only much later that I came to understand that "holding hands" was his euphemism for making love. At the time, what I could tell from Louis' answer was that he too wanted our relationship to advance. He was unmistakably asking me out on a "date." This was a quantum leap from inviting me and my friends to dine at the Forum whenever we pleased. He wanted me to dine with him and his lawyer —not something I imagined he'd want a casual acquaintance to do. And I thought "hold my hand" just referred to becoming a friend, although from the way he leaned close to me, fixing me with a seductive gaze, I knew that sex was very much on his mind, as it was on mine. I felt a deliquescence, a liquefaction in my pelvis which made even breathing difficult, let alone rational thinking. Reckless with desire, I agreed to come to dinner that night.

❦

Louis was a bundle of contradictions. In private, he had no compunctions about calling a spade a spade in sexual matters. In public, his speech and actions were always proper, bordering on courtly. Although alleged to be high up in the Mafia's hierarchy, he numbered among his friends some of the most powerful and respected men in the state, including the lieutenant governor, Tom DiLuglio, Sr., and a host of other lawyers and physicians, not all of whom were Italian-Americans. I was later to hear firsthand from people in law enforcement that Louis was "different," a "real gentleman," "not your

average mobster" —whatever that meant. I only knew that he fascinated me, that I was attracted by his aura of power, and by his open
and frank admiration for me.

My feelings about his alleged mob connections were complex. On
the one hand, any relationship I had with Louis, if it became public
knowledge, would do me great harm. On the other hand, Louis, unlike most men I might become involved with (and being Raymond's
doctor made it very hard to get a date!), saw my defense of Raymond
as something admirable, something courageous. In some ways, I felt
like a pariah after becoming Raymond's physician. But to Louis and
his friends, I was a heroine.

So, for a number of complex reasons I said "Yes" to Louis' invitation, and all that might flow from it. That afternoon, as the festival
gathered strength outside, a pact was sealed; the windmill of fate lum-
bered into creaky motion. The slow revolution of the millstones that
would grind us in their blind embrace commenced. We were oblivi-
ous, which was a mercy.

At home, I made dinner for the children and then headed back to
the Forum. I remember little of what we discussed at the table that
night. I did learn that Marty Leppo was representing Louis in the case
that had led to his fleeing the jurisdiction more than ten years before.
Louis' return was orchestrated by Tom DiLuglio, Jr., another of Louis'
lawyers and the son of the lieutenant governor. He negotiated a deal
with prosecutors that allowed Louis to surrender to the authorities
but remain free on bail pending trial. At the time, I knew none of the
details of the case, but Louis had been back in the country for two
years, with no trial looming.

Before meeting the others, Louis asked me if I'd like to wait for him
in his apartment after dinner until he could get free. A small studio,
it had one entrance from the plaza, and another from a hallway leading off the restaurant's second floor dining room. I said that I would,
fearing all that my acquiescence might entail, but unwilling—and unable—to say no. I was being wrenched by an emotional tug-of-war
unlike any I had ever experienced, trepidation equally balanced by
my fascinated attraction to this mysterious man. After dinner, I bade

goodnight to the Leppos, and Louis escorted me from the restaurant. Instead of going to my car, we ducked into the entranceway next door, and he led me up the stairs to his apartment.

A long, narrow corridor lined with closets led to a small bedroom. Beside the bed was a nightstand, and on the wall a shelf contained a stereo, tuned to a classical music station. The bathroom was walled with ecru-colored tiles and contained the only bidet I had seen outside of France. We kissed for a long, lingering moment, and then he pulled away, saying he'd be back shortly. I undressed and got under the covers, by now shivering uncontrollably from a potent combination of nerves and horniness. I had drunk two glasses of wine with dinner, enough so that I was only half sober. Lying there I began to fantasize, and fear, that any moment armed gunmen would burst through the door, pistols spitting death. I wanted to run, but lust and longing pinned me to the bed more securely than any handcuff.

Louis returned and undressed unselfconsciously. I noticed scars on his shoulder and abdomen. He had the sinewy figure of a distance runner, which he was. He pulled back the covers, which I was clutching to my chin and gazed at my body with open admiration. "I can't believe it," he said, "you're a thirty-seven-year old mother of three and you have the body of a teenager." He then proceeded to tell me what he would and wouldn't do, sexually, with a frankness that astounded me. Everyone who has watched *The Sopranos* on HBO knows that there is a sexual practice that at least the older generation of mafiosi considers unmanly. I learned of this belief that night, long before Uncle Junior's travails on the hit show. "That's fine with me," I replied, "I'm a meat and potatoes kind of woman myself, when it comes to sex."

And so, our affair began. I knew that what I was doing was wrong, not for any reasons relating to sexual morality, but because my first responsibility was to my children, who would be harmed by more notoriety, and my second was to Raymond, who could be subjected to trial if my credibility were damaged. I can only say that I paid a heavy price, one that pushed me to the brink of madness, and left me, for a time, shattered and maimed and inconsolable.

Over the next few weeks, Louis and I met once or twice a week, always at the Forum. If anything, Louis was even more concerned about our affair becoming public knowledge than I was. He reiterated often that he didn't want our friendship to add to the problems I already had to deal with. He was confident that his own legal entanglements would be resolved without a trial. These dated back to the Marfeo-Melei double murder in April of 1968. The two men had been shot-gunned to death in a grocery store in the Silver Lake section of Providence, allegedly on Raymond's orders. Pro Lerner, the shooter, was serving a life sentence. Raymond and three other defendants were convicted of conspiracy but acquitted of accessory charges. They had long since completed their sentences.

Louis had heard that he, too, was going to be indicted on conspiracy and accessory charges and, convinced that he would not obtain a fair trial, had fled, eventually spending ten years in hiding. No eyewitness to the shooting ever came forward, and there was no physical evidence linking the crime to any of the defendants. The prosecution's case rested on the testimony of one man, John J. "Red" Kelley, a notorious thief who was the self-proclaimed mastermind of the Plymouth mail robbery that occurred in the early 1960s. In August of 1969, he was arrested for the December 1968 robbery of a Brinks truck in Boston. More than a year after the Marfeo-Melei murders, when faced with the prospect of a long prison term, he turned state's evidence and implicated Pro Lerner, Raymond, Louis, and others.

By the time Louis returned from his ten years in hiding, Red Kelley had developed Alzheimer's disease, and since he was the only prosecution witness, it seemed highly unlikely that Louis would ever be brought to trial.

Louis was sketchy about the details of his years abroad but did say that the experience changed his life. "I spent a lot of time in the Alps and made friends with a lot of climbers there. Talk about real men! Those guys made me realize that all the people I grew up admiring, thinking were tough, were not — they weren't in the same class when it came to toughness. And I realized that the people I'd been looking up to all my life were all nuts!" He seemed to want to reassure me that he was a very different person as a result of his years away. Once, I asked him how he had made his living when he was younger. He hesitated a moment and then said, "I was a thief, that's what I did. I went out every night and stole, like it was my job." I was a bit taken aback that he would admit this to me, but it didn't change how I felt about him.

In general, he was vague or unforthcoming about his life in the years before I met him. He did tell me that when he was in his twenties he'd served two years in prison for armed robbery. It was not terribly important to me, because that was many years in the past. He also told me that when he was younger and would be out riding in a car with his friends, they would often be pulled over by the police and arrested. "But what were you charged with?" I asked. "Oh, I don't know," he replied, "probably with being abroad after sundown." That's the kind of amusing but unhelpful answer I was likely to get if I asked him something he didn't want to answer.

Even before his ten years on the lam, he'd made several trips to Europe on the *Queen Mary*, visiting Italy and France for the most part, giving himself a spotty but adequate education in art and history, reading the great books of Western literature. He knew more about these than most of the Brown medical students I taught over the years. During his years in hiding, he had taught himself French, taking the Metro in Paris to the farthest stop, then walking all the way back to his apartment, engaging people in conversation with the help of a dictionary, painstakingly translating the signs along the way.

In what I took to be an oblique reference to Raymond and newspaper statements about his position in the Mafia hierarchy, he said, "Nobody has ever been my boss, nor do I want to be anyone's boss." While living abroad, he'd become an expert skier and fair mountain climber. At age fifty-four, he had the stamina and physique of a man half his age; he'd run marathons. I learned that his father had died many years before, but that his mother, Mary, was still living — a tiny woman then in her late seventies whose piety drove him to distraction. We were in full agreement on the Catholic Church and the pernicious influence it wielded in our respective ethnic communities.

Louis had an older brother, Andrew, who managed a bar on Federal Hill, and a younger brother, Anthony, who was a gynecologist with a large practice. Anthony and I became good friends, and each other's physician. He had gone to medical school in Bologna, where he met an Italian woman and married her. They had four children and lived in Providence. Although more than ten years younger than Louis, they bore a strong resemblance to each other, and more than once Anthony had been pulled over by the police and had a gun held to his head by officers who mistook him for his brother. Louis never married but had an adult daughter, born out of wedlock to one of his former lovers. He'd missed most of her growing up because he was in hiding, and they were not close.

Louis showered me with gifts, but not the clichéd items that might be expected: no fur coats or gaudy jewels, no trips to Miami or Las Vegas. He gave me a hand-blown glass lamp, pocketbooks, a pair of leather pants—and books, endless books: Boccaccio's *Decameron*, Will and Ariel Durant's multi-volume *The Story of Civilization*, *Roget's Thesaurus*, and *Bartlett's Familiar Quotations*, among many others. And meals—he delighted in feeding me and my children at the Forum. At times, he seemed almost maternal in his solicitude. He telephoned every day. Without words, but with actions (which always speak louder), he made his caring visible, and I felt cherished and, paradoxically, safe.

I didn't examine my feelings too closely. I was content to let the tender sapling of our relationship exist in its hidden recess, away from the hostile, prying eyes that would view it with censure and seek to destroy it. To bring our affair into the light of day would endanger ourselves and others, but keeping it hidden away stunted its growth in ways we only vaguely intuited, while sharpening the edge of pleasure we stole in the lengthening nights.

10 · MOTHERHOOD ON TRIAL

If there were no bad people, there would be no good lawyers.
—Charles Dickens

By this time, the fall of 1981, a problem I'd been refusing to examine closely was clamoring for attention. Of all the children, Dory, now approaching her sixteenth birthday, seemed most affected by the notoriety of my role as Raymond's cardiologist. She was subjected to ridicule and taunts from schoolmates every time my name was mentioned in the newspapers. She still missed her father, but he was rarely around on her visits to him, which were now confined to the summer, and she was left to spend time with her stepmother, whom she despised and resented. She blamed Nancy for the fact that her visits were so infrequent and felt that Nancy slighted her and young Archie in favor of her own children. I called Archie on more than one occasion to tell him that the children missed him and wanted to spend more time with him. His reply was, "I can't. I don't have the time. My patients come first." He freely admitted he was a neglectful father, which he blamed on the long hours he spent at work as a cardiac surgeon.

Now, at the start of her junior year in high school, Dory was a different person from the beautiful, bright, brash child she had been a few years before. She withdrew from her friends and stopped inviting them to our home. She spent hours closeted in her room and came to dinner disheveled, her hair hanging in front of her eyes. She defied me and was verbally abusive. I was in denial; I kept telling myself this was just adolescent rebellion and would pass. But then, my sister Donna came for a visit; appalled at the change she saw immediately in the niece she had cared for as a baby and watched grow up in the intervening years, she took me aside. "Barbara," she said, "this is more than teenage rebellion. There is something seriously wrong with Dory."

Until Donna said that, I just could not admit to myself that Dory was ill—and getting more so every day. In medical school, in the 1960s, I'd been taught that mental illness in a child was always the result of poor mothering. Those were the days when psychiatrists still talked about the "schizophrenogenic mother"—mothers who caused their child's schizophrenia. I refused to allow myself to see what was truly going on with Dory, because to do so would indict me as a "bad" mother. When I finally could no longer deny the reality of Dory's illness, I was overwhelmed with grief and guilt. I literally felt my heart break. I was helpless, terrified that she would descend into madness and never again be the child I knew and loved.

Would her illness have happened if I'd stayed married to her father? Would this have happened if Ned and I had been able to come to some kind of *modus vivendi*? Would this have happened if I had not invited my former boyfriend George Gregory into our home? Would this have happened if I had not agreed to take on Raymond's care, subjecting myself and by extension the children to the glare of unwanted publicity? I tortured myself with these questions but was unable to come up with any answers.

At the time, our health insurance was with the first HMO in Rhode Island, the Rhode Island Group Health Association, or RIGHA. I called the counseling department and described Dory's behavior, her withdrawal and disheveled appearance. I was told that the earliest appointment was in three weeks. I said that my daughter was having serious problems and shouldn't be made to wait that long, but the secretary refused to give me an earlier appointment. Of course, I should have marched Dory down there and not left until she was evaluated, but I was strangely and uncharacteristically passive. I was in a state of shock at the notion that my daughter was mentally ill. I felt emotionally paralyzed. Yet I had to keep functioning.

During those weeks waiting for Dory to be seen, I continued to work as usual, testified on Raymond's health for five hours in court on October 22nd, had dinner with Louis often at the Forum, and gave a fifth birthday party for Meagan on Halloween—but I was operating on automatic pilot. Perhaps my passivity also resulted from the fact that once Dory was seen by a professional and diagnosed, denial would no longer be an option, and I would have to deal with the fact of her illness. Whatever the case, another three weeks went by. During that time, Dory slid into the abyss, finally hallucinating that football players were congregating in the driveway, wanting her to leave with them.

On the evening of November 3, I brought Dory to RIGHA for her screening appointment with a mental health counselor. Within minutes, she beckoned me outside the room and told me, "Your daughter needs to be admitted to Bradley Hospital tonight. She is a very sick young girl."

I exploded in anger and grief: "That's what I told you people three weeks ago, but no one would give me an earlier appointment!"

Anguish such as I had never before felt skewered my heart, so intense that whole parts of my brain shut down, emotional fuses blown by the surge of fear and guilt that flooded the circuitry. I couldn't think rationally. I alternated between intense anger, and grief, and numbness. I felt like a rat trapped in a maze from which there was no escape. But there was no way out. I had to go *through*.

What would become of my daughter? Was I to blame for her condition? If I'd been a better mother, could this nightmare have been avoided? What effect would Dory's breakdown have on Archie and Meagan? Would Ned find out and use Dory's illness as proof of my unfitness as a mother in the upcoming custody trial? The questions scurried around in my head like rats looking for escape from a sinking ship. And none of the answers was palatable.

We arrived at Bradley, a children's psychiatric hospital in East Providence after 9:30 p.m. I telephoned Archie's home, but Nancy told me he was at the hospital. I called there and had him paged, telling him as best I could between sobs what had happened. He was cold and accusing. "It's your life-style that caused this you know," he said, "you have no one to blame but yourself. I have to go, I have an emergency." I was stricken again, incredulous that he could be so unsympathetic and uncaring. Part of me feared he was correct, and part of me raged at his cruelty and callousness. I called him several more times that night, paging him at the hospital, but each time he cut me off abruptly, saying he was busy with a patient.

I called Louis at the Forum, and he urged me to come see him when Dory had been checked in. I gave an exhaustive history to the psychiatric resident on call, detailing all of the stresses that we had faced recently between Ned's custody struggle and harassment and the publicity over my testimony on Raymond's behalf. He said that it was far too early to make a diagnosis and that Dory would be having psychologic testing; she would undoubtedly need to be treated with medication. Dory, for her part, was furious at me, insisting that I take her home. I don't remember what I said to her; I just tried to reassure her that admitting her to hospital was for her own good and that I would be back to see her the next day. I left the hospital feeling that I had aged a hundred years in one evening.

Over the next few weeks, while Dory was hospitalized, Louis insisted that I bring the two younger children and have dinner every night at the Forum. "You have enough to do without having to cook also," he said. And my family rallied around. All of my siblings had visited us in Providence over the years, but now they came more often, and stayed longer. My mother and Aunt Bea arrived two days after Dory's admission to hospital, without my father who had stopped speaking to me three years before, when I broke up with Ned. We visited Dory, who was refusing to take any of the medications her doctors wanted to prescribe and was verbally abusing all of us, as well as the hospital staff. Bea and my mother stayed for almost a week.

A few days after they left, Dory's father arrived from Florida and we met with Dory's psychiatrists and counselors. They were unable to give us a diagnosis, but wanted to put her on potent tranquilizers and anti-psychotics. Archie tried to persuade her to take the medicines, but to no avail. I knew that Dory needed medication, but I feared the side effects. Some of these were minor, like dry mouth or blurred vision, but others were more severe and could be permanent. One of these was tardive dyskinesia, a syndrome consisting of involuntary movements of the tongue, face, mouth, and jaw. So, although I too urged Dory to take the medicines the doctors wanted to prescribe, I did so with mixed emotions. I attended endless meetings with the staff in those weeks, some with the other children. Young Archie remembers little about these sessions, but Meagan remembers hating them—"Because I knew none of my friends had to go through that shit!"

The meetings were headed by Dr. Charles Staunton, who led the team that took care of Dory during and after her hospitalization. He had severely crossed eyes, curling gray hair, was of middling height, and never inspired me with confidence in his abilities. Perhaps Sigmund Freud himself would not have impressed me at that stage, but I found Staunton to be singularly lacking in the ability to instill confidence or optimism. He was vague about what he thought the diagnosis was, saying only that Dory had an "atypical psychosis" and would require long-term therapy and medication. Dory despised him and to his face called him "Old Googly-Eyes." The rest of the team included a social worker, Mr. Kline, and a Dr. Welch. The team met with me and the children on a regular basis, during and for many months after Dory's hospitalization. We discussed our feelings about the custody suit, my pending felony charge, their fathers, and the publicity surrounding my care of Raymond—without, as far as I could tell, resolving anything. They didn't even offer any helpful advice in dealing with the myriad stresses we faced.

Not long after the counseling started, I was told by Dory's therapists that Ned wanted to be included in the "family" meetings. I don't know how he learned that Dory was in Bradley Hospital, but I adamantly refused to allow this. The children were also opposed to Ned's involvement in our family therapy, but it would become a recurring theme over the ensuing months. None of us wanted to sit and listen to Ned's twisting of the facts. My lawyer advised against allowing Ned in on these sessions. We feared that Ned would try to use Dory's nervous breakdown against me in the looming custody trial, and we were correct.

I visited Dory every day, wrenching, heartbreaking visits in which she pleaded with me to take her home. I had to tell her over and over again that I couldn't, that she had to stay until she got better. Eventually, I convinced her that if she took the medication, she would get better sooner and be able to come home. I also had to juggle my practice, the various legal battles, and the younger children, who were frightened and uncomprehending of what was happening to their big sister. For young Archie, it was a painful and confusing time. It was hard for him to see his big sister in the hospital. He worried that she would not get better. Meagan, at five, was less aware of how sick her sister was, but it was the first time in her life that either of her siblings had been hospitalized. I was depressed beyond anything I had experienced before, and waded like an automaton through quagmire days and tearful nights. Louis was my solace and respite from the sorrows that dragged me down. He assured me daily that Dory would recover and that all of us would survive and be happy once again.

After a few weeks, Dory reluctantly agreed to take medication and, with infinitesimal slowness, began to improve. Her doctors allowed me to take her on a day pass to my Aunt Bea's home in Mystic, Connecticut for Thanksgiving. At the end of the day, Dory wanted to come home with us, and cried and pleaded with me not to take her back to the hospital. I was in anguish but unable to give in to her entreaties. Young Archie flew to Florida to spend Thanksgiving with his father. Meagan was supposed to spend the day with Ned but became hysterical when I told her this and refused to go, insisting on accompanying us to Mystic. I called Ned to inform him of this, but there was no answer at his apartment.

As Christmas neared, the improvement in Dory was apparent. She took an interest in her appearance, she no longer cursed and yelled at the staff, she had no recurrence of hallucinations, and she wanted to return to school. She begged me to take her home from the hospital. Her psychiatrists were adamant that she needed many more weeks of inpatient therapy, but Dory beseeched me not to leave her in the hospital over Christmas. It was always a special time in our house. I started baking cookies each year in late November, freezing them for the holidays. We always trimmed a big blue spruce tree, which was girdled with the gifts we exchanged on Christmas morning. Her pleading wore me down, and a few days before Christmas, I signed her out of the hospital against medical advice.

Ned had court-ordered visitation on Christmas Day but Meagan refused to even consider going to his tiny one-bedroom apartment, the scene of her infamous rescue that March. So, two days before Christmas, we left for my parent's home in Pearl River. I feared that if we stayed in Providence there would be another dramatic confrontation with Ned over Meagan. And there was another reason I was anxious to leave: My father's drinking had reached the crisis point in November, and he was admitted to a hospital in Pomona, New York for detoxification. He'd been on a prolonged binge. He'd not only been drinking heavily but had developed a dependence on tranquilizers. The combination finally made him so sick that he agreed to be admitted. While in the hospital, he confronted his alcoholism for the first time, began attending Alcoholics Anonymous meetings, and told my mother that he wanted to reconcile with me.

My mother desperately wanted me and the children to visit. It would be our first Christmas as a united family in four years. I knew that I was defying a court order by taking Meagan with us, but I decided that traveling to Pearl River would be better for me and my children than staying in Providence. And so we left. When we got there, nothing was said by my father about why we'd had no contact in four years. It was as if our estrangement had never happened; our "issues" were not confronted. It's the way alcoholic families work.

The children and I stayed at my parent's house on Christmas Eve, and the next day had dinner with the rest of the family. That evening, Louis arrived from Providence, and we stayed at the apartment in Nyack where my brothers Edwin and Matt lived. The children stayed with my sister Rosa, her husband Fernando, and their son Andre, who was two years younger than Meagan and her closest friend among the cousins.

The children thought that Louis was just a friend of mine. They didn't look upon him as a "boyfriend." Their experience of my boyfriends was that they lived with us. Louis rarely came to our home, and then only after the children had gone to bed. My parents and siblings assumed we were lovers because they knew we stayed together at times in an apartment in New York City that Louis had the use of. I gave them the phone number there in case they had to reach me. But we didn't fear that our affair would become public knowledge because of our visits to New York. We didn't think that we would be under surveillance in New York, and we usually traveled there separately from Rhode Island.

On December 26th, Louis and I, my sister Mary, and her husband Jack Holland had dinner at a restaurant in Little Italy. Louis was an immediate hit with my family, though I had told them about his background. That night, the two of us stayed in the vacant apartment of a friend of Louis's not far from the United Nations. The telephone rang early on the morning of the 27th. It was my father telling me that I had to return to Pearl River quickly because a social worker from the New York State Child Protective Services wanted to interview me and the children.

At 12:30 the previous night, my parents were awakened by the doorbell ringing. Going downstairs to answer it, my father saw a policeman standing on the step. Instantly seized with dread, he could barely respond when the officer asked if he had a daughter named Barbara Roberts, certain he was about to be told that I'd been killed in a car accident. When he answered in the affirmative, the policeman told him that they had received a call from a Mr. Ned Bresnahan, who claimed to be my estranged husband. Ned told the police that I was

facing felony charges in Rhode Island and that I had fled the jurisdiction to escape prosecution. Ned said that he had been awarded
custody of Meagan, and that I had taken her out of state in defiance
of court orders. He claimed that my oldest daughter was seriously ill,
that I had physically abused Dory in the past, and that I was threatening to kill myself and the children. He said that my parents were both
alcoholics and that several of my siblings were drug addicts.

My father was dumbfounded but intensely relieved that I was not
lying dead in some morgue. He somehow convinced the officer that
the accusations were untrue, but the police said that they were required by law to send a social worker to investigate and determine
that the children were in no danger. I told Louis that our little vacation
was over. He wasn't angry; he just thought that Ned must be out of his
mind. The accusations were so off the wall to anyone who knew me.
I was both angry and frightened, because his actions seemed to indicate that Ned was losing any shred of restraint that might remain. He
was pulling out all the stops and would do anything he could to harm
me and get revenge for my breaking up with him several years before.

I drove back to Pearl River after bringing Louis to the train station
in White Plains for his trip back to Rhode Island. I later found out that
Ned had also called my ex-husband, and Dr. Staunton, Dory's psychiatrist, with similar wild accusations.

That afternoon, I gathered the children and brought them to my
parents' house. Roslyn Portnoy, an investigator for the New York
State Child Protective Services, came and spoke to us for over an hour.
From her questions, it was apparent to at least Dory and Archie that
something Ned did was the reason behind her visit. The social worker
left convinced that all of the accusations were unfounded but told me
that she would have to file a report with the New York State Child
Abuse and Maltreatment Register, and that this report would be for-
warded to the local child protective agency in Rhode Island. My parents, sisters, and brothers were quietly furious at this latest outrage
from Ned. Like Louis, they kept repeating that he must be out of his
mind. There seemed to be no other explanation for such outrageous
behavior. The children were shaken. Meagan didn't want to talk about

it. Dory and Archie were bewildered. "Why does Ned do things like that?" they asked. I had no good answer.

The next day, we drove back to Rhode Island and met for the first of many outpatient family therapy sessions at Bradley Hospital. Dory's therapeutic team was upset that I'd signed Dory out against medical advice. They presented an unremittingly bleak prognosis to me when discussing Dory and were slow to pick up on the side effects she was having to medication. She complained bitterly of dry mouth and blurred vision. Ned telephoned Dory's therapists frequently and they persisted in suggesting that he be included in the "family" therapy. About the only useful thing Dr. Staunton did during this period was to send a letter to Family Court, in which he said: "...I have been advised by Dr. Roberts that she expects the upcoming custody hearing to precipitate considerable media coverage of the proceedings. In my opinion, such publicity would impede Dory's continued progress in hospital treatment. At the time of Dory's admission to Bradley, many of her difficulties were accentuated by family turmoil and the extensive media coverage that made the turmoil public knowledge. Regardless of the significance of the publicity as to the etiology of Dory's difficulties, I remain convinced that continued publicity would complicate her continued treatment..."

Indeed, the custody trial, which had been postponed time and again for over three years, was looming on the horizon. I now had another lawyer. Albert Lepore, Jr. was considered the premier litigator then active in the Family Court and was the first of my lawyers who could be considered a specialist in that field. Although Jack Cicilline and John Bevilacqua were outstanding criminal lawyers, they had little experience in Family Court. I had seen Albert often on my many forays into the Family Court's Dantesque precincts. He was hard to miss. He looked like a sturdy tree stump with legs, and he dressed in suits that, while well cut, were likely to be any color of the rainbow. (At one point, Albert was named by the *Providence Journal* as the second worst-dressed lawyer in the state. The lawyer they named the worst-dressed, Raoul Lovett, wore cowboy boots and string ties and had a gray beard of biblical proportions that hung to his expansive waist. His entire office was filled with Mickey Mouse memorabilia because he liked to tell people that he was "just a Mickey Mouse lawyer.")

Albert had a swarthy complexion and masses of marcelled gray hair. Like Jack, a cigarette was rarely far from his mouth. He had a raspy voice that sounded as if he gargled with emery boards. He never called me anything but "Doc," which was barked at a decibel count that could be heard fifty yards away. But I came to love him dearly, as he proved himself to be my unlikely knight in shining armor.

Albert was born in 1941 to Albert Lepore Sr. and Rose Palmieri Lepore, both children of immigrants from southern Italy. His father, who had been dead for a number of years, and his four paternal uncles were all gamblers. Albert's father, who was nicknamed "Keystone," was a friend and associate of Raymond Patriarca. The Patriarca and Lepore families were close friends, and Albert had also known Louis Manocchio since childhood.

Albert's father wanted him to get an education. "Be a lawyer, Albert," he told him, "it's like having a license to steal!" When Albert Jr. quit school at sixteen, his father kicked him out of the house and took away his car keys.

It wasn't long before Albert saw the advantages of continuing his education. He met his future wife, Celia Pontarelli, when they were both sixteen, and they married when they were twenty-one, in 1962. They had a son, Albert Lepore III, the following year, and a daughter, Sheri, in 1968. Albert worked for a Providence law firm for four years after graduating from Suffolk Law, where he met Jack Cicilline, who'd graduated two years before Albert. In 1970, he formed the law firm of Coia and Lepore with Arthur A. Coia, whose father, Arthur E. Coia, was, by 1981, the secretary-treasurer of the 900,000-member Laborers' International Union of North America.

I knew that both Coias, Albert, and Raymond Patriarca were indicted by a federal grand jury in Miami on charges of violating the Racketeer Influenced and Corrupt Organizations (RICO) Act in connection with alleged misuse of funds from the union. Grand juries in Boston and Miami had been investigating the union, and other underworld figures, including Santo Trafficante and Anthony "Big Tuna"

Accardo, were indicted along with the men from Rhode Island. The main government witness in this case was Joseph Hauser, another paid informant who was described by Marty Leppo, who was defending Albert and Arthur, as "a con man, a swindler, a compulsive liar, a paid informant, and one who has traded whatever integrity he ever had for personal gain." The younger Coia claimed that Hauser was trying to avoid jail by building "a scenario nationwide that includes an organized-crime figure in each scenario."

I learned about these pending charges against my latest lawyer because I had to testify about the health implications of flying Raymond to Miami to be arraigned, but they did not dissuade me from wanting Albert to represent me. I was firmly in the camp of the Italian-Americans and mistrusted everything the prosecutors did. I was convinced that I would never have been arrested on the felony charge if I were not Raymond's doctor. I thought that the government would go to any lengths to "get" the people they wanted to prosecute, for whatever reason. It sometimes seemed to me that they were two sides to the same coin; that on some level, both the criminals and the prosecutors looked upon their dance around each other as a big game. A game with no rules that couldn't be broken, except perhaps the one that decreed that you didn't physically harm any family members of the other side. And they needed each other. The existence of the Mafia justified the tax money spent on the salaries of the law enforcers, and the fact that they were pursued conferred status on the mobsters. It was the childhood game of cops and robbers, played by grown-ups.

Albert came to be my lawyer through his life-long friendship with the Patriarcas. One day, Albert was talking to Raymond Jr., and he asked, "What the fuck is she doing with these lawyers who have no expertise in Family Court?" When I spoke to Albert for the first time, on December 29, 1981, I immediately sensed that I was finally in the hands of someone who would end my four-year ordeal once and for all.

On New Year's Eve, Ned came to the house to pick up Meagan for court-ordered visitation. No doubt remembering the upset and turmoil at her grandparents' house the previous week, Meagan refused to go with Ned. She shrieked, "I don't want to go with my Daddy," repeating this over and over. She wouldn't tell me why. I called Albert on the telephone and he spoke to Meg, but she continued to sob and told him that she didn't care what he said, she was not going with her father. Albert said that it was useless to force her, and in fact, I had no intention of forcing her to go in the state she was in. Ned left when it became apparent that Meagan would not go with him. He stormed off, saying he would be contacting his lawyer. Albert suggested that I talk with Meagan and try to convince her to go with her father the next afternoon.

That night, the children and I had a quiet dinner with Louis at the Forum and then went home early, emotionally exhausted. Meagan continued adamant in her refusal to visit her father despite all of our entreaties. On the 4th of January, Ned came to the house again, and again Meagan became hysterical and refused to leave with him. I knew that I would be accused in court of poisoning her mind against her father. But Ned's own actions had caused Meagan to turn against him, and Albert went to court requesting a temporary suspension of visitation. A hearing on the matter was set for late January. On January 14, Ned came to the house again, prompting another hysterical outburst from Meg. As he yelled and screamed and pounded on the outside door, demanding to be let into the house, Meagan wailed in the solarium. Afraid that he would break the door down, I sent Archie and Meg upstairs and told them to lock themselves in a bathroom. Ned finally gave up and drove off with a friend. Over the next few days, Ned's lawyer entered a flurry of motions in Family Court, including ones to hold me in contempt and to grant Ned custody.

In the intervening months, I'd repeatedly refused to go to Superior Court to be arraigned on the felony breaking and entering charge from the previous March and Jack was forced to come up with excuses for my non-appearance. "Jack," I said, "this is rank persecution. If I weren't Raymond's doctor, there is no way they would be trying to arraign me on this bogus charge. If they ever try to put me on trial, I'll have Gloria Steinem, Bella Abzug, and every other feminist I can get my hands on up here picketing the Court House." Both Jack and Albert agreed with my analysis. Ned had called the police many times and had accused me of assault before, but it was only after I became Raymond's doctor that I was arrested as a result of one of his complaints.

Hard as it was for me to believe, my fitness as a mother was about to be put on trial, and I likely would face another trial on felony charges of breaking and entering. It was absurd; it was inconceivable. How had my life come to this?

On December 9, 1981, about six weeks before the trial to determine who would have custody of Meagan was due to commence, Jack succeeded in getting my breaking and entering case transferred to Family Court. This was duly noted under a blaring headline "Judge Shifts Charge Against Dr. Roberts to the Family Court" in the *Providence Journal*. Along with the usual unflattering picture, the article noted that this transfer effectively decriminalized the felony charge and quoted various prosecutors to the effect that they didn't know anything about the decision. " 'We are trying to determine exactly what happened or why,' said a spokesman for the Attorney General." The article identified me yet again as "one of New England crime boss Raymond L. S. Patriarca's physicians."

The next day, the *Providence Journal* headline read: "Dr. Roberts' Break Charge Returned to Jurisdiction of Superior Court." The article noted that Superior Court Judge Almeida had vacated his own ruling after "discovering" that he had no power under Rhode Island law to transfer the case to Family Court. The Attorney General's office claimed that they didn't know that one of their prosecutors had agreed to the transfer. The judge denied that he had been contacted by anyone from the Attorney General's office concerning the transfer, saying only that: "This case is just not the type of case that can be transferred."

We learned that Ned and Jerry McIntyre, his lawyer, were repeatedly calling the Federal prosecutor, claiming that it was only "mob influence" that was keeping me from being arraigned. Knowing they would appear to be persecuting me in what was clearly a domestic dispute, the state hoped that the case would die a quiet death, but Ned and his lawyer kept demanding to know why I had not been arraigned. The Federal prosecutor was threatening to investigate the matter, and so I finally caved in and agreed to be arraigned.

On February 3, 1982, in the midst of my custody trial, Jack and Albert escorted me to the building where the Superior Court is housed, between morning and afternoon sessions at Family Court, and I pleaded not guilty to the felony charge of breaking and entering. The arraignment was as mortifying as my arrest had been. It was clearly a victory for Ned. Getting arraigned on a felony charge is not something any physician wants to have happen. It doesn't inspire confidence in patients or referring physicians. When asked how I pleaded, I responded, "Not guilty." I was released on personal recognizance and Albert accompanied me back to Family Court.

Ned's lawyer, Mr. McIntyre, was then with the law firm of Edwards & Angell, one of the most expensive and best-known law firms in the state. In what I was certain was no coincidence, Edwards & Angell also represented the *Providence Journal* newspaper. I knew that Ned did not have the money to pursue his custody suit. Almost ten years later, Ned wrote me a letter in which he talked about a suit he had pending after being hit by a truck. He wrote:

> ...*I know it [the suit] will settle and I don't want Jerry McIntyre to try to grab it, although I think too much time has gone by for him to sue, and he did tell me in front of John Dunn that he would take the case for $1,000 period and that it would go all the way to the Supreme Court without me giving Edwards & Angell another cent, which I never did. When the criminal charges against you and George Gregory vanished he told me that if 'you don't stir the pot, I'll forget about your $30,000 bill to [Edwards & Angell]....'*

Edwards & Angell were not in the habit of taking on expensive cases and then foregoing payment. I wondered if the *Providence Journal* had any hand in their doing so, but I never found out.

The trial finally began on January 26, 1982. It would last until March 29. At the time, it was one of the longest-running contested custody cases in the history of Rhode Island. The transcript of the trial would occupy four thousand pages. It was heard by Judge Thomas Fay, a handsome, sandy-haired man of about my age, who resembled the actor Donald Sutherland. Before being appointed to the Family Court bench, he had been a Rhode Island State Representative, having been elected the same year Albert was. Because of all the horrendous allegations Ned had made against me and my fitness as a mother, the Court appointed a guardian ad litem, Richard Jessup, who sat next to Ned's lawyer throughout the proceedings. Whenever there are allegations by a parent that the other parent is unfit, a guardian ad litem is appointed to represent the best interests of the child.

On Albert's advice, I retained separate counsel for Meagan, a lawyer named George McDonald. McIntyre immediately filed a motion asking for a "Protective Order restraining and otherwise of prohibiting the Plaintiff or any Agent of the Plaintiff from employing counsel on behalf of the minor child of the parties." He also filed a motion requesting child support be awarded to Ned, "he being without sufficient means to support her," which seemed to support my contention that this whole trial was about revenge and money, and not about my fitness as a mother. Judge Fay denied the first motion and passed on the second motion pending the outcome of the trial.

On the day before the trial was scheduled to begin, Albert called me down to a meeting in his office. "Doc," he rasped, we've got a problem." I panicked, dreading whatever came next. "You know how the FBI has their informants?" he inquired, "Well, we've got ours too, and one of them told us they saw a 302 (FBI surveillance form) putting you with Louie Manocchio. Is that true?"

"Yes, it is," I replied.

"Jesus, Doc," he barked, "Why didn't you tell me about this? Do you know how bad it would be if that came up during the trial and I didn't know about it?"

"Albert," I said, "I really thought you knew. I mean, Marty Leppo is your lawyer, and he's Louis' lawyer. I just thought you knew."

"Doc," he exclaimed, "do you think we sit around like broads talking about who's dating who, who's doing who? No, we don't. Just try to keep it very discreet, and we'll hope that Ned doesn't know about it."

Albert wasn't forthcoming about how he got the information. He implied that some clerical worker in the FBI office told him about the surveillance. It wasn't the type of thing he would tell me—who the informant actually was, or what that person's job was that allowed them access to the information. I assumed the "we" was Albert and any other lawyers who might have had an interest in me or Louis. I was not surprised that the surveillance report existed; I assumed that Louis, who was free on bail, was periodically under surveillance. I was a bit surprised that there was someone in the FBI office who would feed this information to Albert, but I was mainly concerned that the information would somehow find its way to McIntyre. In the event, my relationship with Louis never came up during the trial, which to me was proof that Ned had no knowledge of it.

His motion to deny Meagan her own counsel only increased my loathing for Jerry McIntyre. A tall, overweight, florid-faced man with sparse blond hair and porcine features, he set about trying to destroy what was left of my reputation by drawing Ned out on every outrageous accusation his fevered brain could conjure up. These ran the gamut from lesbian relationships with Gloria Steinem and every other feminist he could think of, to heterosexual promiscuity, to drug dealing, stating at one point that I gave frequent parties in which bowls of cocaine were scattered all over my house. In a whispered aside, Albert told Meagan's lawyer George McDonald, "The Doc does OK, but she's not rich enough to have bowls of cocaine lying around!" Needless to say, Ned never found anyone to corroborate these accusations.

I hit upon a tactic I was fairly sure would disconcert McIntyre. The entire time I spent on the witness stand, hours that seemed to last an eternity, I kept my eyes fixed on his crotch while I answered his questions. My nurse friend Rita Greene agreed to be a character witness for me, and when she told me how nervous she was, never having testified under oath before, I reassured her and said, "Just stare at his crotch the whole time you're up there. He hates it."

McIntyre requested that Dory's confidential medical records from Bradley be introduced as evidence. I shuddered to think what the impact on Dory would be if these were made public. It didn't bear thinking about. By now, I hated Ned with an intensity that should have had him spontaneously combusting in the witness chair.

On the very first day of the trial, Tracey Breton, a *Providence Journal* reporter, was there in the courtroom taking notes. Albert and George McDonald tried to have the press barred, but Judge Fay denied the motion. She did approach me, however, and told me she knew how delicate the situation was, and that she would wait until the trial was over before writing her article. I was not terribly reassured. Having one's fitness as a mother put to a public trial is a unique form of crucifixion.

It was a bleak time, in which I tried to juggle taking care of my children and my patients with attending court room proceedings that played out alternately as farce or tragedy. I rose early each morning and made hurried hospital rounds after getting the children off to school. Court started at 10 a.m. and usually recessed for the day at 2 p.m. My secretary, Donna, whose loyalty never wavered, rearranged my office hours to start at 2:30, and afterward, if we weren't eating dinner with Louis at the Forum, I cooked dinner at home. I tried to keep up a cheerful front for the children, but they knew the trial was ongoing and were as anxious as I was about the outcome.

Dory had been home from the hospital since I'd signed her out just before Christmas. She was back in school and seemed almost to be her usual self, but I worried that the stress of the trial would cause a relapse. My own feelings during the trial alternated between rage, fear, and guilt. Ned spent days testifying under oath, and even though I knew he was lying, when you hear over and over again that you did something you knew you hadn't, you begin to question your own sanity, and wonder what is wrong with you that someone feels compelled to hurt you in such a fashion. I had chosen to live with this man and have a child by him. How big a jerk was I? Really, there had to be some very grave flaw in me to allow such a situation to come to pass. And so, I was consumed with guilt and sadness over the trauma the trial was causing the children. All through the trial, we met the therapists at Bradley on a weekly basis. We discussed the trial and the children's reaction to it. But what we actually said at these meetings I've erased from the memory banks, as have the children.

Every week, one or another of my siblings came to visit, and the care I had taken of them as children was amply repaid. Their love quite simply kept us all going. As he had during Dory's hospitalization, Louis was another source of comfort and strength, never wavering in his conviction that I would be vindicated. And then there was Albert, who was a rock. He found out that Meagan liked Barbie dolls and the next day he showed up at court with not one, but four different Barbies for her. He would tease me, saying, "Doc, you have nothing to worry about. George McDonald's wife is the Head Warden at the Women's' Prison. If you have to do some time, she'll make sure no one bothers you." His constant refrain was, "Doc, you're going to be fine. Just stay cool."

At one point, he was cross-examining me to refute Ned's accusations of multiple lesbian affairs. Going down the list of names of each woman I was alleged to have been intimate with, he asked me what my relationship was, and I replied that we had worked together in the women's movement. I replied negatively each time he asked me if I'd had a sexual affair with the woman. Finally, out of patience, I exclaimed, "Look, I'm hopelessly heterosexual!"

"OBJECTION, your Honor," McIntyre shouted, erupting from his seat as if he'd been stung by a bee on his ample butt.

Judge Fay raised his eyebrows quizzically and considered his answer for a few seconds. "Sustained," he ruled, "I guess it's never hopeless."

"You mean there's hope for me, your Honor?" Albert inquired innocently, while everyone in the court room laughed out loud. Somehow the image of Albert discovering he was homosexual was comical in the extreme.

Ned accused me of being the only woman in the crew on a few over-night sail boat races, which was true, but also said that these had turned into orgies, which only proved his ignorance of sailboat racing. A common definition has it akin to standing in a cold shower tearing up hundred-dollar bills.

The owner of one of the boats on which I'd crewed was subpoenaed to testify. When Albert asked him if anything untoward had occurred during the race he replied, "Yes, sir."

"And what was that?" Albert asked.

"We came in dead last," was the reply.

But the laughs were few and far between. For the most part the raw, cold weather mirrored the bleakness in my heart and I trudged through the winter days like an overburdened pack animal.

Midway through the trial, Judge Fay decided he wanted to meet with Meagan privately in his chambers. I prepared her for this as best I could, telling her that the judge was a nice man who was trying to do what was best for all of us. I told her to answer his questions truthfully, and she did not seem unduly frightened to have to speak with yet another stranger about the events of her brief but turbulent life. She was a few months past her fifth birthday. Ned had testified repeatedly that I smoked marijuana in front of the children on many occasions—a blatant falsehood. I was particularly pleased to learn therefore that Judge Fay asked Meg if he could smoke during their meeting, and Meagan, in her piping, bossy little voice, told him, "No, no, you shouldn't smoke. My mommy hates smoking. It's *very* bad!"

A parade of psychologic experts testified, including a court-appointed psychologist, and Dr. Staunton. Much was made of Dory's breakdown, the fault for which Ned's lawyer tried to lay at my door. McIntyre hammered away at Meagan's unwillingness to visit with her father and again accused me of poisoning her mind against him. And so we continued, as did Ned's shenanigans outside the courtroom. Even during the trial, Ned was making telephone calls to my parents, siblings, and ex-husband, repeating the accusations he was making on the stand. My family eventually refused to speak with him, but there was nothing at that point we could do to stop him.

Richard Jessup, the court-appointed guardian ad litem, made a comprehensive report. He had interviewed all of the Bradley therapists, Meagan's teachers at the Montessori school, Dory, who was sixteen, and young Archie, who was then twelve. Archie told him that once Ned had attempted to have him smoke cigarettes and marijuana when he was six. I had no prior knowledge of this incident, and it didn't help Ned's case. Both of the children told Jessup that Ned was physically abusive towards me on occasion, but never towards them. Dory told him that she felt Ned was "unable to live by any rules," and they both stated their opposition to his being involved in the family counseling at Bradley Hospital. They denied that George Gregory had ever been abusive towards them or Meagan while he was living with us, although Dory made no bones about her dislike of George, characterizing him as a "parasite." They both adamantly denied that I had ever smoked marijuana or used cocaine, despite Ned's allegation that I did both, in front of the children.

Jessup wrote that both Ned and I led "unconventional lives." His report continued:

> While Dr. Roberts must, of course, make her own decisions regarding her professional practice, it is undisputed that her treatment of Raymond Patriarca gained for her certain notoriety in the community at large. Her continued association with this figure and the publicity she received has certainly not been a stabilizing influence on her children's lives. On the other hand, Dr. Roberts has maintained a high standard of living for her family. In addition, setting aside Dory's recent emotional difficulties, the children appear to be reasonably well adjusted. They are all very bright, do well in school, and are involved in activities appropriate for their age and development.
>
> Mr. Bresnahan, for whatever reasons, has chosen, over the past several years, to emphasize what he considers to be inappropriate behavior on the part of Dr. Roberts. In my opinion, his conduct has been very destructive and inappropriate in view of the presenting circumstances. I would cite his numerous complaints to social agencies, which have been investigated, and which have not resulted in any action being taken by the said agencies. The effect, however, has been to add a great deal of upset and turmoil to the lives of Dory, Archie and Meagan... He has not re-

ally suggested how he could better provide for Meagan in a meaningful, emotional and developmental way... I must wonder, based on all of the circumstances, whether Mr. Bresnahan is truly desirous of maintaining a long-standing, healthy relationship with his daughter, or whether he is more concerned with what his relationship with Meagan can do for him..."

He strongly recommended that "the present family unit" not be disturbed, that the children and I continue family therapy at Bradley Hospital, and that Ned be constrained from further reports to social agencies.

Finally, after seventeen days of testimony spread over two months, Judge Fay rendered his decision. When transcribed it was thirty-nine pages long. At the very outset, the judge ordered that all investigative and hospital reports be sealed, not to be opened without permission of the Court. "...I don't think the public has any interest, nor should they, in some of the personal matters that have been brought out in the case, and substantial numbers of which are completely unsubstantiated..." This removed a huge burden of worry that Dory's medical records would find their way into a newspaper article. As for allegations of alcohol abuse, he found that these were amply proven by Ned's own medical records and that "...the only testimony before the Court, with regard to drugs, would lead one clearly to believe that the only person who might have a drug problem in this case is, in fact, Mr. Bresnahan."

He found that my home was "fit and proper for the raising of children," contrasting it to Ned's one-room apartment, in which the only furniture was a mattress on the floor. He, therefore, denied Ned's motion for change of custody. He touched upon the numerous times Ned called the Department of Children and Families, with horrendous accusations against me and George Gregory, all of which were summarily dismissed as groundless. But he noted the hostility that these visits from social workers must have caused the children. He denied Ned's motion to suspend the order requiring him to pay $5.00 a week child support. Ned had claimed, falsely, that I had an agreement with him that he didn't have to pay. Judge Fay said, "Quite frankly, as I said before, I can't believe these two would agree on anything."

Ned was ordered to pay the child support and was found in contempt because he had not done so. Judge Fay did not deny my motion to terminate Ned's parental rights, but without prejudice, allowed it to pass. He continued: "...Mr. Bresnahan, you are restrained and enjoined from annoying, molesting or threatening the Plaintiff, Dr. Roberts, at home or elsewhere. You are restrained from calling her at any of her places of employment. You are restrained, in fact, from calling the Department of Children and Their Families with allegations of child abuse, and I am making that restraining order—I see Mr. McIntyre looking up at me; since he is the non-custodial parent, one would hope if they obey the restraining orders, they will have little to see or do with each other. I can't conceive of any instances where he would have enough knowledge on his own to even make a complaint to the Department of Children and Their Families from this point in time on, pending the next hearing in this case, because, quite frankly, I am going to, at this time, suspend his visitation until further order of the Court."

It was at this point that I realized that I had won on every point that was important for the children's well-being. I had to restrain myself from jumping up and down with joy or at least shooting my fist in the air and shouting "Right on!"

Regarding the various motions to hold me in contempt of court for visitations that were ordered but did not occur, Judge Fay bent over backwards to be fair. He concluded: "...while I find the Plaintiff in contempt of those orders, I will not in fact sentence her as a result of her contempt..."

Hurray! I was not going to jail. However, I was ordered to pay Mr. McIntyre legal fees of $4,000 to "purge" myself of the contempt—and I almost would have preferred to be incarcerated. Except for the contempt finding, Albert had won every round of the bout, and I clung to him, crying with relief, telling him over and over again how grateful I was. He grinned from ear to ear, telling me, "I told you so." From the corner of my eye, I saw Ned stalk out of the courtroom, without custody, additional money, or any foreseeable visitation with Meagan.

My only remaining qualm was how the trial and its outcome would be reported by my old nemesis, the *Providence Journal*. The next day, March 30, 1982, the article was headlined: "Dr. Roberts Retains Custody of her Child," and it repeated Ned's allegations about my fitness, and about physical and emotional abuse. I was livid, but it was in keeping with their desire to inflict damage on anyone assisting Raymond Patriarca, even if that person was only discharging professional obligations. Raymond himself was fully aware of this and reiterated how bad he felt that my defense of him had resulted in so much unwanted press attention and notoriety. He repeated what he'd said before: "I owe my life to you, I know that. I couldn't love you more if you were my own daughter."

11 · Assault in a Cemetery

Trauma ruptures and hollows.
Compassion mends and fills; love heals.
—Na'ama Yehuda

With the burden of the trial lifted from my shoulders, and Ned's harassment in abeyance, I had unlimited reserves of energy, and life was suddenly peaceful in a way it hadn't been for many years. Louis and I continued our clandestine affair, never meeting publicly in Rhode Island except at the Forum. Marty Leppo sometimes joined us for dinner, and he was of the opinion that it was unlikely that the state would prosecute Louis on the Marfeo-Melei murder charge, though because the state had not dropped the case, a trial remained possible.

I did not examine my feelings about Louis very closely. I lived one day at a time. We never talked of love or of a future together, but his care and devotion enveloped me in a cocoon where I felt safe and cherished.

It was around this time that I had a dream. In the dream, Louis had died, and I walked into the room where his coffin lay. I didn't know whether he had died of natural causes or had been killed, but the grief I felt at seeing him dead was so intense I awoke in tears. The dream made me realize how much I had come to depend on him and hinted at the devastation I would feel were I to lose him.

This dependence had crept up on me. He was always there when I needed him, with a comforting word, or a gift, or an invitation to bring the children to the Forum for dinner. Whether he was in Rhode Island or out of town, he telephoned every day. Our sexual relationship nourished me too. It was only in the throes of orgasm that all of my problems were erased from my mind. I found sex to be *the* great stress reducer and used to joke, before I started working out when I was thirty-eight, that for years sex was the only aerobic exercise I got.

In late April of 1982, the children and I drove to Nyack for my brother Matty's wedding. Louis traveled separately by train and I picked him up in Rye, New York. Matty was now almost 29, with the impish, implacably sunny disposition he had retained since childhood. He was almost six feet tall, dark-haired, mustachioed, and devilishly handsome. He was rarely serious, except in play. Luckily, both he and Edwin had drawn high draft numbers during the Vietnam War era and neither was drafted, but he would parody the super patriots of that era, pounding on his chest in mock machismo, bellowing, "Ah'm an Uh-merican. Let's kill the gooks!"

His bride was Amy Lehman, a petite, blond dancer from State College, Pennsylvania, where her father was an administrator at Pennsylvania State University. They met and fell in love while working at Benny's, a restaurant in Irvington where Matt bartended. Amy worked as a waitress to support her dancing. She was a protégé of Jacques D'Amboise, himself a protégé of George Balanchine, and Jacques was a guest at the wedding.

All ten of the Hudson siblings were in attendance, and all six of my parents' grandchildren. Mary, Jack, and their daughter Jenny had moved from Dublin to Brooklyn, and for the first time in many years all of us were reunited. Meagan whirled around the floor, dancing for hours. At one point, Jacques D'Amboise came up to me and made a courtly little bow saying, "Madame, your daughter is a very talented dancer. If you ever want her to study the dance, please send her to me."

The wedding ushered in a summer of sunshine, sailing, and peace for me and the children—the first in years that was not shadowed by Ned's harassment. Dory seemed fully recovered from her breakdown of the previous year. She passed all her courses and was taking ice-skating lessons. She had blossomed into a beautiful young woman. My practice had miraculously survived and prospered. I was still being referred new patients, usually by family members already in my care. Bob Indeglia and a few other physicians also continued to send me patients. As I approached my thirty-eighth birthday, I was reasonably content with my life.

Raymond's medical condition had stabilized, but he still suffered from easily provoked angina. He had surgery to correct nerve damage in his wrist, which was performed under local anesthesia—less risky, given his heart condition. Various state and federal prosecutors were still intent on bringing him to trial. That summer, I had to testify in New Bedford concerning the likely health risks if this came about. Again, Dr. Most, testifying for the state of Massachusetts, concurred that Raymond would run a significant risk of heart attack if he stood trial. Because of our testimony, his trial was again postponed. The rest of the summer passed uneventfully. Cousin Bernie visited in June, and we sailed with the children to Block Island for a week. Later in the summer, he came back with his children, Tom and Marah, and we all sailed to Block Island again. Meagan particularly loved it there, pointing out all the honeysuckle to her cousins, but she called it "*sunny-hunkle*."

Several times each week, we had dinner with Louis at the Forum. Chairs and tables were set up outdoors in the warm weather and music was piped outside. Meagan danced around the fountain while we relaxed after eating, and before long, people were giving her money for her performances. She began informing people, very seriously: "I have a job dancing on Federal Hill." She seemed unscarred by the custody battle and relieved that she no longer had to visit her father.

To no one's surprise, Ned filed an appeal of Judge Fay's decision to the Rhode Island Supreme Court and requested that he not have to pay the fee to have the transcript typed. He also did not pay the five-dollar weekly child support that was ordered, nor one half of the guardian ad litem fee. Because of this, during a hearing six months after the conclusion of the trial, Judge Fay refused to reinstate any visitation.

Yet despite appearances, my legal problems were far from over. The felony charge of breaking and entering still had not been tried. The state appointed Stephen Famiglietti, an attorney famous because of his role as a prosecutor in the Claus von Bulow trial, to prosecute my case. The von Bulow trials were sensational, and after them, Famiglietti was appointed head of the Major Crimes division of the attorney general's office.

How my rescue of Meagan qualified as a major crime was a mystery to me. Again, I could only assume that my notoriety as Raymond's doctor entered into the decision to assign the case to the most prominent prosecutor in the state. It quickly became apparent that he was no more eager to put me on the stand than I was to stand trial. The district attorney's office suggested to Jack that if I accepted "diversion" and did several hundred hours of community service, the case would be settled without going to trial. Jack assured me that it was not the same as pleading no contest, but I refused to accept "diversion." This was a way of resolving cases that did not involve testimony or trial but was not the same as being found innocent.

"Jack, I'm innocent," I insisted. "Tell them they can take their diversion and shove it where the sun never shines." Jack rolled his eyes and tried to change my mind, but I was adamant. And so the standoff continued, for many months. Most of the time, I could forget that the charge still loomed over my head like the sword of Damocles, but the children knew it was pending. It was one of the issues that came up in our family therapy sessions at Bradley.

The resolution of the felony charge did not occur for many more months. On January 30, 1983, almost two years after the incident, the *Providence Journal* broke the news, even before Jack had a chance to inform me, that the charges had been dropped. The article stated: "Over the objection of the attorney general's department, Superior Court Judge Joseph F. Rogers yesterday dismissed breaking and entering charges against Dr. Barbara Roberts—a cardiologist who has treated New England crime boss Raymond L.S. Patriarca—and a friend of Dr. Roberts." It recounted the story of the "breaking and entering" and repeated the false allegation about George using a tire iron. The *Journal* reported that "Rogers yesterday dismissed the charges at the request of defense lawyers John F. Cicilline and John F. Sheehan because the state and police say they can't locate Bresnahan to testify at trial. Asst. Atty. Gen. Stephen R. Famiglietti said the state didn't have prosecutable cases against Dr. Roberts or Gregory unless Bresnahan were in court to testify. He said that the Providence Police Department... " 'has been looking assiduously' for Bresnahan for 'quite some time, most intensively in the last several days, and can't find him.' " As usual, the *Journal* was unable to resist taking another swipe at me, by printing their totally gratuitous rehash of Ned's accusation that I was an unfit mother. Even more galling was the implication that Ned had disappeared. I was amazed they didn't come right out and suggest that he was the victim of foul play, planted on the bottom of the Seekonk River in a pair of concrete boots.

In fact, the police and prosecution were well aware of Ned's whereabouts. In an affidavit filed in Family Court three months before this article appeared, Ned testified that he was working as a personal aide to a retired industrialist, even giving the Providence address of his employer, where he could have been found on most days of the week. Pretending that the only prosecution witness was nowhere to be found was just a ploy for the attorney general's office to save face and drop the charges at the same time. And if once again, my reputation was dragged through the mud, so much the better.

Two months later, very much alive, Ned withdrew his appeal of the custody decision to the Rhode Island Supreme Court but continued in his refusal to pay counsel fees or child support and to undergo psychiatric counseling. The last hearing in this tortured saga occurred on September 14, 1983, five years after it began. Eventually, when Judge Fay threatened him with incarceration for disobeying orders of the court, Ned dropped out of sight, leaving the state and not returning for many years.

❧

After returning to Rhode Island from a Christmas 1982 visit to my family, I admitted Raymond once more to the hospital. Over the previous months, he'd noted increasing angina, and I'd suggested hospitalization to him on several occasions. Finally, he agreed so that I could treat him with a new, recently approved anti-anginal medication. The medicine caused him to have abnormalities in his liver function tests, which fortunately were only transient. His diabetes was also becoming more difficult to control, with wild swings in his blood sugar. His heart rhythm continued to concern me, raising the specter of sudden death. A federal judge had recently ruled that he was too ill to be flown to Florida to be arraigned on racketeering charges, but prosecutors in Massachusetts and Rhode Island were still trying to press ahead with trials on the murder conspiracy charges that had prompted his arrest two years before. Over the course of the first six months of 1983, he would need to be hospitalized six times. All of these were duly reported in the newspapers, and all required that I report regularly to the various jurisdictions where he was facing charges. Presented with these further proofs of how fragile he was, none of the judges was willing to set a date for trial.

By March of 1983, I'd been involved with Louis for a year and a half. He was my closest confidante, as well as my lover. Apart from my family, there was no one else who knew me so thoroughly or who cared about me so much. When he was away, I missed him terribly. In the winters he often left to ski for a week or two at a time. He asked me to come with him, but I was unwilling to leave the practice and the children. His physical presence had become like a drug to me. And although we almost never argued, I was beginning to chafe at the need for secrecy.

I always feared that our affair would become public knowledge. We could not do something as simple as walk down the street in Providence holding hands. We could not attend medical functions together. As far as the doctors I worked with knew, I was a single mother with no man in my life. This fear of exposure blighted our relationship to an extent that became clear to me only in retrospect.

There were also whole areas of his past and present of which I was ignorant and would remain so. For Louis, the habit of secrecy was the habit of a lifetime, and deeply ingrained. I felt that I did not truly know him, nor ever would. I was reminded of the words of a Joan Baez song: "You're mainly a mystery with violins filling in space." The secrecy, the "unknowing," were not things I felt could continue indefinitely. And yet, there did not appear to be any alternative.

The previous summer, I'd had a brief dalliance with one of the young men who crewed for me on *Boadicea*. He was twenty-one to my thirty-eight. It involved nothing more than lust and affection, laughter and long, sun-drenched cruises to Block Island and Nantucket. My heart was engaged elsewhere; that my body strayed did not feel like a betrayal. I did not reveal this brief fling to Louis. I didn't want to risk hurting his feelings. We'd never discussed whether or not our relationship would or should be exclusive.

Shortly after our affair began, Louis had given me the key to his apartment, so that I could let myself in without his having to accompany me. Not long after, I had some unexpected free time one afternoon and decided to surprise him. I went to the apartment, unlocked the door and stepped into the entrance hallway that led to the bedroom. I immediately heard a woman's voice say, "Shh — I just heard something." Then Louis responded, "No, I don't think so." My heart plunged towards my feet. I backed out as quickly and silently as I could. I was more mortified that I'd almost walked in on him in bed with another woman than I was angry at him. It was just a few weeks after we'd become lovers, and we'd never discussed monogamy. But I was upset and somewhat hurt.

Neither of us ever mentioned the episode, although Louis must have known it was me who'd almost walked in on them. Over the course of the next two years, it was my impression that he was not sleeping with any other women. And with the one exception, I was not physically involved with any other men. In truth, no other man excited me as Louis did.

Years before, I had read a book in which the author, writing about erotic attraction, made an analogy. He likened it to what happens when two electrically charged wires are brought closer and closer. When they are too far apart, no charge and no spark flows between them. As they approach closer and closer, at a certain critical distance, a spark ignites and bridges the gap. Then, as the distance between them lessens still further, the spark disappears but a current of electricity now courses between the two wires. And so it is with erotic attraction between two people: Too far apart and there is no spark, too close and the spark dies, to be replaced, if they are lucky, by the powerful flow of energy that is mature love. But I was addicted to the spark, and the unbridgeable distance between us, the lacunae of unknowing, the words that could not be spoken, all served to keep the spark crackling between us. I was as hooked as any junkie—and this half-acknowledged, half-denied fact festered in my brain, setting up a low-level thrum of foreboding.

⚹

The morning of March 5, a Saturday, was sunny but brisk. I had, at Louis' urging, begun jogging the previous summer. He thought that regular physical exercise was crucial to maintaining physical and mental health, and I thought that it would be tacky if I waited, as so many did, to turn forty before taking better care of my body. That morning, rather than jogging, I felt like taking a long walk, wanting to mull over our relationship. I was dressed in an old pair of jeans, a sweater, and a black jacket.

About a half-mile from my house, I turned into the grounds of Swan Point Cemetery. Founded in the nineteenth century, it covers some dozen acres on Providence's east side and contains many beautiful mausoleums and headstones. I wandered down the manicured pathways towards the back of the cemetery, where it borders on the Seekonk River.

I had just passed the headstone of someone named Kirby, which I noted because it was my grandmother's maiden name, when I heard a sound. I turned and beheld a sight straight out of a nightmare, or some schlocky horror movie.

A white man wearing no clothes—nothing but sneakers and a ski mask, which covered his face—jumped out from behind a headstone and began beating me. In an instant, I was seized with such terror that hot urine gushed down my legs. I began screaming like a banshee, half expecting to see the dead rise up from their graves as I flailed my arms in an ineffective attempt to protect myself and fight him off. All I could think was, "My poor children, my poor children, I'm all they have and now they'll have no one." The only thing my attacker said, as I continued to scream and fight back, was, "Shut up or I'll kill you." His voice was absolutely uninflected, almost robotic, in stark contrast to the violence he was inflicting; it whiffed of the death I was sure would sink its talons in me. My terror redoubled; I had no doubt he meant to kill me, I only wondered if he meant to rape me before or after.

Time is very elastic, and I have no idea how long our struggle went on before he succeeded in beating me to the ground, breaking my sunglasses in the process. I kicked up at him, frantically trying to avoid being pinned down, screaming the whole while. Suddenly, he backed off and I jumped up. He bent down to pick something up and I thought, "He's getting a rock and he's going to bludgeon me to death with it." I mentally bid my children farewell, in an agony of grief that they would be left motherless and started to run as fast as I could towards the cemetery entrance. When I looked over my shoulder, he had disappeared into the woods bordering the river.

An older couple, alerted by my screams, hurried up and asked what had happened. Still hysterical, I told them I had been attacked, and they walked me to the administration building. The guard on duty insisted I accompany him as he drove around the cemetery trying to spot my assailant, but I knew that he was long gone, nor would I have been able to recognize him if he weren't. I debated whether or not I should report the incident to the police. I was fearful that it would be reported in the newspaper, but since it was clearly a sexual assault, I thought that even if it were, my name would not be mentioned.

And so, knowing that a murderous woman-hater was on the loose, I called the police. An officer came to the cemetery and took a statement from me. I then telephoned Louis, who came and brought me to his apartment so I could clean the blood from my face. The inside of my mouth had several cuts, but luckily there were none on the outside, only some bruises. He was shaken and furious, grimmer than I had ever seen him. I wondered, very briefly, if my attacker could have been someone in law enforcement, but quickly dismissed that as an impossibility. They would not stoop to something so bizarre and evil. This was a random event; I hadn't known I was going to be in the cemetery that morning, so no one else could have known either. I didn't tell the children what had happened, but said that I had fallen and that's how my face came to be bruised. They had been through enough turmoil, and I was desperate to keep this latest disaster from them, but my personal sense of safety was shattered forever.

Suddenly, the world had become a dangerous place; if this attack could happen in broad daylight, so close to my home, then no place was safe. I became obsessive about locking doors, and my life-long insomnia worsened, as even the slightest sound caused me to wake up terrified. I began to lift weights to increase my upper body strength. I had floodlights installed around the house and acquired a handgun. Louis offered to sleep at the house, which he had never done, but he insisted on sleeping on the living room floor. He was far too proper to share a bed with me while my children slept under the same roof. I had no doubt that he would kill anyone who threatened me or the children.

As the nightmare scene replayed itself endlessly on the screen of my mind, I re-wrote the script. In my new version I was not a terrified, pants-wetting, ineffectual victim but a vengeful virago, turning on my attacker with fists honed into weapons by hours of sweaty weight-lifting, beating him to the ground and stomping on his testicles until they were bloody pancakes.

That Monday, I had to appear in Family Court once more at a hearing about Ned's appeal of Judge Fay's decision. After work, I took the children with me to the Brown University gymnasium, where I often jogged on the indoor track. A Superior Court sheriff, whom I had gotten to know from my many appearances on Raymond's behalf, came up to me and said, "Dr. Roberts, I'm sorry to hear what happened to you." I was surprised that he knew but thought that perhaps he had heard the story from Jack Cicilline, or Albert Lepore, both of whom I had informed. When I looked at him questioningly, he asked, "Haven't you seen the newspaper today?" I hadn't, but when I saw the *Journal* article that described the whole incident, I was aghast—and furious.

I now had no hope of keeping this incident from the children. I sat Dory and Archie down and told them what had happened, playing down the violence and how traumatized I was. They were stunned and frightened—and furious that the *Journal* had once again violated our privacy.

"You know what, kids?" I told them, "I think we all need a vacation. Spring break starts next week, and we're all going to Mexico." In the meantime, I had a bone to pick with the *Journal*—and the police. The latter told me that police reports were a matter of public record and that they could not prevent the newspaper from writing articles about incidents that were reported in them. Then, incredibly, they said they wanted me to come down to police headquarters and take a lie detector test. I said I would do so, but when I told Jack and Albert, they had a fit and they told me not to be so naive.

"I can just see the headlines," Albert said. "Those tests are very inaccurate and the next thing you know the *Journal* would be saying that you had flunked the lie detector. There's no way we'd let you take it. You couldn't even pick this guy out of a lineup if they had a suspect, which they don't. So forget about it." Jack heard from a police source that a similar attack had taken place in a park in another part of Providence, but the *Journal* had not seen fit to print an article about that episode.

I learned that the city editor decides what articles will appear in the newspaper. At 7 o'clock the next morning, I went to the city room and asked to have him pointed out to me. He was a skinny, mousy, dark-haired man, who appeared to be about my own age. I stormed up to him with all the rage of the Valkyries, Furies, Harpies and Amazons rolled into one tight bundle. When he saw me bearing down on him, he paled the precise shade of a beached flounder and his mouth flopped like a wind sock in a freshening breeze.

"I'm Dr. Barbara Roberts, and you are SCUM," I hissed. "You are the *lowest* form of scum. How dare you print my name and home address in the newspaper when I was the victim of a sexual assault! If this maniac comes back to finish the job because now he knows where I live, you'll be in trouble—you'll be in *serious* trouble!"

He began to stutter a half-assed explanation: "That is the newspaper's policy and has been since the last century. In a sexual assault, unless penetration occurs, we print the name of the victim. It's done to discourage false allegations of sexual assault. That's our policy."

"Do you mean to tell me that if I hadn't resisted, if I'd let this maniac rape me, you wouldn't have published my name?" I asked, incredulous. He averred that that was the case. "That's insane," I replied. "You haven't heard the last of this. And just remember what I said." With that, I stalked out of the city room, happy that I had frightened him, if nothing else.

There were no follow-up articles in the newspaper about the attack on me, but several women's groups expressed their outrage at the *Journal*'s policy with regard to "unsuccessful" rape attempts, and the local television stations carried the story. However, the *Journal*, in its arrogant fashion, refused to change the policy, discouraging many women, I'm sure, from reporting sexual assaults. Louis slept on the living room floor for ten days, until the children and I flew to Acapulco for a much-needed rest. No one was ever arrested or charged with the cemetery assault.

12·LOUIS ON TRIAL

Sooner or later, we all go through a crucible.
—Marc Guggenheim

Unfortunately, the courts continued to play an important role in my life. Louis tried to shield me from his own legal entanglements, but as the spring of 1983 approached, he told me that the state was going to bring him to trial on the Marfeo and Melei murder charges. Despite the fact that the only prosecution witness, Red Kelley, was suffering from early Alzheimer's disease, David Leach, the prosecutor, persuaded a Superior Court judge to set a court date for May. Marty Leppo, Louis' lawyer, had assured him that this day would never come, but in this he was mistaken. Leppo continued to be certain that the State's case was fatally flawed. Not only was Kelley now mildly demented, he admitted under oath that he had perjured himself in previous testimony about the murders.

I was not as confident as Louis' lawyer. He was based in Boston, not Providence. He was an outsider and would be seen as such by a Rhode Island jury. I had no doubt that he was competent—after all, he was defending Albert in the racketeering charges that were pending in Florida—but I mistrusted his strategy, which was to hammer away at the credibility of the state's only witness and ignore the fact that Louis had fled the jurisdiction for ten years, which in the insular world of Rhode Island would be well known to all the jurors. I was convinced that not addressing those years when Louis was a fugitive was a grave error. What juror would not wonder if Louis fled because he was guilty, not because he was convinced he could not obtain a fair trial?

Louis was adamant that he did not want me to attend the trial. I was in agreement, but I could not avoid being involved because the prosecution was intent on establishing that Louis was an associate of Raymond's. The prosecutor subpoenaed Raymond, and the three other defendants in the case who were still living. Jack called me with the news of the subpoena on Raymond. I had been dreading the call: I knew that this was one more court appearance I would have to try to save Raymond from making. At the same time, I knew that if I failed, then Raymond's testimony about any dealings he'd had with Louis would be additional nails in the coffin the prosecution was determined to bury Louis in.

The fact that I was Louis' mistress made the whole scenario even more nightmarish. What if I were subpoenaed to testify? I envisioned a prosecutor asking me, "Why should we believe anything you say about Mr. Patriarca's health, Doctor Roberts. Haven't you been having an affair for the last two years with Louis Manocchio, the defendant in this case?" It was Kafkaesque, it was terrifying, it was inconceivable that my life had arrived at this point. If the subpoena were not quashed, Raymond would have to appear in court, not at his own trial but at my lover's, and I would have to be there while the state tried to prove that the two of them had conspired, fifteen years before, to commit two murders.

On May 3, 1983, at a pre-trial hearing, Superior Court Judge Joseph Rogers, who that day was hearing miscellaneous petitions, granted Jack Cicilline's motion to quash the subpoena summoning Raymond to testify. Jack asserted that complying with the subpoena would present a "clear and present danger of death" and as such would constitute a "reckless disregard for human life." Judge Rogers based his decision on the wealth of "uncontradicted medical testimony" that Raymond was too ill to take the witness stand.

Unfortunately, he left open the possibility that the state could obtain his testimony another way—for example, by taking a deposition from him at his home. Judge Rogers was not the judge who would preside over the trial, which began the following day. The trial was assigned to Judge Francis M. Kiely, who before his appointment had been an insurance company lawyer, and whose cases were reversed for judicial error with greater frequency than average. Judge Kiely denied requests from lawyers for Pro Lerner and Rudolph Sciarra to squash the subpoenas requiring them to testify. And throughout the trial, almost without exception, his rulings were favorable to the prosecution, and damning to the defense.

I never came out and asked Louis if he were guilty. I blocked out the question of his guilt or innocence. The only statements he volunteered was that "things didn't happen the way Kelly said" and that the reason he'd fled the state in 1969 was that he was convinced he could not get a fair trial. I didn't ask him to elaborate. All I cared about was that he not be taken away from me and sent to prison, and that Raymond not be forced to testify about his relationship with Louis, perhaps sealing his fate.

Jury selection began in early May and continued for almost two weeks. The state used six of its first seven peremptory challenges to strike prospective jurors of Italian descent. Marty Leppo became alarmed by this and moved for a hearing, alleging that the State was deliberately using its peremptory challenges to exclude a recognizable class of prospective jurors in violation of Louis' constitutional rights. The judge denied this request, terming it frivolous because "This is America. It's an American courtroom, and it's an American trial, with an American defendant, and that's all that's here." The final panel contained one Italian-American. The jury would be sequestered for the duration of the trial.

On May 23, the testimony portion of the trial commenced. The owners of the market where the murders occurred, a customer in the store at the time, the police officers who reported to the crime scene, and a former girlfriend of one of the victims gave testimony about the day in April 1968 when the murders took place. Later that night, Louis came to my house for tea after the children were in bed. Our mood was grim. It was already apparent that the trial judge was bending over backwards to grant every prosecution request and to deny every defense motion. I believed in my heart that Louis had not been involved in the planning of the murders, but there was overwhelming evidence that he knew Raymond and all the other defendants.

The prosecution was allowed to treat the jury to a veritable buffet of street gossip about the mob, of who was fighting with whom in those days—most of which was totally irrelevant, but still allowed by the Judge. The prosecution was also requesting that Raymond be compelled to give a deposition about his association with Louis.

On the second day of testimony, Jack asked me to come to court in case Judge Kiely wanted my sworn testimony about Raymond's condition. The day's session had not yet begun, while the lawyers and judge conferred in chambers. I stood outside the courtroom (potential witnesses are not allowed to be present at a trial in which they might testify), pacing back and forth while I waited to find out whether my testimony would be required. Suddenly, Louis rounded the corner of the hallway. Seeing me, he stopped as abruptly as if he'd slammed into an invisible wall. Our eyes met for an instant, and then he whirled around and rushed off in the opposite direction. I realized that anyone watching this scene would have known the truth of our relationship in a moment. In the event, I was not called to testify in court that day, or on any other day of Louis' trial, but the judge did grant the prosecution's motion to compel Raymond to give a deposition.

Two days later, Raymond had another prolonged attack of angina, and I admitted him again to the hospital. The state requested another evaluation from Dr. Most, who concluded that "depending on the degree of stress which deposition testimony entails in this instance, the risks may be sufficient to make this course of action ill-advised from a medical point of view." But the state ignored the advice of its own consultant and scheduled the deposition for the 4th of June, one week after Raymond's most recent hospitalization.

At this point, he was on ten different medications and was still severely limited by angina and shortness of breath. I don't know which of us dreaded his deposition more. I'd never told him of my involvement with Louis; I'd told no one other than my closest friends and family. Jack's wife Sabra cottoned on to our affair when she saw Louis eat food off my plate one day when Sabra and I were lunching at the Forum. I never learned who told Raymond Sr., but as the trial started, he tried to reassure me. "Louie will be alright," he said, "he's a good man." Raymond said that loving me as he did, he would prefer to go to jail himself rather than contribute to Louis' predicament. I realized that he was not upset about our involvement. He trusted us to be discreet enough so that it wouldn't interfere with my care of him.

At times, the hardest part was trying to lead what passed for a "normal" life with the children. On the last weekend in May, Meagan was the flower girl at the wedding of one of the cardiac catheterization lab technicians. The ceremony was held at a spare, typically New England church in Barrington, Rhode Island, located on a salt pond that was home to flocks of swans and egrets. Its pristine white steeple rose into a sky whose limpid blue is found only near the sea. The wedding reception was held at the Blithewold estate in Bristol, a stately mansion with exquisite gardens and sweeping views of Narragansett Bay. Meagan was beautiful in her lilac gown and flowered tiara, the image of a sprite out of some fairy tale. She almost stole the show from the bride. As I moved through the day, reaping praise for my daughter's beauty and poise, I longed to have Louis at my side, but that, of course, was impossible. I realized, not for the first time, how much I resented the secrecy our situation required.

My life ran on two parallel but very separate tracks; I inhabited two very different worlds. In one, I was a single mother and busy physician, a teacher, a mentor, a stalwart of the local Planned Parenthood where I performed abortions one day a week, an attendee at my children's theater and sports performances, and a sailboat racer. In that world, I was a respected physician, if somewhat controversial.

In my other world, I was the secret lover of an alleged organized crime figure, and the physician whose testimony was preventing the head of the New England Mafia from having to go to trial and, almost certainly, to prison. In that world, I was looked up to and admired for my defense of Raymond; I was a Federal Hill folk-heroine.

The "straight" world was where I spent most of my time. It was a world whose rules I knew without having to be told. The Federal Hill world was one of secrets, of mobsters and FBI agents, a world carrying with it the possibility of sudden violence, of arrests, of prison terms—a world whose rules I groped to understand.

In one life, I socialized with some of the most prominent, respected Rhode Islanders, and in the other I slept with, and loved, one of its most notorious criminal figures. I was considered a heroine by people whose presence in the same room with "straight" citizens would have frightened and scandalized them. In effect, I was suspended over the abyss separating these two tracks, in danger at any moment of losing my footing and being annihilated.

⚐

That Monday, Memorial Day, we raced *Boadicea* in the J-30 Memorial Day Regatta, and we took first place, due entirely to my young, talented crew of sailors. I let them run the show and just went along for the ride. More than anywhere else, I was able to leave the complexity of my private life behind while racing and sailing. It was comforting to have to worry about wind shifts, tidal currents, and race tactics, rather than murder and mayhem, prosecutors and police, testimony and trials.

When Louis' trial resumed on the next day, Red Kelley broke down in tears on the witness stand, admitting that his ability to remember events was impaired by Alzheimer's disease. The jury was not in the courtroom at the time, but Judge Kiely ruled that his memory problems were no reason to disallow his testimony. He also denied Marty Leppo's request to have a physician examine Kelley to determine whether or not he was competent to testify. Once the jury was back in the courtroom, the judge overruled every attempt by the defense to explore the issue of Kelley's memory loss, leaving the jury with no real knowledge of its extent. Just before the trial was recessed for the long weekend, Kelley admitted that he had lied under oath at the earlier trials of Raymond and the other four defendants thirteen years earlier. This perjury was prompted, he said, by an FBI agent, Paul Rico. But Judge Kiely ruled that this perjury was insufficient cause to declare a mistrial in the current trial.

On the following day of Louis' trial, Kiely ruled that Raymond was healthy enough to answer questions about his association with Louis in his own home. A court stenographer was to take down the testimony and transcribe it so that it could be read to the jurors. Jack Cicilline had tried to block the taking of Raymond's deposition by asking Supreme Court justice Joseph Weisberger to stay Kiely's order, but he refused to do so after a thirty-minute meeting in his chambers with Jack and the prosecutor, David Leach.

Some days I read about the trial in the *Providence Journal*. At other times, Louis or Jack filled me in on what was transpiring. When Jack told me that Raymond would have to give a deposition, I was filled with dread. I knew that any testifying was extremely stressful for Raymond. I'd observed the effects on his EKG just from being present in a courtroom in New Bedford. That he knew about my affair with Louis would only compound the stress of answering questions about their association. As a later lawyer would point out, Louis' case was tried on the theory of "Give a dog an ill name and hang him." Showing that Louis was associated with Raymond was the surest way to give that particular dog an ill name.

On the night before the deposition, I stayed home; I slept poorly. The next morning, I drove to Johnston, arriving before the others. I gave Raymond a mild sedative and put him on nasal oxygen. "Don't worry about the questions," I told him, "you know that Jack will be here, and I'll be here, and we won't let anything bad happen to you, or Louis."

I doubt I was very convincing, and he kept shaking his head, his voice choked with tears as he repeated, "This isn't right, they have no right to do this to me. They'll never leave me alone, never." Rita bustled around, reminding me of a tea kettle about to let off steam. I thought if I looked closely, I would see wisps of smoke curling out of her ears. The den gradually filled up with policemen, prosecution lawyers, Judge Kiely, Jack and I, a court stenographer, and by 9:30 everyone was present, and the questioning began.

Raymond was sworn in. He was dressed in his pajamas, his feet up on an ottoman placed at the foot of his reclining chair. His skin was its usual dusky hue, despite the extra oxygen, and he intermittently shivered, his hands wasted and tremulous as he adjusted the nasal cannula which kept slipping out of his nose. I had syringes filled with cardiac medications and a portable defibrillator at the ready. Jack allowed Raymond to answer with his name, but when David Leach began to question him about his relationship with others, including Louis, he objected based on the Fifth Amendment right against self-incrimination. Judge Kiely overruled Jack's objection and stated that Raymond had no such right in this case, ordering him to answer the questions.

I stared at Raymond as the seconds ticked by with infinite slowness. He became visibly more and more agitated. Suddenly he erupted with rage, and everyone in the room jumped, startled at the hoarse, raging cries that burst from his lips. "You're trying to kill me," he screamed, "you won't be happy till I'm dead, will you? You want me in jail or dead and you won't stop until it happens. This is persecution, this is persecution."

He continued in the same vein, becoming cyanotic, spittle flying from his mouth, and collapsing in tears. His chest was heaving as he struggled to breathe. I turned up the oxygen and put a nitroglycerine tablet under his tongue. My hands were shaking as I administered the medicine, but it was all I could do not to smile. I had no doubt that Raymond was sincere, that he was not play-acting, but I also knew that he had out-foxed the prosecution. They would get nothing to buttress their case against Louis. Raymond continued to keen and sob, hysterical. I hooked him up to a portable cardiac monitor, which revealed signs of severe ischemia. His heart rhythm was frightening, with runs of the ventricular tachycardia that is a harbinger of sudden death.

Raymond was writhing with chest pain by now, despite additional nitroglycerine. "That's it, this deposition is over," I told the judge, "I'm calling Rescue and taking him to the hospital. He's about a minute away from a fatal heart attack." The judge, shaken himself, acquiesced without argument.

Rita came into the room, furious, and railed at them, "Are you happy now? Does this make you feel good, doing this to a sick old man? You're all sons of bitches and I want you out of my house, get out of my house this minute!" With two furious women castigating them, various police and court officials left the room quickly. When they all had slunk out with their tails between their legs, I knew they would not be back. But events would show that it was a short-lived victory.

The ambulance came, and Rita and I got in with Raymond for the ten-mile ride to the Miriam Hospital. I gave Raymond some intravenous sedation and he fell asleep. By the time we reached the hospital, his lungs sounded wet, showing signs of congestive heart failure. This responded to medication, and miraculously, his EKG and blood tests showed no evidence of another heart attack.

The aborted deposition was front-page news the next day. Judge Kiely was quoted as saying, "We didn't cancel it. We simply continued it." But I was determined to prevent the deposition from occurring. If there was nothing else I could do for Louis, I would make certain that the state would not use Raymond's testimony as a weapon against him.

Two days after Raymond's deposition, Louis and I drove to Boston and attended the opera at Symphony Hall. The touring company of the New York Metropolitan Opera was putting on Puccini's *La Boheme*, which I'd loved since childhood. Louis would turn fifty-six on June 23rd, and this outing was my birthday present to him. I have never *not* cried at the final scene when Mimi dies of consumption in Rudolfo's arms, but that night the tears wouldn't stop, and all the way back to Providence they made silent runnels down my cheeks. The irony of the situation was not lost on me; I had kept Raymond out of the clutches of the courts for almost three years, but was unable to do the same for the man who was my lover. Fortunately, or unfortunately, Louis' heart was robust, and not in need of my services as a doctor.

The next day, my parents came to visit, and the day after that, Archie graduated from eighth grade. He had transferred from the Wheeler School to Moses Brown, a Quaker private school not far from our home, in the fall of '81 in order to be able to play football. Dory graduated from Classical high school the same day, June 8th, in the afternoon. My parents came, as did Dory and Archie's father, step-mother, and step and half siblings. All of them came to the schools for the ceremonies, but the Roberts side of the family declined my invitation to come to the party I gave at the house. Louis, of course, was not in attendance. On the day after graduation, Dory and Archie left with their father for a visit to his parents in Holyoke. My parents departed also, leaving Meagan and me alone for what promised to be a somber weekend.

Louis' trial came to a close on Friday, June 10. Meagan, Louis, and I had dinner at the Forum that Friday night, and we met there again for lunch the next day. Saturday night, after Meg was asleep, Louis came to the house and we made love. It was the only time in our almost two years together that we made love in my home. We both were in the grip of dread, fearing that he was going to be convicted, though we said nothing out loud; his previous scruples about making love at my house went out the window. Our lovemaking had a bittersweet intensity, and I clung to him like a frightened child in the grip of a nightmare.

The next day, Sunday, Meg and I went to a party at Jack and Sabra Cicilline's house in Narragansett. We ate dinner with Louis at the Forum and then went home. After the restaurant closed, Louis came by for tea. We knew that it might be our last night together, but as if to deny that, we did not make love again, just sat in the kitchen holding hands, for the most part silently. I have no memory of our conversation, just the atmosphere of quiet sadness that clung to the night like a deadly miasma.

Monday was a beautiful late spring day. I made a house call on Raymond at noontime, after making hospital rounds in the morning.

Each time my beeper went off, I froze in dread that it would be news from the courthouse. I performed some stress tests in my office during the afternoon, then went home before three o'clock, no longer able to concentrate. Louis' brother Anthony promised that he would call me as soon as there was any news. Before the trial, I saw Anthony infrequently. He had a large gynecologic practice and four children to occupy his time.

But as the trial approached, and during the trial, Anthony came more and more often to the Forum and would sit with me and discuss his brother's predicament. We were both very uneasy with Leppo's handling of the case and thought he was optimistic without any basis in fact. We looked upon him as an outsider, one who would not have a handle on Rhode Islanders and how they thought. We thought it a mistake not to confront Louis' absence for ten years head on. If the rare juror didn't know that Louis had been on the lam for ten years, they certainly must have wondered why the State took fourteen years after the original indictments to bring Louis to trial. But this fact was never addressed.

Anthony and I both spotted what we thought were unmarked police cars parked outside our homes during the trial, and plainclothes cops began appearing in the Brown University gymnasium where I went to jog almost every night. I recognized them as police because I'd become familiar with the faces of many law officers during my many court appearances. Our telephone calls were often accompanied by strange clicks, and we assumed that our phones were bugged. We wondered if the police imagined we were planning to assist Louis to escape once again if he was convicted.

When I mentioned these sightings to Jack and Albert, they just shrugged them off as something to be expected. During this same period, Jack's garbage was being picked up by the police, and he later learned that his office and office telephones were bugged. Anthony and Bob Indeglia were my only doctor friends who knew what I was going through. In front of everyone else, I had to conceal all evidence of the effect the ordeal was having on me. I expected that the jury might deliberate for several days and wondered how I would be able to bear the suspense if they did.

At 3:00 p.m. the telephone rang. I answered it on the extension in my den. Anthony said one word: "Barbara," and I knew instantly that we had lost. His voice was drenched in anguish as he said, "It's bad—it's very bad." I began to scream "No, no," reeling around the room in an agony of disbelief, clutching the phone to my chest while pain such as I had never experienced tore a gaping wound in my heart. I knew that madness lurked just around the bend in time, that only madness or death would be the end result of this grief. It didn't seem possible that I could be in so much pain, and yet go on living.

I have no idea how long I screamed in impotent denial. The rest of that afternoon is gone from my mind. What I remember next is picking up Meagan from day camp then driving us to the Brown University gym. She recalls knowing that Louis was on trial and realizing that he must have been convicted just by looking at me when I came to get her. I began running laps and soon spotted two undercover cops. They were also running around the track, and I was grimly determined that they would not see any evidence of the devastation I felt.

While Meagan played with other children in the gymnasium, I ran the track, soundlessly repeating the refrain, "There is no pain I can't endure, there is no pain I can't endure." I ran until I could run no more, and then Meagan and I went home. She tells me she heard what sounded like me throwing pots and pans around the kitchen, but I have no recollection of doing so. Later, I lay in bed, unable to sleep, tears coursing down my face through the endless hours of the night. I tried not to envision Louis in a prison cell, behind bars, but that image kept battering on the fragile defenses I erected. At some point I may have slept. I can't recall.

In the morning I got up and went to the hospital to make rounds, operating on automatic pilot. I was in terror of seeing the verdict being read on television, and averted my eyes from the newspaper, which I knew would carry the story on the front page. I was certain that my fragile composure would be shattered if these reminders were shoved under my nose. No one in the hospital seemed to notice any difference, but it was inconceivable to me that my wound was invisible. I imagined how my colleagues would recoil in horror if I said, "Oh, by the way, my lover was just convicted of conspiracy and accessory to murder."

The loss I felt was a physical ache, centered in my throat and chest. I had known for many years that patients in severe emotional distress often somaticized their pain, developing aches in various parts of the body, certain that it had some organic cause, that it boded the onset of some dread disease. And now I was experiencing the same thing. I knew that I was not in the throes of a heart attack, or suffering from gastritis, but the physical pain was no less real.

In the office, I tried to concentrate on my patients—but every now and then, thoughts of Louis would intrude, and I would excuse myself and hurry into the restroom to regain my composure. I longed to be able to curl up in a ball and grieve, undisturbed, but that was impossible. I had a practice to run and children to raise; a nervous breakdown was not an option, though whether force of will could prevent one was an open question. I lived in a place of utter desolation. One of the dictionary definitions of the prefix "de-" is "remove from," and "sol" is the Latin word for sun. My sun had been removed from me, the man who was my lover, my best friend, my protector.

On one of those sleepless nights, at about 4 a.m., I felt my bed shake from side to side. There was no wind or storm at the time and I thought, "Well, that's it. You're hallucinating. You're losing your mind." I was disappointed later on in the day to learn that a slight earthquake, a very rare occurrence in New England, but registerable on the Richter scale, had occurred at the exact moment I felt my bed tremble. I was dismayed that I hadn't been hallucinating. If I had, it would confirm that I was losing my mind and would be forced to go into hospital, where I expected I would be given drugs that would relieve the hurt that was driving me mad. But whatever solace insanity might bring, that too was denied to me.

Two days after Louis was convicted, my crew and I raced *Boadicea* on Narragansett Bay. Just after the start, the sky turned black, and a violent squall charged down from its northern reaches. The winds went from barely detectable to gusts of fifty knots in a matter of seconds. The fleet was scattered, spinnakers blowing out when they were not taken down fast enough. Under bare poles, we had a wild ride while the storm lasted; I realized that I was not frightened at all, that I was indifferent to the danger, that death no longer seemed a catastrophe. Louis had called me from the prison that day, his first phone call. I was overjoyed to hear his voice, but my heart broke again when, in answer to my imploring him to put me on his visitor's list, he said, "No, you can't come to visit me. There's too big a risk that our relationship will become known. I can't take that chance." Above all else, he didn't want that harm to befall me. I begged and pleaded with him to change his mind, but he was adamant.

On my first house call to Raymond after the conviction, we both burst into tears when he tried to console me. Rita hurried into the den and hugged me to her ample bosom, murmuring words of comfort, telling me she knew what I was going through. She was one of the few who did.

In my imaginings about what my life would be like when I was a child, it had never occurred to me that someone I loved would be imprisoned. In many ways, death seemed preferable. At least the dead didn't suffer, were not penned in, were not chained, were not at the mercy of guards. I knew how fastidious Louis was about food, about clothing, about hygiene. I knew how proud he was. I could only imagine his suffering, which would be compounded by the pain he knew his conviction and imprisonment caused me. We were powerless to comfort one another. When the verdict was read, he was taken from the court in shackles and Judge Kiely ordered him held without bail.

Marty Leppo was appealing the revocation of bail and held out the faint hope that Louis would be released pending the outcome of an appeal, but I was certain that bail would be denied. On June 16, three days after his conviction, Leppo was quoted in the newspaper as saying that Louis had turned down a plea-bargaining agreement that would have required him to serve about two years in prison. Louis did this, Leppo said, putting his fate in the hands of a jury, because he was innocent of the charges against him. Leppo and Tom DiLuglio, Jr. called a news conference to outline their strategy for an appeal.

Leppo had not been available for comment since the jury's verdict on Monday, which came after only three and a half hours of deliberation, because he described himself as "devastated" by the outcome and too upset to discuss it for several days.

Anthony and I, however, had lost all faith in Louis' defense team, especially after learning of the rejected plea-bargain. Now, instead of two years in prison, Louis faced a possible life sentence. We suspected that Leppo had urged the far more dangerous option of trial in order to garner the fame (and money) that a high-profile Mafia case bestowed on lawyers. We had nothing concrete on which to base this suspicion, but we believed it nonetheless.

Anthony and I met with Jack Cicilline and asked him who, in his opinion, was the best appeals lawyer in the state. He recommended John MacFadyen, called Terry by his friends. Then in his early thirties, he only took cases on appeal and was highly regarded throughout the legal community. I learned other things about him that increased my liking for him. He lived with another lawyer, Rose, with whom he had three sons. They had never formalized their union with a legal marriage, not feeling it necessary. Rose said, "I want Terry to be with me because he wants to be, not because he has to be." Rose worked as a labor lawyer.

We met with Terry and he agreed to handle Louis' appeal. He did not hold out a lot of hope. "With an appeal, you are starting out at the bottom of a well. The worst has happened. You've been convicted, and unless there were egregious errors made during the course of the trial, you are going to remain at the bottom of that well. And nothing will happen quickly. We are talking about years here, not months." After Leppo's bluster and unfounded confidence, his honesty was welcome, if not comforting.

In the meantime, the march of bad news continued unabated. The Rhode Island Supreme Court heard arguments on Louis' request for bail pending the outcome of his appeal on June 21st, a week after his conviction. The Attorney General's office opposed the granting of bail. Not surprisingly, two days later the Supreme Court denied Louis' request for bail, terming it "premature" because there had yet to be a hearing on his motion for a new trial. The high court wrote that Judge Kiely had scheduled the hearing for a new trial for the following Monday and "it is conceivable the he will grant the motion and eradicate the jury's guilty verdict." Right. The odds of that happening were slim and none.

On June 30th, Judge Kiely denied the motion for a new trial, to no one's surprise, and put off a decision on bail until August 10th, after his return from vacation. "I fail to see why I should disturb my vacation to hear something that should have been disposed of last week," he said. He also set sentencing for August 24th. Bail was, of course, denied, and on the appointed day in late August, Judge Kiely sentenced Louis to two consecutive life terms, plus ten years in prison, the maximum allowable sentence.

This was the same sentence that had been meted out to the trigger man in the case, Pro Lerner, and far in excess of the sentences served by Raymond and the other defendants who'd been found guilty of the same charges. With the consecutive life sentences, Louis would be 86 years old before the state's Parole Board could even consider paroling him. Though we had feared this sentence, the finality of it was stunning, and my depression gathered strength, sapping my energy like some hidden but voracious parasite.

By now, Louis had changed his mind and put my name down on the list of allowed visitors. My entreaties had worn him down. I begged everyone who was on the visiting list to intercede with Louis on my behalf. I was less concerned about keeping our relationship secret than I was about being able to visit him. I'd been writing daily letters to him, which we knew were opened and read by the prison authorities. He was able to telephone often. Eventually, Louis decided that if our relationship had not made the newspapers, despite telephone calls and letters, it was unlikely to be written about if I visited him. Visiting days brought a sad parade of wives, children, relatives and loved ones to the prison. Many were too poor to own cars and came by bus.

There was an unchanging protocol for visiting the prison. After being checked in, I put my pocketbook into a locker and passed through a metal detector. All visitors were then led up a worn flight of stairs. On rainy days, this became an obstacle course of buckets set out to catch the water that leaked through the ancient roof. The prison smell was indescribable, redolent of sweat, urine, boiled vegetables and what I could only presume was the reek of barely contained violence admixed with boredom and fear. We met at tables in a large open room, the cafeteria, unlike all the prisons I had seen in the movies where the prisoner sat across from the visitor, separated by a glass barrier. We were not supposed to touch, but the guards ignored quick embraces on greeting and discreet hand-holding.

Children raced up and down between the tables, raising the noise level to a deafening roar. Louis, a bit thinner and paler than usual, seemed to be holding up better than Anthony and I were. But he held out no false hope. "Barbara," he admonished, "I'm buried alive here. I may never get out. You have to go on with your life."

I took this to mean that I had his tacit blessing to seek out other romantic involvements. I intuited, however, that if I did so, he did not want to hear about it. In reply, I protested my love and vowed that I would wait, no matter how long it took. But as the months passed, I began to doubt my ability to do this. It seemed a needless cruelty to admit this to him, and I never did.

He told us that the food was almost inedible, consisting of starches, boiled vegetables and unidentifiable meat. There was almost nothing to do, and he was confined to a cell for up to 20 hours a day. Eventually, he was able to take a ceramics class, and he gave me some of the pieces he made: a small Christmas tree, a vase with three kittens cavorting on the side, and serving bowls. Some people had Wedgewood, or Lenox ware. I had prison ware, and I cherished it; it was now all Louis could give me.

I brought him news of my family, who had been shocked by the verdict and were worried about my mental state. In June, my sister Donna set a new women's world record in a one-hundred-mile ultra-marathon. She had taken up running five years before in order to keep from gaining weight when she gave up a ten-year smoking habit. Donna was Louis' favorite among my sisters because of her feistiness and their shared love of running. The course for the race consisted of 100 laps around the Shea Stadium parking lot. Donna broke the previous record by over three hours, finishing in 15 hours, 31 minutes and 57 seconds. This feat made the Guinness Book of World Records the following year.

In July, I sent Archie and Dory on a trip to Italy with Donna as a graduation present. Mary, Jack, and their daughter Jenny had moved to a little town outside of Rome, Trevignano Romano, where Jack was writing a novel based on the life of Boadicea. In August, my niece Maris was born to brother Matty and his wife Amy. I traveled to Nyack to visit and photograph the new arrival. But none of these events could assuage my sadness for more than a few moments. Grief at Louis' imprisonment was a perpetual dirge playing doleful background music.

I still broke into tears at times when thoughts of him crept unbidden into my consciousness. I would be listening to a patient's heart, and suddenly a vision of Louis in a cell would invade my mind. Tears welled up, threatening to course down my cheeks. I would excuse myself hurriedly and rush to the bathroom, putting cold water compresses on my eyes to get rid of the evidence of tears. I had a constant ache in my chest. Getting through the days felt like slogging through a quagmire. Exhaustion was my constant companion.

I told Anthony that I thought I needed to see a psychiatrist, but he was opposed to this, for reasons that were never clear to me. It just wasn't done. I was supposed to buck up and weather this on my own. The children and I were no longer required to attend family therapy sessions at Bradley. The psychiatrists there had never inspired confidence in me anyway. But surely there were other therapists who might be more competent, who could help me deal with my loss. Time, which is supposed to heal all wounds, was not bringing relief from the crushing sadness I felt. I tried to distract myself with reading, and sailing, but sleep was almost impossible. I would doze off for a few hours and awaken about 2 or 3 am with tears seeping out of my eyes, my pillow sodden.

Finally, after about six months of unremitting depression, I put myself on an antidepressant and immediately began to sleep better. Within a few weeks the blackness that had invaded my mind began to lighten somewhat, and although still often sad, I cried less, and was able to concentrate better. The toxic tide began to recede. I could, occasionally, find humor in the events of the day. I said to Anthony one day, while we waited for visiting hours to begin, "You know, for two such renegade Catholics, we sure seem to spend a lot of time performing two of the cardinal works of mercy: healing the sick and visiting the imprisoned." The irony was not lost on him. He too performed abortions, and his office was frequently targeted by protesters.

Below my level of awareness, as the days shortened, and the nights grew longer, as the year died, along with my hopes for Louis' release, the love that had become a torment began to shrivel and die. Longing that goes too long unmet becomes a poison, an acid that corrodes the heart and love leaks out in little rivulets of loss. I was unaware on a conscious level that this was happening—I was only aware of my pain. And as the weeks turned to months and the months to years, I was powerless to stop it.

Many years later, I was to read these words in a book entitled *Melancholia and Depression* by Stanley W. Jackson:

> ...*reality makes clear to the bereaved person that the loved one is gone, not to return. The grief-stricken person gradually works over the memories and attachments to the lost loved one, clinging to the person and yet slowly giving him up and eventually accepting the realities of the loss. To varying extents, the person is eventually free to go on with his or her life, to reinvest interest and energy in other activities and other people. This work of mourning is an important process of adaptation whereby the bereaved person, to varying degrees, withdraws feelings from the mental image of the loved one who is gone.*

This passage helped me understand the feelings I grappled with during those years Louis spent in prison, and what came later.

13 · A DEATH FORETOLD

Death is not the worst that can happen to men.
—Plato

In the fall, Dory enrolled at Emerson College in Boston. When we were no longer required by court order to attend family therapy at Bradley, I found a new psychiatrist for her. Unlike the Bradley therapists, Dr. Massouda won her trust; he was always upbeat and optimistic. He urged her to attend college, and because she liked him, she took his advice. Archie began high school at the Moses Brown School, and Meg started second grade at the local Montessori school. My three closest girlfriends, Ginny, Rita, and Patty, all moved out of state during that autumn, leaving me even more lonely. The high points of my week were the visits to Louis, and these were always bittersweet meetings, during which he was often more optimistic than I about the outcome of the appeal, or at least fooled me into thinking that he was.

In October, I enrolled in a fiction writing workshop at the Brown Learning Connection. We were required to write a short story, or the first chapter of a novel, and I wrote a short story based on an incident

Louis had related to me from his youth. When he was fifteen, a local bookie named Joe-Joe the Wild Man took him on his first visit to a brothel. He wore a fedora and pasted on a fake mustache to look older, but the madam was still leery of letting him in until Joe-Joe swore up and down that he was of age. My first foray into fiction since high school was well received by my classmates, who wrote comments such as "fun story once we hit the brothel," and "you write well; I would imagine you are published." The teacher was more measured in her response, complimenting me on my sense of style and pacing, but she felt that there was nothing special about the protagonist's first sexual experience, at least as I had imagined it. There was no way I could have written about my own affair with Louis. That wound was still too raw and painful. It was still necessary to keep it secret, and so it festered out of sight—a constant, gnawing malaise.

My parents and siblings visited often in those months after Louis went to prison. As it had in the past, their love and support propped me up and helped me to survive. In November, there was a hearing about alleged jury misconduct and outside influence that occurred during the trial, which Marty Leppo and Tom DiLuglio felt warranted the granting of a new trial. One of the jurors informed them that another juror, a woman, had sexual relations with the sheriff assigned to supervise the jury while it was sequestered. The sheriff and juror denied this, but what was incontrovertible was another incident in which the jurors saw, on the floor of the bus transporting them to court, an article in the newspaper that discussed the fact that Raymond Patriarca was unavailable to testify at the trial. In a separate incident, the bus driver told a juror that he was related to one of the victims. None of these incidents was reported by the sheriff to the judge or the lawyers during the trial. After several subsequent hearings on the alleged jury improprieties, Louis' application for post-conviction relief was denied.

Now his only hope of release rested on the lengthy appeals process, which Terry MacFadyen undertook. He spent almost a year writing the brief that set forth the arguments for overturning Louis' conviction. The brief was filed with the Rhode Island Supreme Court on May 2, 1984. Terry kept us abreast of what was going on with the appeals process via telephone calls. Once again, I remembered what I'd been told about the legal system. Don't expect "speed, justice, or logic, because you won't find them."

Gradually, as the months passed and the antidepressant took effect, my libido re-awakened. Louis had urged me to get on with my life, although we never discussed just exactly what that meant. At the Brown gym where I ran almost every night, while Meg played with other children whose parents were working out, I struck up a friendship with another of the regular joggers. Don was also a single parent, a slight, attractive sandy-haired man, often accompanied by his adopted son, who was black. What was more important to me was his profession. He was a Protestant minister. Here was one man who was not going to be sent to prison for life!

We began dating, and a week before Christmas, I even attended a carol service at his church. The next day I made one of my usual twice-weekly visits to Louis in prison. In fact, because of Christmas, the prisoners were allowed an extra visit that week, and between the visits, I had Don and his son Matthew to dinner at our house. This was becoming a bit bizarre even by my standards. Another future I had never imagined: being simultaneously involved with a prisoner and a minister. I told neither about the other, and Don and I were not yet intimate. In fact, he made no sexual advances at all.

I knew by now that he was divorced and that he had a daughter who lived with his ex-wife. After almost a month, I was beginning to wonder if we would ever wind up in bed. Finally, in early January, as we sat on the floor in front of the fireplace in my living room, I asked him, "Don, do you want to bed me?" When he admitted that he did, I seduced him there on the living room floor. Unfortunately, images of Louis in his prison cell kept invading my head, and it was not the most uplifting sex I ever had. Quite the contrary. Or maybe the months of celibacy had left me out of shape. In any event, we did not have an exciting sexual relationship.

I made no secret of my distaste for the institution of marriage. Don believed that pre-marital or extra-marital sex was sinful. Finally, his guilt became overwhelming, and we agreed to part amicably. For my part, I'd felt a smidgen of guilt too, no so much because I had sex with another man, but because I had sex while Louis couldn't. As I began to date other men, the version I gave Louis of my activities was a very edited one. It was one more thing that drove a wedge between us.

I met other runners at the Brown gym and within a few weeks was dating one who had no sexual compunctions. We had an affair that lasted into that summer when it fizzled out from a mutual lack of interest. On a conscious level, I still loved Louis and longed for his release. Subconsciously, the emotional scars caused by my grief were slowly strangling that love, as I prepared myself for the possibility that his appeal would be unsuccessful and he would spend the rest of his life in prison. When and if that time came, it would be unbearable, were I still to love him. But I could not admit any of this to myself consciously. And to assuage my libido at least, I slept with several other men as the months and years went by, often without any feeling but lust.

I continued to visit Louis, and we never discussed this aspect of my life. When it came to my lovers, I chose people as far removed from the world of Federal Hill as it was possible to find in a small state. One of the men I became involved with was Italian-American, and he got wind of the fact that I was somehow connected with Louis Manocchio. He confronted me and asked if it was true. When I admitted that I had been Louis' mistress, he turned pale and asked, "Am I in some kind of trouble here?"

"Don't be an asshole," I replied. "Of course not," but the relationship was effectively over.

⋈

On March 17, 1984 Raymond turned 76. He had not required hospitalization since the previous June, during Louis' trial. He was no better, but there had been no acute exacerbations of his angina and no further need for any surgery. Earlier during his birthday week, Superior Court Judge Elizabeth Dolan denied a prosecution motion to bring him to trial for the 1968 Candos murder. She was ruling on a motion to expedite the trial but said in her decision that it was unlikely that the trial would ever be held because doctors in two states had shown, based on extensive medical tests, that Raymond was suffering from multiple life-threatening ailments.

She noted that it might appear to the public that Raymond was being given special status in the judicial system, but she denied that this was so. She said that the only point of dispute was the amount of stress that was necessary to trigger a heart attack. Judge Dolan said this could not be determined with any degree of medical certainty and that Raymond had the right to participate actively in his own defense. She ruled that his "benign presence" in the courtroom was not sufficient. It would prove to be the last attempt that a state court would make to bring Raymond Patriarca to trial.

The Special Attorney for the U.S. Department of Justice, Edwin Gale, sent Dr. Albert Most to evaluate Raymond once more, in May of 1984. Gale was still hopeful of arraigning Raymond on the federal labor racketeering charge. Dr. Most reported that "...it is my opinion that the risk 'to Mr. Patriarca's medical condition that is posed by travel to Florida for the stated purpose' is sufficient to render such transportation and subsequent arraignment ill-advised from the medical standpoint.' " After the expenditure of thousands of dollars, neither Rhode Island nor Massachusetts, nor even the federal government, was able to find a physician whose testimony about the seriousness of Raymond's condition contradicted my own.

I continued my weekly house calls to check on Raymond at his home in Johnston, and my twice-weekly visits to Louis at the prison. My practice was growing, despite all the publicity, and I was actively involved in teaching the Brown medical students, the residents, and the cardiology trainees at the Miriam Hospital. Ned had dropped from sight after withdrawing his appeal of Judge Fay's decision. I was making new friends among the runners at the Brown gymnasium and the female residents at the Miriam. All of the children were doing well in school and didn't lack for friends, despite their mother's notoriety.

With infinite slowness, the pain of losing Louis to the maw of prison was lessening.

On Monday, July 9, 1984, I made my usual weekly house call on Raymond. He appeared much the same: a shrunken, frail, elderly man. It seemed impossible that he ruled what law enforcement called a "vast criminal enterprise." The man I knew could barely walk from his den to his kitchen without stopping to catch his breath. His feet and hands were in almost constant pain from diabetic neuropathy. That visit was no different from any of the others I made in the years since I had become his physician. We talked about how he was feeling; I examined him, taking his pulse and blood pressure, listening to his heart and lungs, and checked his feet for signs of ulcers or gangrene. Rita made us a heart healthy lunch, but what she served I no longer recall. It was the last time I saw Raymond alive.

Two days later, I was at the Miriam Hospital when my beeper went off. It was Jack Cicilline's office calling to tell me that Raymond had collapsed and been taken by the Rescue Squad to Rhode Island Hospital. I ran out to my car and drove across town. In the emergency room, I was led to the cubicle where the ER physicians were performing CPR. Raymond was intubated on a respirator, and his electrocardiogram varied between ventricular fibrillation and a flat line.

Ventricular fibrillation is the most common fatal abnormal heart rhythm. The term refers to very rapid and disorganized electrical activity in the ventricle, such that the heart cannot pump blood effectively. Unless corrected, it leads to circulatory arrest and death. But for the most part, Raymond's EKG was a flat line. Intravenous lines ran into both his arms, which lay flaccid on the stretcher. There was no circulation, except what was induced by external cardiac massage.

I did not have admitting privileges at Rhode Island Hospital and my request to put in a temporary pacemaker was refused for that reason. Furious, I rounded on the ER physician, "Either let me put in a pacemaker or get one of the cardiologists on staff down here IMMEDIATELY. Otherwise this man is going to die." He replied, "We've paged the cardiologist on-call, and he should be here any minute." Perhaps another five minutes went by before the pacemaker was finally inserted, but all efforts to restore a normal heart rhythm were in vain. After the attempted resuscitation had lasted about an hour, at 1 p.m. on July 11, 1984, Raymond was pronounced dead.

The event I had been predicting for almost four years had occurred. He had escaped the judgment of the courts, thanks to my efforts and those of his lawyers. I doubted that he now stood in some celestial dock. He lay there naked and alone, still as only the dead are still, the inexorable dissolution of his physical body already underway; his next stop a coffin, and the grave. Sadness invaded me as I realized that Raymond was beyond our ministrations. My sadness had in it a portion of the grief that death occasions even when the patient is elderly. Who does not glimpse a pale presentiment of her own death, in the death of another? Who is not a little affrighted by the abrupt passage from living, breathing, thinking human to a cold, still lump of meat? Who can look on a newly inanimate body and not wonder what eyes will someday gaze at them in death? The physician who is inured to death is one who has lost the ability to feel empathy.

We had formed a unique alliance, Raymond and I, against the forces of "law and order" —the ex-Catholic schoolgirl and Public Enemy Number 1. But life had taught me nothing if not this: that some who are held up as epitomes of evil contain much that is good, and some who are held up as exemplars of virtue wreak evil with abandon and impunity. If something other than the testimony of various snitches had been the reason he was arrested, and if his health did not make a trial unsafe and potentially deadly, I would not have disagreed that Raymond should be tried. The judicial system, as flawed as it is, is a place where wrongs can be righted, crime punished, and the weak protected. But I never regretted my decision to become Raymond's doctor, and thus his defender.

As I gazed at his body, along with my sadness, a tremendous weight was lifted from my shoulders. I had kept him out of an earthly prison, and the ground to which he was being consigned in a few days was the common destination of all of us. My responsibility to him was discharged. An era was coming to an end.

❧

Raymond's body was taken to Berarducci's Funeral Home on Providence's Federal Hill. This impressive Victorian pile squats like a dowager on a chamber pot in a small lot, a testament to immigrants who made good by dint of sacrifice and hard labor. It quickly filled with dozens of floral tributes. The medical examiner elected not to perform an autopsy. Raymond Junior and Rita decided on a closed casket—and this occasioned another dispute between law enforcement and the Patriarca family. No one from the police had seen the body and ascertained that Raymond Senior was indeed dead.

Lt. Richard Tamburini, who had been instrumental in developing the evidence that led to Raymond's arrest in 1980, called Jack Cicilline from the squad room at the police station. He told Jack that he wanted to see the body.

Jack refused, "It's a closed coffin and the family doesn't want to open it."

"Fine," Tamburini replied, "then I'll just get a court order and have the body exhumed."

"No way," Jack said. "Try me," Richard replied.

There was a long moment of silence, and then Jack asked him to hold on. When he came back to the phone, Jack told him "Okay, come on over." Richard pulled a mirror out of his desk. The other cops who'd been eavesdropping on this conversation asked, "What's that for?" He replied, "I'm no doctor. I can't take a pulse. I'll hold this under his nose and if it doesn't fog up, I'll know he's dead." At the funeral home, after the room had been cleared of onlookers, the coffin was opened, and Tamburini—without needing the mirror—was satisfied that Raymond Patriarca was dead, just as the newspapers had reported.

The next day, the front-page *Providence Journal* headline read, "Crime Boss Patriarca Dies at 76 of Heart Attack." The article was accompanied by five photographs on page one and two additional photos inside, dating from a head shot in 1938 to the picture of Raymond being wheeled into court in New Bedford on a stretcher in 1981, an intravenous line dripping into his left arm, his head wrapped in a towel. He was described by the ER physician as having arrived "in full cardiac arrest, with no blood pressure, no pulse and no spontaneous respirations." The ER doctor was asked whether the staff knew whom they were treating, and he replied, "Initially, no, but it became clear as the tension in the surrounding atmosphere began to mount."

The newspaper noted that I was in attendance. It went on to say that Raymond had been brought to the hospital by members of the North Providence rescue squad, who had responded to a call from 1605 Douglas Avenue in that town at 11:37 a.m. By the time of their arrival, three minutes later, his skin was cool and clammy, he was cyanotic (blue), unconscious, and his pupils were dilated, a sign of brain damage. Reporters tried to interview the woman at the apartment, who was described as teary-eyed, but she refused to answer questions and told them to leave.

This was the first I knew of her existence, and the first I learned that Raymond had not collapsed at home. There was much speculation in the press about her, and it was implied that she was Raymond's mistress. Her name was Toni DeMaio. She was a real estate agent with an office on Federal Hill. Lt. Tamburini was quoted as saying that "she was associated with him, definitely involved with him." It was reported that Raymond was clothed only in "boxer shorts" when the Rescue Squad arrived. *The Providence Journal* reported: "It was unclear what Patriarca was doing at the apartment, one of a row of apartments in a brick building, the Twin Rivers Apartments. Two women at the apartment, one of them with teary eyes and a tissue in her hand, later denied that Patriarca had been there and told a reporter to leave."

I learned that when Raymond took sick in her apartment, Ms. DeMaio panicked and called friends and family first, wasting precious minutes before calling Rescue. Whether Raymond would have lived if Toni DeMaio had called Rescue immediately is an unanswerable question. The delay could not be construed as beneficial. But knowing his medical condition as well as I did, I was certain that whatever else their relationship may have been, it was not sexual.

The article gave an extensive review of Raymond's life, noting that the police were convinced that he maintained "tight control of a complex web of bookmaking, loansharking, hijacking and other criminal interests that netted millions of dollars annually." On the other hand, the newspaper reported that he was:

> *...well-liked by his neighbors, in part for favors such as his ability to quickly recover stolen cars and goods taken in housebreaks — just for the asking.*
>
> *Likewise, first- and second-generation residents of Federal Hill remember him favorably. Food was supplied to the hungry, condolences (often in cash) were sent to funerals, and more than one brighter-than-average young man got a 'Patriarca scholarship' to college. These scholarships resulted in the education of doctors, lawyers and others — men who could scarcely hesitate later in their careers when they were asked for favors."*

Also mentioned was a story that became public as a result of testimony by Vincent "Big Vinny" Teresa, a mobster turned informant. Teresa reported in a deposition in 1978 that Raymond was contacted by the CIA to enlist his aid in assassinating Cuban Premier Fidel Castro. Raymond allegedly assigned Pro Lerner to do the job. Raymond, of course, denied the allegation, saying, "You people [reporters] are crazier than he [Teresa] is." And Castro stayed very much alive whatever the truth of the matter.

An article on page four of the *Journal* the same day was headlined: "No clear successor to Patriarca seen; lawmen say N.Y. mob may step in." Over pictures of seven men, the caption read "New England successor could be one of these men." Those pictured were New York boss Paul Castellano, Louis Manocchio, Rudolph Sciarra, Nicholas Bianco, Gennaro Angiulo, Edward Romano, and Stephen Broccoli. The article said that Raymond's death left behind "a crime family in chaos." Jerry O'Sullivan, the Boston-based head of the Justice Department's campaign against organized crime in New England, was quoted as saying: "The top leadership is either recently deceased, serving a lengthy prison sentence, or currently under indictment." He predicted that the five New York crime families would "have a large say on the future direction of the crime family."

O'Sullivan raised the likelihood that if this occurred, "traditional activities of the New England mob like loansharking, gambling and pornography will be supplemented by the more favored activities of the New York families like heroin and labor racketeering."

I told Meagan about Raymond's death that afternoon when she came home from day camp. She climbed onto my lap and cried. This was her first brush with the death of someone she knew, the man she called "Uncle Raymond," a man whose eyes lit up every time she entered his den. Being younger than her siblings, she was less affected by the publicity surrounding him and my involvement as his physician. She would miss visiting him, and the money he pressed into her waiting hand when we left. I asked if she wanted to come with me to his wake, but she decided she didn't. She gave no reason, and I didn't press her. Dory and Archie were still visiting their father's family in Holyoke and learned of Raymond's death from the newspapers.

On Friday the 13th, I drove to Federal Hill to pay my respects to the family and to bid Raymond farewell. An estimated 400 people, including lawyers, alleged mobsters, priests, businessmen, and neighbors, were in attendance. The Berarducci Funeral Home contained intricately hand-carved wood paneling and solid mahogany furniture. That day, the cloying odor of thousands of flowers crowded into too small a space made breathing a chore. The closed casket was almost buried in elaborate floral tributes. The sidewalk outside the funeral home was crowded with curious spectators, newspaper and television reporters, uniformed and plainclothes cops, and FBI agents.

Following me up the steps was Jim Taricani, a reporter for Channel 10 who had covered organized crime for years. I ignored his request for an interview, but he continued right behind me as I went up to embrace Rita and Raymond Junior. The latter hugged me tightly, tearfully, saying, "You're like a sister to me. I'll never, ever forget what you did for my father." As far as I know, Taricani did not repeat this comment on the evening news.

The next day, July 14, 1984, the day of the funeral, an incident took place that was subsequently reported in the *Journal* on the 15th of July. The article contained pictures of Raymond Junior, the pallbearers, and

Rita. Several mourners were noted to be carrying long-stemmed red roses. The *Journal* reported:

...unlike Friday afternoon's wake, when the younger Patriarca hurriedly ducked out a side entrance to avoid the cameras, he marched straight out the front door of the funeral home toward a score of cameras and reporters. He is a solidly built man with strong, dark features, and in his hand was one of the long-stemmed roses. Walking between the limousines and right up to the press, he thrust the rose out to them and said, 'For waiting so long, I'm sure he'd want you to have it. Sincerely.' The meaning was unclear, and there were no takers at first. He held it out to Jim Taricani... and Taricani took it.

Kneeling at the closed coffin, I bade Raymond farewell. Head bowed, I reflected on this man who had so radically altered my life. I did not know the pitiless executioner, the grasping loan shark, the mastermind of a huge criminal enterprise. I knew a sick, elderly, depressed man, uncomplaining though in frequent pain, pitifully grateful for my efforts to keep him out of prison, a father who worried and fretted about his son, a husband utterly dependent on his wife even for something so simple as cutting his food or buttoning his shirts. He had loved me and treated me like a daughter. I had been his physician, his protector, his friend. I would miss our lunches, I would miss him as a person, but I longed now to be left in peace, to raise my children without worrying that they would be taunted by their schoolmates over some snide newspaper article.

Raymond was dead, and Louis was imprisoned, perhaps forever. I wanted to build a life far removed from the drama, intrigue, and controversy of the previous four years. But I could not abandon Louis to the isolation of his cell, at least not yet. He was adamant that if his appeal were unsuccessful, I had to stop visiting him and get on with my life. I have no recollection of his actual words, the actual exchanges between us. I was loath to discuss the possibility that he would never be released from prison. When he brought it up, I quickly steered our conversation elsewhere. And so, the second summer of his incarceration began, with no resolution on the horizon.

I decided not to attend Raymond's funeral. Dory and Archie returned from Holyoke. We'd planned a cruise to Martha's Vineyard before all the recent events. Cousin Bernie came to help me sail the boat. With him and the five children—my own three and two of their friends—plus a new puppy, we set sail that Saturday from Bristol. After a two-day sail to Martha's Vineyard, we tied up at a private dock in Edgartown. The house was a beautiful old whaling captain's home, owned by Alan and Pat Symonds, whose youngest son, Alan Jr., was a friend of my son Archie.

After a week on the island, we drove to Nyack, where my parents and siblings threw a 40th birthday party for me at sister Rosa's house. Mary and Jack were in Italy, but all of the rest of the family were there, including my youngest brother Mark. With fifteen years in age separating us, we had not been close growing up. He was living in the suburbs of Washington, D.C. and working for IBM, in sales. When he had graduated high school several years earlier, Ned and I were still living together, and Ned urged him to go away to college. Mark attended American University in the Capitol, graduating in 1980. He'd recently broken up with his college sweetheart and was at loose ends. We spent hours together at the birthday party, bringing each other up to date on our lives, getting to know each other for the first time. After that, he became a regular visitor to Providence, flying up at least once a month for the weekend.

That autumn, young Archie, now a sophomore at Moses Brown, began playing varsity football at the quarterback position, despite being at least twenty pounds lighter than anyone else on the team. He loved football with a passion, and despite my misgivings I did not try to dissuade him from playing. Like his father, he was a talented passer and never suffered a serious injury.

On Saturdays, Meg and I, along with several female doctor friends, attended the games and cheered the Moses Brown team. Among the new friends I'd made since Louis' incarceration was Silvia DegliEsposti. She was born and raised in Bologna, Italy. While in medical school there she met and married a fellow student who was American. Like me, she was pregnant during her internship year, and knowing what she was going through, I sought her out and we became, and remain, close friends.

In November, I flew to Miami for the annual meeting of the American Heart Association. Two friends accompanied me. They were Mary Frances Nevin, a resident in Internal Medicine at the Miriam Hospital and Candi McCulloch, a Brown medical student. Mary was a brilliant redhead who had majored in Latin and Greek at Fordham University in the Bronx. Candi, a vivacious blond, was one of those women to whom members of the opposite sex are instantly attracted. She was thin but large breasted, with long-lashed hazel eyes and high cheekbones; men took one look at her and their brains and penises rushed by each other at warp speed, heading in opposite directions—and I don't mean to imply that they suddenly became geniuses. Quite the opposite, in fact. It was always fun to watch the effect she had on men as they almost fell over one another to attract her attention.

She had a steady boyfriend, Russell Long, who was a well-known sailboat racer. In 1980 he was the youngest person to compete in the races to determine the American entry into the America's Cup, losing out to Ted Turner in the elimination matches. Russell's father was a multi-millionaire, a shipping magnate who was considered the American equivalent of Aristotle Onassis. His mother was a Reynolds heiress, both tobacco and aluminum. He and Candi lived in an apartment in a colonial era house just off Benefit Street in Providence. Once a slum where successive waves of immigrants lived, Benefit Street underwent gentrification in the 1970s, and now contained some of the most expensive real estate in the city.

That autumn, Albert Lepore and the Coias went on trial in Miami for labor racketeering and misappropriation of union funds. They rented an entire floor of the Fontainebleau Hotel for the duration of the trial and leased several limousines. So when Mary Frances, Candi and I attended the American Heart Association annual meeting, Albert let us stay in one of the hotel suites, and we interspersed lectures on the latest developments in cardiology with festive dinners, trips to the pool to swim and sun bathe, and reunions with Greg Brown who was also attending the cardiology meetings. I wanted to attend the trial, for no other reason than because I knew that if I walked into the courtroom, the prosecution would immediately assume I was there to testify that Albert, who was my patient, was too sick to stand trial—and it would freak them out. Albert was not, in fact, ill at all, and the trial was recessed that week, so I never got to unnerve the Feds. On December 6th, 1984, they were acquitted of all the charges.

I filled my life with the children, my practice, working out, and my new friends. I dated sporadically but could never reclaim the happiness I had known with Louis. I continued to make at least weekly visits to the prison. The trips became increasingly difficult as the months wore on. I grew to detest the sight of the grim, gray fortress, with its aura of brooding despair. The possibility that it would be Louis' permanent abode was never far from my thoughts, and that seemed as unspeakable and unimaginable as it had on the day he was convicted.

※※※

On February 6, 1985 Terry MacFadyen argued Louis' appeal before the Rhode Island Supreme Court. He warned me and Anthony that it would be months before a decision was handed down.

The months crawled by. I tried hard to distract myself from the looming decision. I worked out more and more. I grew to love weightlifting and took demanding aerobics classes. Having made a whole new set of friends, I gradually saw less and less of Jack, Junior, Albert, and the other people I'd associated with while Raymond was alive. I yearned for Louis to be freed on appeal, and I hoped that I would have the same feelings for him that I'd had before. But as the months went by, I feared that even if Louis were freed I would not be able to integrate our relationship into the life I was now leading. Although I still cared deeply for him and craved his release, I knew that the love I felt for him had undergone some subtle metamorphosis; it had become a burden rather than a comfort. I foresaw that I would never again be able to give myself wholeheartedly to him, because in doing so once, I'd suffered a blow that almost destroyed my sanity. Without my conscious volition, in the years since his conviction, I'd armored myself against that happening again.

In March 1985, during their spring break, I took the children on vacation to the Club Med in Ixtapa, Mexico. I had the second floor of our home renovated. I took on additional teaching and mentoring duties at the hospital. I worked out frenetically; I did everything I could think of to distract myself from the looming decision. I spun through the days like a whirling dervish, never still except when I slept.

On a visit to the prison in late April, Louis told me Terry Mac-Fadyen had heard rumors that his appeal was going to be granted. I was afraid to get my hopes up, afraid that the rumors would prove false. Time ground almost to a halt over the ensuing weeks as we awaited the decision. I alternated between elation, convinced that the appeal would be successful, and despair when I became certain that this final chance for Louis' freedom would be denied.

On Friday, June 28, 1985, Terry telephoned with the news that Louis' conviction had been overturned. But he cautioned that Louis' release was still not assured. The prosecution intended to file a petition to re-argue the case before the Rhode Island Supreme Court. Until that issue was decided, Louis would remain in prison, where he had now spent over two years. The delay, the uncertainty, were excruciating. My only comfort was that the worst had not happened. There remained a chance—in fact, a good chance—that Louis would ultimately be free.

By now, I dreaded my trips to the prison. The chaos and squalor of the room where we sat, the lack of privacy, the inability to even hold hands except for brief seconds, had become unendurable. Whatever the outcome of the appeal, my visits there were coming to an end. If the appeal was re-argued and failed, if Louis was condemned to spend the rest of his life in prison, he was going to strike everyone off his visitor's list. I agreed to this because the visits would be even more unendurable if there were no possibility of Louis leaving prison for another thirty-odd years. I knew that adjusting to such an eventuality would take all of his emotional strength—and having to see the effect on me would sap that strength and double his pain. If his appeal failed, I would in all probability never see him again. In the meantime, until the decision was final, he urged me to stop coming to visit, to enjoy my summer as best I could. On July 19th, I made my last pilgrimage to the ACI. My brother Mark came with me, but I remember nothing else about that visit.

The last few years of my life had been painful in the extreme. At times, I wondered if I'd made the right decision to move to Rhode Island in 1977, when I left my first job out of fellowship. Had I been able to foresee the events that would from that decision, I might have chosen to move elsewhere, and my life would have been unimaginably different.

14. THE END OF THE AFFAIR

*At some point you have to realize that some people can
stay in your heart but not in your life...*
—Sandi Lynn

Usually, the summer months fly by in New England, perhaps because the winters seem so interminable. But the summer of 1985 inched by with stultifying languor. Cousin Bernie and my brother Mark visited, and we cruised on *Boadicea* for a week. I crewed for Russell Long in dinghy races in Newport. In August, Meagan and I flew to Seattle to attend Greg Brown's wedding. Over the years, Greg and I had stayed in touch by telephone and letter. Every few years, we ran into each other at national cardiology meetings. He was marrying a medical researcher whom he'd met at the University of Washington where he was on the medical school faculty. Our relationship had evolved into friendship: the unique friendship that occurs between a man and a woman who have been lovers and who still maintain a liking and respect and affection for one another.

Meg was only an infant when Greg and I had last been lovers. She did not know Greg as anything other than an old friend of her mother's but was delighted to be asked to be in the wedding. Once more she carried out her role of flower girl impeccably. Our mutual friend Dr. Walter Henry flew up from Irvine, California, where he was now Dean at the University of California's medical school there. We gorged on salmon and caught up on each other's lives.

On August 6th, the Rhode Island Supreme Court announced its decision. It reversed Louis' conviction and ordered a new trial, stating that Superior Court trial judge, Francis Kiely, "impermissibly limited Manocchio's cross-examination of a key witness." The article in *The Providence Journal* the following day recounted how Kelley had testified at a pre-trial hearing that he suffered from Alzheimer's disease. But when Kelley took the witness stand in front of the jury, Judge Kiely refused to allow Louis' lawyer to explore Kelley's memory problems and mental diseases.

> *Each time counsel broached this subject ... he found inquiry foreclosed when the trial justice sustained the prosecutor's objections. Therefore, all the jurors knew when they went to deliberate Manocchio's case was that the state's chief witness had 'a problem' with his memory, but not the extent of that problem," according to Justice Thomas Kelleher, who wrote the opinion. "In this case, said Kelleher, 'an exploration of Kelley's possible memory defects was especially warranted.' He was the only witness before the jury 'who could link Manocchio with the 15-year-old murders of Melei and Marfeo. It is readily apparent to us that Kelley's credibility was the only real issue before the jury....'*

This was at least the fourth time since the murders had occurred that Kelley had been required to relate his story under oath, admitting for the first time on the eve of Manocchio's trial that all of his prior testimony had been tainted in significant respects with perjury. 'There was an obvious danger here that Kelley's testimony involved far more recitation than recollection,' Kelleher concluded."

The high court declined to consider the other issues raised in Louis' appeal, dealing only with his constitutional right to confrontation.

Kelleher said that Judge Kiely's "unwarranted restriction of defense counsel's cross-examination of Kelley on the issue of Kelley's memory deficiencies and mental diseases denied the defendant his federal and state rights to confront his accusers."

The article also quoted a spokesperson from the Attorney General's Office on the state's intention to file a petition to re-argue the appeal before the Rhode Island Supreme Court. "We feel that's a more successful approach than trying to re-try Mr. Manocchio," given the fact that Kelley was now 70 years old and suffering from Alzheimer's. If that approach were to fail, the Attorney General "might consider asking the U.S. Supreme Court to review the case."

A dim light was beginning to be visible at the end of the tunnel, but it was clear that the battle was far from over, and that the state would use every weapon in its armamentarium to keep Louis behind bars.

On September 9, the Rhode Island Supreme Court refused to re-argue Louis' appeal, and a bail hearing was set for September 25th. By that day, however, Hurricane Gloria was heading for the New England coastline, and the hearing was postponed as Rhode Island braced for the storm. Low-lying areas were ordered evacuated. My J-30 sailboat, *Boadicea*, chaffed through her mooring lines and was blown ashore, narrowing missing the rocks and sustaining minor damage. We lost electrical power for three days. Even Mother Nature seemed to be conspiring against Louis' release.

Finally, the original pre-trial bail of $50,000 was reinstated by a Superior Court judge, and Louis was freed on September 30, 1985.

Terry MacFadyen picked him up at the prison and brought Louis to his brother Anthony's house in the Mount Pleasant section of Providence. Meagan and I drove there to meet him. I flew into his arms, shaking like a victim of advanced Parkinsonism. I was a jumble of conflicting emotions, ecstatic at his release, fearful that the ordeal had changed him irrevocably, alternately longing for and dreading the time when we would be alone together for the first time in over two years. I had not been with a man in almost a year. Louis had been celibate for twice that amount of time. He was now 58 years old, and I was 41.

But my fears were groundless. Later that night, at my home in the canopy bed I'd bought while he was away, Louis proved that he had lost neither his ardor nor his ability. I tried to ignore the niggling voice in my head that warned, "Don't get used to this. He could be taken away from you again at any time."

And indeed, the newspaper the next day, in reporting his release, noted that he was "released on bail... pending a new trial... No date for a new trial was set." None of the lawyers thought it likely that the case would be re-tried, but then, no one thought that Louis would be brought to trial in the first place. We saw each other almost every night, after I got through with work, but he would not spend the night except on rare occasions when my children were away.

Louis was staying at his mother's house, on the other side of the city. The Forum, and his apartment over the restaurant, had long since passed into other hands. Although we no longer had to worry that knowledge of our relationship would destroy the credibility of my testimony about Raymond, Louis was still leery of being seen with me in public, at least in situations where people would realize that we were a couple. He feared that it would get into the newspaper, or that the gossip would cause physicians to stop referring patients to me. It was a reasonable fear. And so, when we could, we left Providence, usually going to New York, where Meagan could visit with her cousins, and my family could watch her for me.

Archie was now a junior in high school. On Sunday, October 20, 1985, an advertisement appeared in the *Providence Journal*. It showed a picture of my son, in his football uniform and helmet, under the headline TOMORROW IN SPORTS MONDAY: Maybe the Pats Should Sign Him. The text read:

> With the high-flying Jets invading Sullivan Stadium today, the Patriots will need all the help they can get. If Archie Roberts, Jr., quarterback for Moses Brown, is anything like his famous dad, he could be a real help. Young Archie will be featured in a Sports Spotlight.

The next day's article was headlined: "The name's the same, and so's the game." There was a 6-by-4-inch close-up photograph of his face, looking too young to belong to a high school junior. The article began:

> It's a question Archie Roberts knows he will be answering as long as he plays football. 'Every place we play, people ask me if I'm any relation to the *Archie Roberts,*' said the Moses Brown quarterback. 'It doesn't bother me. I'm thrilled when people ask me about my dad.' Archie Roberts, Sr. was an All-American quarterback at Columbia University 21 years ago. For three seasons, from 1962-64 he put Eastern football in the national spotlight with his sensational passing. Now, Archie Roberts, Jr. is making his own name on the football field...

The article recounts how his passing was instrumental in two recent victories, noting that he had a pass completion rate of 62%. It touched on his acting career at Trinity Rep and quoted young Archie extensively on his love of the game, and the fact that he felt no pressure from his father to play. What was most important to me, though, was that the article made no mention of his mother; only noting that Archie's parents were divorced when he was very young. I hoped this meant that the *Journal* had lost interest in me. He tried to appear blasé, but Archie was delighted with the article, despite the ribbing he took from his teammates.

Louis met my friends Mary Frances, Candi and Russell, Silvia and her husband, and a few others I was closest to and knew I could trust. For the most part, they were all a decade younger than I, which made Louis almost 30 years their senior. During a dinner at Silvia's one night, her little daughter Francesca, the child she'd carried as an intern, pointed to Louis and called him "Nonno" or grandfather. Although he got on well with most of my new friends, particularly Silvia, who was a brilliant cook and with whom he could brush up on his Italian, he had little in common with them. And we could only go to small, private gatherings together; other social functions I had to attend alone.

The need for discretion and secrecy was more irksome now than it had been previously. I was out of the habit of looking over my shoulder, of wondering if I was under surveillance, of assuming my telephone was tapped. I also wanted to know more about Louis—his past, which was still largely unknown to me, and what we could expect in the future.

While he was in prison, I had become friendly with Francesca Bianco, wife of Nicky, the alleged "Number 2" man in the New England mob while Raymond was alive. Her son Angelo and my son Archie were good friends and football teammates at Moses Brown. Francesca and I met at a football dinner in which we sat at a table with other divorced, separated, or otherwise solo mothers. At that time, her husband Nicky was not imprisoned, but he did not usually attend school functions. I'm not sure why; I guess so as not to make any of the other parents and students feel uncomfortable to be in the presence of a notorious mobster.

One night, in the restaurant she owned, Francesca told me that many years before, Louis had shot her husband, wounding him in the shoulder. One day, not long after his release, I turned to Louis and said, "May I ask you a question?"

"Sure," he replied.

"Why did you shoot Nicky Bianco?" I inquired.

There was a long hesitation. "Well, you know how it is," he said. "One guy says one thing, then another guy says another thing, and before you know it..." finishing up with an eloquent Gallic shrug meant to imply who knew what. I most assuredly *did not* "know how it is." I couldn't even begin to imagine "how it is." The abyss that yawned between our lives was never more graphically on display.

And gradually, I became aware that Louis was increasingly unhappy. Except for evenings, and then only if there was no emergency, I was busy with either my patients or the children. Dory was living in Boston, and Archie was now a teenager, but Meg was only nine and I was her only parent. Ned was off in parts unknown. She was used to having me to herself, and I worried that she would resent the attention I gave to Louis. After being seemingly upbeat and optimistic while in prison, his increasing negativity was a shock. Nothing pleased him. His lips seemed permanently curled in disdain. He disparaged Candi's boyfriend Russell Long because he'd inherited loads of money; he'd never had to work for it. In restaurants, Louis sent meals back for trivial reasons and criticized waiters. Once, young Archie made a slurping noise with a straw while drinking soda, and Louis reprimanded him. Archie felt that Louis didn't like him for some reason, but he never realized that Louis and I were lovers until he was himself an adult. None of the children at that time knew we were lovers. I had many male friends, and the children thought Louis was just another.

I kept telling myself that Louis' ill-humor was a delayed reaction to his imprisonment, and the horrors of the past few years. And it may have been largely that. But it might prove to be permanent. Perhaps the trauma of his incarceration had warped his personality irreversibly, coiling it into a Gordian knot of insoluble contradiction.

What I could not doubt, and did not doubt, was his love for me. I knew that as deeply as I knew that *no other* man had ever loved me as much. Increasingly he chafed at being in Providence and wanted to move away, to either California or Europe. And he wanted me to come with him.

We spent hours and hours talking around the problem. I tried to explain to him that I could not uproot my children and having devoted so much time and energy to it, I was not ready to give up my practice. The next ten or fifteen years would likely be my peak years, professionally. I was unwilling to forgo them. I was coming to realize that we did not have a future together, at least not as lovers. Louis was out of prison, yes, but the bubble of unreality we'd floated in before his incarceration had burst. I was, and would remain, a mother and physician, a respected if somewhat controversial member of the community. He was, and would remain, an "alleged organized crime figure;" he would never be free of that stigma. He would never NOT be the subject of investigations and surveillance.

And I didn't want to live with that anymore. Louis became more and more withdrawn and spoke bitterly about his persecution by law enforcement. "They'll never leave me alone here. You're fooling yourself if you think they will. The only way we'll have any peace is to move." I could not give him the answer he sought. And as the winter winds swept down from their Arctic home, as darkness encroached more and more on the light, a chill foreboding invaded my heart. Something was dying along with the year, and I could only stand by helplessly, and watch.

I looked forward to the holidays, to spending them with Louis and the children, but just before Thanksgiving, he abruptly decided to leave town. Dory and Archie visited their father, who was now living in Massachusetts. He'd been appointed Chief of Cardiac Surgery at the Boston University Medical Center. Meg and I celebrated Thanksgiving at our house with Candi and Russell, and several other residents from the hospital. The next day, the older children returned from Boston. Dory, Meagan, and I drove to Nyack in Louis' car. I lent my car to Archie, and he stayed home to attend parties with his friends. Louis took the train to White Plains, where I picked him up. While Dory and Meg visited with their cousins, Louis and I had dinner at a restaurant where my brother Matty bartended. We spent that night at my brother Eddie's house in Nyack. Saturday night we drove to New York City and had dinner with sister Mary and her husband Jack.

After dinner, while we were driving to Manhattan, we got a flat tire—and Louis was furious, far out of proportion to the situation. We left the car at a gas station and took a cab to the apartment he had the use of near the United Nations. The next day, I rented a car and drove Dory and Meg back to Rhode Island. Louis stayed on in New York. Archie had his end-of-the-season football dinner that Sunday night at the Brown University Faculty Club, which I attended alone. To no one's surprise, he was elected co-captain of the team for his upcoming senior year.

I hoped that we could spend Christmas together, but on December 22, Louis left again, this time for a trip to New York and Florida. The children and I spent a quiet Christmas day, a Wednesday, in Providence. That weekend, we visited my family in Nyack. On New Year's Eve, Candi and Russell had a party, which I attended with Meagan. Archie was there too, serving as the bartender. I was quietly sad to be spending another New Year's Eve without a lover at my side, but I had come to a decision. My New Year's resolution was to tell Louis that I could not go on as his lover. I'd arrived at the decision gradually. It was painful process, so painful that I've suppressed the memory of how exactly I arrived at this resolution. But I knew that I could no longer lead a double life.

I did not have whatever it took to live a life in the shadows, hiding important truths from all but the closest of friends. I wanted to be able to go anywhere and do anything with my lover, yet I also wanted to stay in Rhode Island and continue to care for my patients and children. They were my anchors and had kept me safe from the storms surging about me after the fateful night when I became Raymond's doctor. There, in the Scituate State Police barracks, all unknowing, I entered a looking-glass world, a parallel universe, where the real became unreal, where nothing was quite as it seemed, and I, a clueless Alice in an underworld Wonderland, was lucky to escape with my head. Above all, I wanted to be free of the constant fear that my lover would once again be caged like an animal, locked away from the sight of all he held dear.

I was overwhelmed with guilt. I had promised Louis over and over again, in letters when he first went to prison, that I would love him forever, that no matter how many years went by, I would still love him. What I had to face now was the knowledge that I had killed a large part of that love. Maybe the alternative was madness, but maybe I was fooling myself, attempting to assuage the guilt I felt over inflicting a terrible blow on the man who cherished me as no one else ever had.

He returned to Rhode Island on Friday, January 3, 1986, and we had dinner at L'Oasis, Francesca Bianco's restaurant, a rare public foray together. On the way home, I told him that I wanted to end our affair. I felt no fear, only an obliterating sadness, and the tears I tried to stem flowed ceaselessly. A dam in my heart was broached. The pent-up pain of all that had happened to me in my life welled up and spilled over in a salty flood. Louis, shocked almost speechless, was dry-eyed. Many years later, he told me that it felt as if molten metal were being poured over his head, and that hearing my words was more painful than hearing his guilty verdict read out by the jury fore-man a few years before. To have learned this at the time would have been unbearable, and he spared me that knowledge until a time when I could absorb it without agony.

The next day I wrote him a letter, trying to explain why I had to end our affair; the night before I had been tongue-tied, able only to weep. We talked a few times on the phone and met for a few lunches and dinners, bleak meetings that left us both uncomforted. Within a few weeks he left, going to Italy to ski, calling from there about once a week. I was glad that he was back on the mountains he loved, free once more to go careening down them, carving tracks in the pristine alpine snow.

The months went by. I was often lonely, wondering if I would ever find a man to share my life. A girlfriend who believed in psychics begged me to go with her one night, convinced the woman could tell her what lay in the future. I tagged along, feeling smugly certain that the psychic was a charlatan. I was a scientist, mildly superstitious since leaving the Church, but deeply skeptical of all "paranormal" phenomenon. On the spur of the moment I decided to pay her fee and hear what she predicted for me.

She was a small woman, living in a non-descript apartment in West Warwick, a town about fifteen miles from Providence. She had no crys-tal ball, or Ouija board, she just took my hand and held it loosely in her own. "You have just ended a relationship," she told me. I thought this was a lucky guess. She told me other generic things about myself I no longer recall. She then asked me if I knew someone named Joe, and I replied that I had an uncle Joe and a cousin Joe, but she said no, this was a different man, someone with whom I would be involved intimately.

Just before our session ended she told me that I would move from my home; she saw me living in a house by the water. At this I was frankly disbelieving and promptly forgot her predictions for many years. There was no way I was going to move. My home was my nest, and the last of the fledglings had many years to go before she could fly away. Meagan loved our house too and told me that she never wanted me to sell it. Over the years, I remodeled it extensively. When I bought it, the yard, almost a quarter of an acre in size, contained plantings of rhododendrons, and azaleas. There was a pink dogwood tree just outside the solarium, with a wisteria shrub standing next to it. With my own hands, I dug rose beds and planted them with antique English roses. Outside the back door, the one we used almost exclusively, I planted hydrangea and lilac bushes. I turned a long strip of land just inside the cedar stockade fence into a sunny perennial bed, and planted it with tulips, daffodils, peonies, irises, lilies, poppies, lupines, and clematis vines. (Meagan christened the latter "clitoris" vines when she was a teenager.) I could never smell the peonies without being transported back to my boarding school years in Goshen. Just outside the dining room window, in the shadow cast by a huge copper beech tree, I planted a shade bed, where I grew columbines, hosta, coral bells, and lilies-of-the-valley.

For many years I had a recurring dream, one that in some form or another is very common. In my dream, I am on my way to take a final exam, and I realize that I have attended none of the lectures and have not studied any of the material. I wake up in a sweat. After I bought the house in Providence, this dream was replaced by another in which I took a job in a faraway city and sold my house. The end result was the same; I startled up into wakefulness, panic-stricken, until I realized it was only a dream.

Our home at 312 Laurel Avenue rang with life, with the raucous shouts of teenage friends of Archie's, and the chirp of Meg's pre-pubertal pals. Every Friday evening, I made homemade white pizza for dinner, so heavily laced with garlic that Archie's friends swore they could still smell it on his breath on Monday. Many of them just "happened" to stop by at dinnertime on Fridays. I was a mother figure and mentor to scores of younger women physicians, never forgetting how keenly I felt the lack of female role models when I was in training. I invited them to my home, I attended their weddings and their baby showers, I listened to their trials and tribulations. I gave them advice on how to take care of patients, and how to deal with their fellow physicians. I held them and hugged them when they cried to me about broken love affairs, and I provided a form of living proof that you could be a physician yet lead a full life as a woman: a life complete with children, and lovers, and travel, a life that contained tears and controversy, but also laughter, and fulfillment. I called my home the "Barbara Roberts Home for Wayward Females," and over the years many women, most but not all physicians, lived with us for weeks or months at a time, in transit between husbands, or lovers, or jobs. Three were married from my home or held their wedding receptions there.

My life was rich and full, lacking only a man to share it. I wanted to find that special person, and I finally confronted my abysmal record in the lists of love. I began to see a therapist. Prompted by some of my siblings, I also attended meetings of Adult Children of Alcoholics and read widely on the subject of alcoholism and addiction. I learned that it is common to attempt to replicate the conditions of one's childhood home in adulthood—only this time around, make everything turn out better. I had tried to choose men who were not alcoholics to father my children, but each of them had been as emotionally unavailable to their children as my own father, in the throes of his addiction, had been to me. Therapy helped me to look at my parents with compassion, and I was able to acknowledge how heroic they had been. It allowed me to forgive my younger self for the errors *she* had made. Armed with new self-knowledge, I met and dated several men in the years after breaking up with Louis, but none of these relationships lasted very long.

15 · A Love and a Life Foretold

Love is the mystery of water and a star.
—Pablo Neruda

Friday, August 4th, 1989 was a hot and sunny day. After work I met my friend Joan D'Agostino for dinner at the Plaza Grille on Federal Hill. We became friends after attending the same aerobics class for several years and discovering that we had an ex-boyfriend in common. In fact, I dated this man shortly after Joan broke up with him, and he spoke of her non-stop, praising her to the skies. Joan was about my age, the divorced mother of two teenage sons. She worked as a housing specialist for the Rhode Island State Department of Elderly Affairs. She was raised in North Providence where she still lived. Endlessly kind, she was somewhat naive, beautiful, and flawlessly feminine. We joked that I taught her how to be assertive, and she taught me how to put on makeup and do my hair.

That night tables were set up outside the Plaza Grille, located on DePasquale Square, a few doors down from Louis' old restaurant, the Forum, which had gone through multiple changes of name and ownership. I still could not enter it without sadness. As we nursed our drinks, three men approached our table. One, Steven, I knew because he and Joan had recently dated. He introduced one of the others as his brother, Paul, and the last as his friend, Joe Avarista. After chatting with them for about fifteen minutes, when they showed no sign of wanting to leave, we invited them to join us for dinner.

I was immediately taken with Joe's looks, guessing his age at about thirty. Just under six feet tall, he was muscular and carried himself with an easy grace. He had abundant black wavy hair, just beginning to show touches of gray, and a mustache. His eyes were hazel, his features perfectly regular. He was a dish, but far too young for me, I thought. When he told me, in answer to my question, that he had just turned forty I was at first unbelieving—he looked so much younger. But then, I was often told that I looked ten years younger than my age of forty-five, and I still *felt* young. I was delighted that there was only a five-year difference in our ages.

He was a sculptor, and he worked at various other jobs to support himself when his art wasn't selling, which happened with regularity. He bartended and built post-and-beam houses. He made period furniture to go with the houses he built. But wood-carving was his passion. He had served a nine-year apprenticeship with Armand LaMontagne, a well-known Rhode Island carver, famous for his life-sized wooden statues of sports figures like Ted Williams, Bobby Orr, and others. Joe was in the midst of carving a series of leather jacket sculptures, so life-like they had to be touched to convince oneself that they were not actual pieces of clothing. We talked for hours, and at the end of the evening, I gave him my business card. Two weeks later, he called and asked me out.

We have been together ever since and have been married for decades. We've traveled over much of the world and have had many adventures, about which I will write in the fullness of time if that time is granted to me. My children are grown and my first grandchild is on the way. Joe and I live in Jamestown, in a house that overlooks the East Passage of Narragansett Bay, and the Newport Bridge. We named the house Suan Croi, pronounced "Sue-in Cree," which is Gaelic for "heart's repose." As I write this morning, a tug boat bustles down the bay towing a heavily laden barge, like a petite mother dragging a recalcitrant adolescent. Song birds are busy at the feeders outside the den; goldfinches, house sparrows, cardinals, red-winged black birds, and blue jays squabble over the sunflower seeds. Hummingbirds dart and hover at their feeder, before alighting to drink. The evocative odor of peonies wafts in from the flower garden. I am at peace.

I am the luckiest woman alive.

Joe Avarista and Barbara Roberts, September 2017.

POSTSCRIPT 1 • HOW I TOOK DOWN THE MAFIA

The man who sits across the table from me in an out-of-the-way corner of Rhode Island shall remain nameless, but his credentials for commenting on the Mafia are impeccable. He has agreed to be interviewed for this book, which has been gestating in my mind for many years now. We have known each other for decades. He is rock solid, honest, and not given to flights of fancy.

"You know, Barbara," he says, leaning towards me and lowering his voice, though no one is nearby, "the mob in New England is dead, kaput, and you're the reason why."

"What do you mean?" I ask, taken aback. His reply astounds me.

"You kept the old man alive too long, that's what I mean. Until the last year of his life, who would succeed him was up in the air. During that last year, he persuaded the heads of the five New York families to let his son take over—and his son just wasn't up to the job. You thought you were doing the right thing by keeping him alive and out of jail, and maybe you were—but because of that, everything he built up was destroyed.

"Look at it now, all the old guys are dead, in prison or out to pasture. Nothing's going on up on Federal Hill; it may as well be a ghost town."

I hear him out. I have no way of knowing if what he says is true.

POSTSCRIPT 2 • CRIMETOWN

Sheila Bentley, the ex-wife of Providence's notorious mayor Buddy Cianci, had bonded with me in the early 1980s over our both being infamous Rhode Island women. Over the ensuing years, we kept in touch and met for lunch. In November of 2016, she told me about a new podcast, *Crimetown*, which was going to examine the intersection of Providence politics and the New England Mafia. *Crimetown's* co-producers were Marc Smerling and Zac Stuart-Pontier. They had co-written an HBO documentary, "The Jinx," which won an Emmy for best documentary in 2015. Sheila said that they were very interested in interviewing me for the podcast and showed me the front-page article about the series in *The Providence Journal*, which featured photos of Buddy Cianci and Raymond L. S. Patriarca. I agreed to meet with Marc but didn't commit to being interviewed.

On November 12, 2016, Marc came to my home in Jamestown, and after listening to the tape of the first episode, I agreed to participate. During the next few months, over the course of many hours, he taped interviews in which I described, for the first time publicly, the story of my years as Raymond's doctor and my affair with Louis. *Crimetown* Chapter 11, *The Doctor Broad*, aired on March 5, 2017. It was downloaded more than 400,000 times in the first 24 hours after its release. The entire podcast series, consisting of 18 chapters and 7 bonus episodes, became an international hit and was downloaded more than 50 million times. It is currently in production as a television series by FX Network.

ACKNOWLEDGMENTS

No book springs into existence fully formed, and *The Doctor Broad* is no exception. Over a prolonged gestation of almost twenty years, many have extended a helping hand, and I would be remiss not to acknowledge their contributions.

My publisher Naomi Rosenblatt believed in me and in my vision for what the book should be. Elizabeth Platt Hamblin is an outstanding editor who helped birth both my first and latest book. My agent Esmond Harmsworth was steadfast and supportive. Thank you all.

Marc Smerling, Zac Stuart-Pontier, John Kusiak, Drew Nelles, Mike Plunkett, Rob Szpko and the rest of the Crimetown crew helped bring the short version of my life story to the 50 million people around the world who downloaded the first season of the Crimetown podcast. I can't thank them enough.

My gratitude goes to the many people who shared their memories with me including Jack Cicilline, Sabra Cicilline, Dr. Robert Indeglia, Johnston Police Chief Richard Tamburini, retired State Police Captain Brian Andrews and retired South Kingstown police chief Vincent Vespia.

The late Bob Leuci, author, professor and friend, encouraged me to tell this story and was the first person who assured me I could write.

A special shout out to Mike Plunkett for coming up with the idea for the book cover and to the following for making it happen: Isabel Almeida Mota, Jorge Almeida, Edward DaSilva, Stephen J. Boyle, Joseph Carroll, Amanda Melo and Brittany LeClerc.

And last but far from least I'd like to acknowledge the debt I owe to my children-in-law, Luis Reis, Stephanie Linakis, and Michael Shine.

CPSIA information can be obtained
at www.ICGtesting.com
Printed in the USA
BVHW030519170819
556030BV00001B/1/P